HIKING &
BACKPACKING

A COMPLETE GUIDE
BY
KAREN BERGER

Introduction

by

John Viehman

A TRAILSIDE SERIES GUIDE

W.W. NORTON & COMPANY

NEW YORK   LONDON

Copyright © 1995 by New Media, Incorporated
All rights reserved
Printed in the United States of America

First Edition

The text of this book is composed in Bodoni Book with the display set in Triplex
Page composition by Tina Christensen
Color separations and prepress by Bergman Graphics, Incorporated
Manufacturing by R. R. Donnelley & Sons
Illustrations by Ron Hildebrand

Book design by Bill Harvey

Library of Congress Cataloging-in-Publication Data

Berger, Karen, 1959—
Hiking & Backpacking : a complete guide / by Karen Berger;
introduction by John Viehman.
p.   cm. — (A Trailside series guide)
A companion volume to the television series, Trailside.
Includes bibliographical references and index.
1. Hiking, 2. Backpacking. I. Title. II. Title: Hiking and backpacking. III. Series.
GV199.5.B47 1995   796.5—dc20   95-5528

ISBN 0-393-31334-4

W. W. Norton & Company, Inc., 500 Fifth Avenue, New York, N.Y. 10110
W. W. Norton & Company Ltd., 10 Coptic Street, London WC1A 1PU

1 2 3 4 5 6 7 8 9 0

C O N T E N T S

INTRODUCTION

My wife and I can't recall how many years we've been married, but we'll never forget our first backpacking trip together. We'd just begun dating and I was her trail-hardened outdoorsman, a knight in shining Cordura, the guy who could handle any wilderness emergency. She was my...well, let's just say I was bent on making a good impression. This was her first backpacking experience and I wanted to have many more with her as my hiking partner.

I'd checked and double-checked everything—trail conditions, equipment, weather forecast. I even bought a new stove for the occasion. We set off under overcast skies with packs loaded and spirits high. There was precipitation in the forecast, but it was November and too early for snow, I assured her. (Did I mention that we were just a few miles south of Mount Washington, home to the worst, most unpredictable weather in the Northeast?) As we climbed the few thousand feet up a granite ridge, the trail steadily steepened and we strained a bit under our loads. On top, a gentle breeze pushed a fluffy, light snowfall. The flakes were big and chunky, the kind you chase with your mouth open. Certainly no threat, I told her matter-of-factly.

After a few miles, the winds picked up and the snowflakes thickened into a swirling soup. The trail all but dissolved into a wall of white, so I pulled out my compass to locate the three-sided shelter that was to be our base for the night. Eventually we found it, tucked alongside a gurgling freshet.

The winds were roaring now, so I pitched our tent inside the shelter for added protection. It was a tight fit, with the tent door only two feet from the log end-wall, but at least we were out of the snowy gale. To ward off the cold and warm my fair belle, I pulled my glittering stove from its pouch, primed it, and confidently christened the burner with a match. She was awestruck by my back-woods wizardry. Color me smug and far too confident. That's when I noticed it: what appeared to be water streaming down the side of the stove.

My new cooker's white-gas fuel was bathing the stove base. It was also drenching the tent floor between us and the doorway—the doorway that was zipped tightly shut. A headline flashed through my mind: "Brainless Hikers Toasted In White Mountains."

The stove burst into flames that ran up the tent wall. I grabbed a wet sock, clutched the stove base with one hand, and unzipped the tent door with the other. I heaved the hissing fireball through the opening, assuming that was the end of the episode, only to hear a thud as it hit the shelter wall before bouncing back inside to melt some more nylon. My now fairly unimpressed belle grabbed a pack towel and doused the inferno. She breathed a huge sigh of relief, while I swallowed a pound or three of pride.

We went on to have a thoroughly disastrous outing. The weather pounded us into submission. A full day of storm later with no letup in sight, we decided to hike out. Fortunately, that slippery, slithery descent down a snowed-up, iced-over trail was merely the end of our first backpacking trip together and not our relationship. But we learned some important lessons in the White Mountains that weekend. For instance, never take an untested stove into the field, especially in winter. And of course, never fire it up inside a tent.

My wife learned that, despite her feelings about me, she shouldn't be lazy about her own safety. That is, common sense told her before I lit the ill-fated stove that this was a dangerous situation. But, being polite and trusting, she assumed I knew what I was doing, when in fact, I didn't. She learned a lot about me on that trip that has since helped us build a strong, loving relationship not just with each other but with the outdoors as well. We now look back on a long list of great shared outdoor experiences.

Our story has a lot to do with how you approach this book. For starters, realize that the information you find here is a first step, albeit a superb first step because author Karen Berger is a seasoned backpacker, Appalachian Trail through-hiker, and someone who truly knows what she's talking about. Karen's expertise is matched by her infectious enthusiasm, which imbues every page of this inspired and inspiring guide. Still, it's only the first step. No matter how much you think you know about a subject after reading a book, you won't really know it until you've had in-the-field experience. You have to feel the tug of pack straps on your shoulders and swallow some trail dust before all of Karen's advice and wisdom become relevant. Only then will they stick to you like wet winter snow.

Second, don't forget to bring your common sense. As sound as Karen's advice is, it should be balanced with your own gut feelings. Give yourself credit for knowing something about what works and doesn't work for your particular needs—like my wife did when she saw gas pouring over the stove and me about to light it. Fortunately for both of us, she knew enough to reach for a towel when I tossed the fire-bomb.

Finally, remember to have fun. An old sage once said, "I don't go into the backcountry to rough it; I'm going there to smooth it." And that is what this book is all about—getting rid of the bumpy spots on the outdoor road ahead of you. Smoothing it.

See you on the trail!

—John Viehman

STARTING
OUT

"**W**hy walk?" a woman asked. "You know, you can drive to the top."

It was the summit of New Hampshire's Mount Washington on a cloudy, blustery day. And indeed, the woman was right: There are other, more convenient ways to the summit. You can drive. You can take the auto coach. You can even ascend by a cog railroad that has been chugging up and down the mountain since 1869.

But I had walked.

The woman asking the question clutched her jacket around her, as though a tighter grip could shut out the cold. She regarded me with a mixture of friendly curiosity and skepticism.

I tried to think of a pat answer, but none came. Because the world looks different at two miles an hour? Because spring comes one flower at a time? Because a mountain reveals itself to those who climb it? Because I like the drama of crags and gullies emerging from behind a curtain of mist and then disappearing again as the fog rolls in and out? Because of the way wind cools the skin, and a snowflake stings the tongue? Because it feels good to stretch muscles, and make them work; to know that they can?

The fog was thick; it often is in the highcountry. I stammered something about liking the mountains.

"But there's nothing to see up

Backpackers experience foreign lands far beyond cities and resorts. New Zealand's Milford Track affords hikers spectacular views along its 33½-mile length.

here," she complained.

That was the last I saw of her. We went our separate ways, she to the road, I to the trail. Mist swirled around me as I descended. Behind me, fog clothed the summit, obscured the road and the restaurant and the crowds in the parking lot. The trail wove among the boulders, and I followed it onward and down. Finally, the clouds parted, or maybe I had just walked through them, and before me was a vertical world of rock and ice, and air so clear it almost sparkled.

Why walk?

There are as many answers as there are hikers.

If you like making new friends, try a couple of weeks on the Appalachian Trail. If you enjoy adventure, set your sights on Alaska's Denali National Park. If you're intrigued by exotic locations, you can hike in France, Spain, Iceland, and Norway. If that list sounds too tame, what about Kenya, India, Nepal, or Ecuador? There is even a trail around Hong Kong. If you are drawn to history, you can follow its path along the Oregon Trail in Wyoming, climb to a Colorado ghost town, trek through the Peruvian Andes to Machu Picchu, or follow in the footsteps of medieval pilgrims who climbed the Pyrenees in search of salvation. If you want to improve your fitness; if you are touched by photographs of pristine wilderness; if you long for peace and solitude in an ever more frenetic world; if your heart answers the call of northcountry ponds and alpine peaks and cool green forests smelling fresh and moist after a night of rain; if you are attracted by the song of a wolf, the sweet smell of spring grass, or the cold, solid feel of granite under-foot; if you seek challenge and achievement; if you relish the sense of independence and self-reliance that comes from removing yourself, if only briefly, from the welter of nonessentials that is modern life — try backpacking.

Away from it all along the John Muir Trail in California's Sierra Nevada Range.

The limits of a backpacking trip are defined by simple things: how far you can, or want to, walk; how much time you have; your imagination. A backpacking trip can be a leisurely overnight in your local county park or a multi-month expedition to the other side of the globe. For many back-packers — whether we go out for a weekend, a week, or several months — hiking is a vital and cherished part of our lives, a chance to reconnect with a simpler world, and with ourselves.

WHERE TO HIKE

First, let's get down to basics. The most basic questions are how do you get started, and where do you go. The fact is that most of us don't live close to some wonderful wilderness area. (I, for one, live adjacent to New York City.) As for planning your first trip, it might sometimes seem as if you've wandered through the looking glass into a world of confusion. Whom do you ask? Do you have to spend a ton of money on high-tech gear before you're even sure you'll like the sport? Where

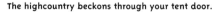

The highcountry beckons through your tent door.

Climbing on a sandstone formation in southern Utah. Much of Utah's "slickrock" country is public BLM land open to hikers and other users.

become a backpacker. From my house — which is 25 miles from midtown Manhattan — I can walk 5 minutes to a trail that goes for more miles than I can, at least in a day. A 45-minute drive takes me to the Appalachian Trail; from there, I can walk south all the way to Georgia or north all the way to Maine. Less than an hour away, Harriman State Park has hundreds of miles of interlocking trails where I can hike and camp. And in the nearby Bronx (yes, the Bronx) the Appalachian Mountain Club has recently completed work on a day-hiking trail in Pelham Bay Park. If there's a place for me to hike, I'm willing to bet that there's a place for you to hike, too. Here are a few specific places to check with.

YOUR LOCAL OUTFITTER. The growing popularity of outdoor recreation has led to a concurrent explosion of specialty shops. There's probably one close to you, and it's the best place to go not just for gear (that comes later) but for information, which is what you need right now. Your local outfitter probably has a selection of publications and maps, including guidebooks for local trails, many of which are published by local outing clubs. Your outfitter may also offer, or know about, seminars on how to backpack. Ask.

LOCAL CLUBS. Outing clubs often post information about their programs, activities, and slide shows on the bulletin boards of outfitting stores. These activities offer the beginner the easiest and safest way to learn about hiking and backpacking. First, a group hike

can you hike? How will you ever choose among wilderness areas — the Bob Marshall and the Scapegoat and the Goat Rocks and the Great Bear and the hundreds of others — none of which means anything to you? You're worried about safety, or bears, or finding your way, and you haven't the slightest idea what a four-season dome-design Northface VE25 is, let alone whether you want or need one.

But stop a moment. It doesn't have to be that complicated.

Start Locally

You don't have to live next door to a wilderness area or a national park to

means that there is a leader to answer your questions and do the basic planning for you. Second, there are other people to learn from and make friends with. Third, you'll get an opportunity to find out about gear before you spend a lot of money. The group scene doesn't work for everyone — in fact, once you've got a couple of trips under your belt, you'll probably want to break away to experience the solitude of wilderness travel. But when you're starting out, local clubs help you avoid some basic mistakes. And outings run by local groups are not the big-ticket adventure travel trips advertised in the glossy magazines. The fees are minimal — enough to cover membership, transportation, and possibly food, rental equipment, or entry fees. The leaders are generally volunteers, but they've usually received some training. OTHER CLUBS. Try chapters of the Sierra Club, the Audubon Society, or other environmental organizations. In the East, local affiliates of the Appalachian Trail Conference have hiking programs. The Appalachian Mountain Club is active in the Northeast; the Potomac Appalachian Trail Club is active in Virginia and surrounding areas. In Colorado, try the Colorado Mountain Club; in the Northwest, the Mountaineers. The American Hiking Society can give you the name of a member club in your area. (See Sources and Resources, page 209, for addresses.)
LAND MANAGEMENT AGENCIES. Check out land management agencies like the USDA Forest Service, the Bureau of

An afternoon nap along the Appalachian Trail in Maine's Barren Chairback Range.

Land Management (BLM), the National Park Service, or state and county parks that manage land in your area. Trails in wilderness areas and national parks are usually better marked and maintained than trails in multiple-use sections of national forests or on BLM land. Well-known trails like the AT

The 100-foot-deep Oneonta Canyon in the Columbia River Gorge National Scenic Area, northern Oregon: a popular trek among dayhikers.

(Appalachian Trail), the PCT (Pacific Crest Trail), the Long Trail (in Vermont), and the Colorado Trail also tend to be well marked and well maintained, which makes them ideal for beginners who aren't sure which end of the compass needle points north. Rangers at national parks and national forests are there to answer questions about trails: Take advantage of their knowledge.

BASIC QUESTIONS, BASIC ANSWERS

I'M NOT IN GREAT PHYSICAL SHAPE. CAN I BACKPACK? Like any other physically demanding activity, backpacking is more enjoyable the fitter you are. But it's also a great way to get in shape. When I started my Appalachian Trail hike of more than 2,000 miles, I was overweight and in terrible shape. Six months later, I had lost 45 pounds and felt terrific.

I'M A SENIOR CITIZEN: AM I TOO OLD TO START? No, most emphatically not! At gatherings of long-distance hikers, there is a large and enthusiastic population of hikers in their sixties, seventies, and even eighties! And many of them didn't start backpacking until they retired. As with any other strenuous activity, discuss your plans with your doctor — then go for it.

I'VE NEVER SLEPT IN THE WOODS BEFORE. SHOULD I BE AFRAID? Most hikers feel that they are safer in the woods than on a city street. But that depends on where in the woods and, I suppose, which city street. You should hike with a partner until you gain confidence and expertise. (Many people always hike with a partner, and, certainly, that is the best way to reduce the risks of wilderness travel.) Backpacking can be dangerous if you ignore common-sense precautions, don't pay attention to your surroundings, or take unnecessary risks. Most wilderness problems occur owing to adverse weather and injuries — and most of them are avoidable. See Chapters 7 and 8 for information on staying healthy, and Chapter 9 for a discussion of wildlife.

ISN'T BACKPACKING TERRIBLY EXPENSIVE? Not really. As with any sport, there is plenty of opportunity to spend money. That's why you should borrow or rent equipment the first few times you go out, so that you can learn what you really need. There are plenty of things lying around your house that you can press into service (see page 55). The basic outlay for boots, sleeping bag, backpack, rain gear, stove, and tent

The Colorado Plateau of southern Utah can make for challenging backpacking up sandstone cliffs.

It means that there are lots of right answers for every question. There are as many ways to backpack as there are backpackers, and, because backpacking is a learning experience, even seasoned hikers constantly experiment with new ideas and techniques.

In this book, I'll try to steer you through the cacophony and confusion by teaching you what questions to ask. I've avoided item-by-item reviews of high-tech gear, charts comparing the weight of one tent to another, and detailed descriptions of insoles, outsoles, and midsoles of hiking boots. That information is readily available from retailers and magazines, and, by the time you read this, a new generation of gear will be on the market.

Instead, the information I give you will be helpful even if you're looking at a piece of gear that hadn't been invented at the time this book was published. How do you assess your needs? What different kinds of products are available to meet those needs?

can be expensive, but you don't have to buy everything all at the same time. And once you have your gear, a backpacking trip is one of the cheapest vacations you can take: There's nothing to spend money on in the woods, and a week's hike may cost no more than your food and your transportation to and from the trailhead!

How Do I Know What I Need? You can check out a couple of magazines, go to an outfitter, or ask a hiker friend. Don't be surprised or alarmed if you get four different answers. If you ask thirty more people, you may get thirty more opinions! But that's a good thing:

End of a day of trekking: equal parts exhaustion and accomplishment.

Starlight over Thousand Island Lake and Ritter Peak, Sierra National Forest, California's Sierra Nevadas.

What can and should you expect gear to do for you? What is the minimum you need to take with you to be safe and comfortable?

Finally, I answer the questions most often asked when my husband, Dan, and I give lectures on back-packing or when we take new back-packers into the woods — not only about gear, but about safety, first aid, minimum-impact camping, navigation, animals, food, and a host of other issues. For those who want further detail, the Sources and Resources section at the back of the book will tell you where to go for information on everything from maps to winter camping to first aid.

Remember: Any place is within walking distance if you have enough time. Happy trails!

DID YOU KNOW

The Appalachian Trail (AT) runs 2,155 miles from Springer Mountain in Georgia to Katahdin in Maine. Each year, 1,200 to 2,000 "through-hikers" attempt to hike the whole thing. Only about 200 finish. The journey takes an average of 6 months. Hikers who complete it will have taken some 5 million steps and climbed up (and down) 470,000 feet. The AT is located an easy drive from most of the major cities in the East, from Atlanta to Boston. It is estimated that about 4 million people hike on some part of the AT every year.

LEARNING TO WALK

There's a reason that the exercise gurus tout walking as one of the best ways to achieve cardiovascular fitness. Assuming a respectable pace, plain old walking—whether around the block, in a park, or even in a shopping mall—is an extremely effective way to build both strength and fitness. Add a pack and a hill, throw in some rocks and roots, and you have yourself a workout every bit as demanding as a class at your local gym.

Novices are sometimes surprised to find their bodies voicing initial objections to the demands of backpacking. The heart beats faster; the lungs work overtime to meet the body's need for more and more oxygen; unused muscles strain as they ascend and descend on unfamiliar terrain.

But there's no reason to be discouraged. Backpacking may pose physical challenges, but for the most part, those challenges are well within the average person's ability to achieve. Grandmothers and grandfathers have walked the entire length of the Appalachian Trail; so have teenagers and children, men and women of all levels of fitness, and even a few handicapped people. My friend Sue Lockwood, forty-nine, is a diabetic. She's on dialysis, she's lost a couple of toes to circulation problems associated with her illness, and she is legally blind. Assisted by her

Terrain that is unpleasant for hikers may provide good habitat for wildlife. Take bogs and swamps. Not only do they perform vital functions for the ecosystem — by purifying water, mitigating flood damage, and recharging groundwater supplies — they also provide feeding and breeding grounds for birds.

You may think that those puncheons — the boardwalks that sometimes traverse bogs — are there for your benefit, but it's more likely that they were put in place to protect the fragile bog vegetation from hikers' bootprints.

brother, Gordon, and her leader dog, Mac, Sue hikes an average of 1,000 miles a summer, but last summer she did a little more. Sue just sent me a postcard from the Northcountry Trail, which runs from New York to South Dakota. The message: "I did it! 2,000 miles! And still going."

THINK POSITIVE!

The first strategy isn't physical at all. It's mental. In fact, many experienced backpackers think that the key to enjoying their sport is as much a matter of attitude as it is a matter of physical strength. The secret lies in learning to deal with — and enjoy — the challenges.

Backpackers who have mastered the art of living comfortably in the wilderness learn to expect the unexpected. They accept the fact that not everything will be easy, or convenient, or fun, or predictable.

They expect to work for a ridgeline or a summit, and they enjoy the feeling of muscles that strain. They know that a view is better when it is earned, and that the experience of climbing a mountain to reach the summit will be different — more intense, more rewarding, more memorable — than the experience of someone who has taken an automobile or a ski lift or a snowmobile to the top.

They also accept that certain things are beyond their control: the weather, the trail conditions, the climbs that the guidebook didn't warn them about. They remember that it's the adventures that make the best stories — including the empty water sources and the week of nonstop rain and the bear that scared them at three o'clock in the morning. They know that there is pleasure in coping with adversity, in gaining confidence in skills and judgment, in being able to say, "I can do that!" They know that the key to getting somewhere is simply to keep going — no matter how slowly.

Backpacking is indeed for everyone, whether fit or fat, couch potato or marathon runner, young or old or somewhere in between. All it

The enjoyment of hiking is at least as much a matter of attitude as it is a matter of physical health.

takes is a desire to try and an openness to new experiences. A sense of humor doesn't hurt. And neither does a little preparation.

BEFORE YOU GO: THE 50-MILE RULE

One of the questions that I am almost invariably asked about backpacking is, "Aren't you afraid?" Generally, people have something specific in mind when they ask the question, and generally, it's something on the order of snakes, bears, or criminals. I'm not particularly afraid of snakes; in most parts of the United States, bears are more of a

66 It's not really walking, is it? Not those first few days. I mean, I certainly wasn't walking; I was lurching from tree to tree. 99

— Edward Mayson, age 54, Ripon, England, on the beginning of his 2,150-mile hike of the Appalachian Trail

nuisance than a threat; and I've never met a criminal in the woods. But for a

A walking stick can save your back, knees, and legs.

DID YOU KNOW

Two Views on Hiking Sticks

According to Leki, a company that manufactures adjustable, shock-absorbing hiking sticks, medical studies have shown that using two hiking sticks results in 250 tons of pressure being transferred from the back, knees, and legs to the arms during an 8-hour hiking day.

But in *The Theory of the Leisure Class*, Thorstein Veblen expounds a different idea: "The walking stick serves the purpose of an advertisement that the bearer's hands are employed otherwise than in useful effort and it therefore has utility as an evidence of leisure."

long time, I was very, very afraid of blisters.

In most cases, fear is founded on the unknown, but in my case, the opposite was true: My fear came from a long and intimate acquaintance. I didn't have to suffer alone. Few are the backpackers who have never opened a package of moleskin: Blisters are probably the number-one cause of backcountry misery. They are not, however, inevitable.

Harden Feet, Soften Boots

The most common cause of blisters is the introduction of tender feet to boots that are brand-spanking new. The trick: to harden feet and soften boots before beginning your hike. When Dan and I invite new hikers to join us for a

backpacking trip, we suggest (some would say we insist) that they put 50 miles on their boots before they show up at the trailhead. The 50-mile rule achieves two important goals. First, it ensures that boots are broken in and that any foot-related problems are identified and corrected. Second, by walking 50 miles, you give your muscles a chance to adjust to a new level of activity.

Fifty miles? Isn't that a lot? After all, this is your recreation, and you don't want to turn it into a chore. Besides, you just bought some of those new, ultra-light hiking boots — the kind you don't have to break in.

Maybe it *is* extreme. I can only point to the results: Neither Dan nor I got a single blister on the entire Appalachian Trail, and most of our novice friends who follow this rule don't get blisters, either. As for boots that don't need breaking in: Just remember that they fit differently and feel different in your living room than they do on the trail. If you need further convincing, ask your fellow hikers whether they've ever gotten blisters from a new pair of lightweights.

Breaking in your boots doesn't have to be a chore: quite the opposite. There's no need to walk 50 miles on pavement to prepare for a leisurely 15-mile loop trail! Take a few weekend dayhikes and the job is done. At home, wear your boots around your neighborhood, mowing the lawn, or going to the store. You can even go on short overnights. Just be sure that your boots are well broken in before you go out for anything longer than a weekend.

Conditioning

Backpackers often say that the best way to get ready to walk up a mountain with a pack is to put on a pack and walk up a mountain. What if your neighborhood lacks a mountain? Don't worry: There are plenty of things you can do to get in shape. Climbing stairs is excellent preparation, and convenient, too: You can do it in your home. I try and work up to 100 flights at a

> 66 Physical combat for the means of subsistence was, for unnumbered centuries, an economic fact. When it disappeared as such, a sound instinct led us to preserve it in the form of athletic sports and games.... Public wilderness areas are, first of all, a means of perpetuating in sport form, the more virile and primitive skills in pioneering travel and subsistence. 99
>
> — Aldo Leopold
> *A Sand County Almanac*

time before a hike. If that's too easy for you, add ankle weights. Or more flights. If 100 flights seems like an impossible goal, start with 20. Or 10. Jogging is good. So is riding a bike. Or aerobics. If you have a regular exercise program, stick with it. Just don't forget those 50 miles of walking.

The "harder" your break-in miles, the better. Trails are better than pavement, hills are better still. If you can, carry a backpack and wear the clothes you intend to take on your hike. That way, you can check for problems such as chafing, rubbing seams, or a poor fit. If you're going to rent or borrow a pack and don't have access to one, carry a daypack and stuff it with telephone books to get used to the feel of lugging a few pounds on your back. I live in suburban New York, and the

Blisters demand attention. If you ignore them, you will pay dearly later. Always carry a blister kit, even on dayhikes.

kids in my neighborhood get a kick out of following me around asking, "Are you going to sleep in the woods?" Their parents may be more reserved, but they're no less curious: As I tromp past each house, I'm greeted by a series of pulled-back curtains and inquisitive, not to say suspicious, stares.

A hint: You want to avoid blisters during your breaking-in period just as much as you want to avoid them on the trail. I carry a blister kit and a pair of running shoes with me when I'm breaking in boots. That way, if I'm far from home, I can treat the blister and, if necessary, change shoes.

GETTING READY

● Put 50 miles on your boots and make sure they are comfortable.
● Check to make sure the clothing you intend to take fits without chafing or rubbing.
● Carry a daypack around to get used to the weight.
● Continue your regular exercise routine. If you don't have one, why not start now?

ON BLISTERS

Once you hit the trail — in your no-longer-brand-new boots — you'll want to pay particular attention to your feet. After all, you're in the backcountry now, and you're going to have to get out the way you came in — on foot. Blisters happen fast, but they do give you a warning. If you feel a hot spot, stop immediately. Don't worry about holding up your hiking partners. A short break to check your feet is far preferable to limping around on blisters, or cutting your hike short — or maybe even having to be evacuated. (It happens.) You're doing everyone a favor by taking care of the problem before it begins.

If, despite all your painstaking attention to your feet, you find a blister, don't panic. First aid treatments make it possible to walk on blisters, in varying degrees of comfort. But don't try to tough it out: Blisters demand attention, and if you ignore them now, they will make you pay dearly later.

First, pierce the blister with a sterile needle (you can hold it to a flame or douse it in rubbing alcohol) and then disinfect it. I use rubbing alcohol and an antibiotic ointment.

Then cover the blister so it can heal. Different people have different

BLISTER-BUSTING TIPS

❶ Make sure your boots fit properly and are broken in.

❷ Treat leather boots with saddle soap, mink oil, or a compound recommended by the manufacturer.

❸ Wear sock liners (do not use cotton; instead, use a wicking fabric like polypropylene or Thermax that moves the moisture away from your skin) and heavy, well-cushioned wool socks. It's best to buy a brand made especially for hiking. Thorlos are popular among long-distance hikers.

❹ If you have a habitual blister spot (the back of the heels is a common one), put a piece of medicine tape or moleskin over it before you even start walking.

❺ Pay attention! If there is any rubbing or soreness, STOP. Don't wait to see if your sock will rearrange itself. It won't. Don't tough it out till lunch. You can't. Don't say, "Maybe this won't turn into a blister." If you don't stop, it will.

❻ Check for the problem. Shake out socks and boots. Make sure the sock isn't folded or creased. Make sure toenails are pared.

❼ If there is any visible irritation, even if it's just a tiny red spot, treat it immediately. I cover the irritation with medicine tape. Some people prefer moleskin or even duct tape.

❽ If the hot spot is very red, or wrinkled, or if the skin has broken, treat it like a blister (see above).

❾ Keep your feet dry. Change socks if necessary. Use gaiters to keep water (and pebbles) out of your boots. In heavy rain, put adhesive tape on both heels before you start walking. Even well-broken-in feet are prone to blister in very wet weather.

❿ Go easy on the mileage.

strategies. Some cover the blister with gauze or a Band-Aid, then cut a hole in a piece of moleskin. Moleskin is adhesive on one side, to stick to your skin, and padded on the other, to provide a cushioning layer between your skin and whatever is irritating it. Molefoam is a thicker variation. The hole goes over the blister. This relieves pressure on the injured area and ensures that the adhesive doesn't stick to it. Some people put another piece of moleskin — without a hole — over the first one for added padding. Band-Aids can be used for blisters on toes.

My own favorite treatment is a product called Second Skin, which is made by Spenco. As far as I'm concerned, it's a miracle product: It relieves the pain of a blister, it helps it heal — and you can walk in reasonable comfort while all this is going on! I must admit, I'm somewhat of a zealot on the subject, but like I said: I've had a long and intimate acquaintance with blisters. Second Skin looks like a thin section of jellyfish, and it works on the theory that a blister is your body's way of protecting itself from an irritation. The Second Skin takes on the function of the blister by acting as a moist cushion; this allows your skin to heal without having to form its own blister. Put the Second Skin directly on the blister or hot spot, then cover it with tape, making sure that all sides of the tape firmly adhere to your skin. Note that medicine tape or moleskin adheres better than the tape provided by Spenco. Unlike moleskin, you'll need to remove this dressing every

> *Now away we go toward the topmost mountains. Many still, small voices, as well as the noon thunder, are calling, 'Come higher, come higher.' Farewell, blessed dell, woods, gardens, streams, birds, squirrels, lizards, and a thousand others. Farewell, farewell.*
>
> — John Muir
> *My First Summer in the Sierra*

night and reapply it every morning. Second Skin is available at most outfitters. Your local pharmacy probably carries Spenco products, so even if they don't have Second Skin, they can probably order it for you.

Warning: Do not hike without an adequate blister kit! When you start out, take moleskin and Second Skin and adhesive tape — even on a day-hike.

MILEAGE

No one ever came into camp crying because the day's hike was too easy. Unfortunately, the opposite happens all the time. Far too often, we cityfolk forget how long a country mile can be.

All miles are not created equal.

City jogging miles are different from uphill-with-a-pack trail miles. Hot desert miles are different from icy mountain miles. Uphill miles are dif-

THE MILEAGE-ELEVATION CONNECTION

How many miles should you plan to hike in a day? That depends on (1) the kind of miles and (2) how hard you want to work. This chart rates the difficulty of different combinations of mileage and elevation. (See Chapter 10 for how to use maps and guidebooks to figure elevation gain.)

LEVEL 1: A couple of days like this will help you break in in comfort.

LEVEL 2: Faster hikers should bring a book — they'll be done by midafternoon. If you're a little slower, don't worry: You'll be in camp in plenty of time for dinner. If you've adhered to the 50-mile rule, you can start at this level.

LEVEL 3: Veteran hikers find this range a nice balance for smelling the flowers while covering some distance. Newer hikers can do the mileage without hating themselves for overreaching — once they are in shape. But you'll want to break in at Level 1 or 2 before you start covering this kind of distance.

LEVEL 4: You're not a fanatic, but you are in good aerobic shape. You don't mind pushing a bit. You don't smell too many flowers.

LEVEL 5: No lollygagging for you. You're a serious backpacker, a regular exerciser, and you're broken in to the trail. Make sure you know what you're getting into: These kinds of days aren't for everyone.

LEVEL 6: You are a marathon runner, a long-distance hiker, or a masochist. Maybe all three.

ELEVATION GAIN (FEET)	Less than 8	8–10	11–13	14–17	More than 17
Less than 1,000	1	1	2	3	4
1,000–2,000	1	2	3	4	4
2,000–3,000	2	3	3	4	5
3,000–4,000	3	4	4	5	5
4,000–5,000	4	5	5	6	6
More than 5,000	5	5	6	6	6

ferent from downhill miles. Miles at the beginning of the day are different from miles at the end of the day. My miles are different from your miles.

It's possible to become obsessed with miles: How many can you do, how far have you come, how fast can you go — especially in our overly competitive, numbers-oriented society.

But backpacking is not about competition or numbers, and mileage is a subject that is best approached slowly, with caution. A long-distance backpacker who has been out on the trail for a couple of months may be doing 20 miles a day by three in the afternoon. That does not mean that you should plan to do 20 miles a day — not at first, anyway. In fact, you should decidedly not plan to do 20 miles a day.

Pacing Yourself

First, you need to get used to what a mile feels like for you. You need to learn how your body will react under different conditions: On a strenuous climb. Carrying a pack. Going downhill. Each of us has a pace that feels right for us: a pace that we can sustain over a long period of time. You'll need to learn what yours is. Do you climb easily? Do your knees hurt going downhill? Do you get tired in the middle of the afternoon? Do you get stiff after a long break? Do you prefer to climb first thing in the morning, or do you like to warm up for a while? Before you start worrying about miles, you need to reacquaint yourself with your body and find out what it has to say about the subject.

Still, in order to plan a hike, you need to have some basic idea of the distance you'll be covering. For some people, 5 miles a day might be more than enough; others might be able to handle 15. For me, 8–10 miles on moderate terrain is quite enough for the first two or three days. After a

couple of days to break in, most people can manage 10–12 miles a day on average terrain. (Warning: "Average terrain" is another term that means different things to different people. For this purpose, let's assume good footway and a total elevation gain of not more than 2,000 feet.) If you're very fit, you'll be able to handle longer distances and bigger climbs.

They say in a marathon that for every minute too fast you go out, you lose two minutes coming in. The idea applies to hiking: Too much mileage too early in your hike will leave you

Grade (in this case steep) and *footway* (in this case slippery) determine *pace* (in this case SLOW).

stiff and sore, as well as more susceptible to blisters and injuries. Start
slow! Give yourself some leeway on
your first couple of trips. Rein in your
initial enthusiasm a bit. You'll soon
learn what feels right. And remember:
This is not a race!

UPS AND DOWNS

Like mileage, all elevation gain is not
equal.

Two factors — grade and footway
— determine whether you jog uphill
with barely a huff or you struggle with
lungs aflame, face red from exertion,
and buckets of sweat pouring from
places you didn't even know perspired.

Grade is a measure of steepness:
how many feet you're going up divided
by how many feet you're going forward.
If you climb 264 feet in a mile (a mile

being 5,280 feet; feel free to round
off), you are climbing 264 feet up
divided by 5,280 feet forward. That
comes out to 0.05, or a 5 percent
grade, which most people find pretty
comfortable.

Gain 528 feet in a mile and
you're climbing at a 10 percent grade.
Now you're starting to work a little,
although once you get the hang of it,
you'll find that it's fairly easy to sustain a comfortable pace. Most national
parks try, whenever possible, to keep
their trails graded at 10 percent or
less.

If you're not huffing and puffing
yet, don't worry: You soon will be if the
grade gets any steeper! Grades of up to
15 percent are not uncommon, and if
you hike long enough over enough different terrain, you'll run into your fair
share of 20 percent climbs as well.

More than 20 percent (that works out to a little more than 1,000 feet of elevation gain in 1 mile) and you're likely to be hauling yourself up with your hands! You'll also slow down: If I'm climbing about 1,000 feet per mile, my pace drops to about a mile an hour.

Footway is the second factor. Trails in some areas — Shenandoah and Rocky Mountain National Parks come to mind — are so clear that you can virtually jog on them with barely a glance at your feet. The hiker glides along, taking in the view, striding without concern for protrusions and protuberances. This is not, however, typical. Far more commonly, the hiker's most memorable view is the front of his boots, and if he sneaks a glance now and then at the scenery, he should be prepared for a quick and brutal encounter with rocks, roots, stumps, and mudholes. In extreme cases — the White Mountains of New Hampshire and the Mahoosucs of Maine being cases in point and extreme indeed — the hiker resigns himself to the fact that his main concern is staying upright. Here, the walking turns to scrambling: over, around, and sometimes under boulders; down slippery slopes of rock and

FIGURING SPEED

"How long will it take to get there?" is a question you'll want to know how to answer, if only to plan your lunch stops or to reassure yourself that you have plenty of time to reach your intended campsite. To guess accurately, you'll need to know both the mileage and the approximate elevation gain. Most guidebook authors suggest that hikers figure their average walking pace at 2 miles per hour plus 1 hour for each 1,000 feet of vertical gain.

Let's apply the formula to see how long it will take us to climb a modest mountain — say, a 4-mile ascent with a total elevation gain of 1,500 feet.

MILES ÷ MILES PER HOUR =
HOURS FOR MILEAGE
$4 \div 2 = 2$ hours

ELEVATION ÷ 1,000 =
HOURS FOR ELEVATION
$1,500 \div 1,000 = 1.5$ hours

Then we add the two together for an estimated hiking time of $3^{1}/_{2}$ hours.

Remember, this is only a guideline! I find the formula a little conservative; experience tells me that once I'm in condition, I'll probably get to the top in just under 3 hours. Some very strong hikers can sustain a 2-mile-per-hour pace or more going uphill. You'll soon find how close you are to the standard and adjust your planning accordingly.

mud and back up the same. It seems merely obvious that such terrain requires more time to traverse.

The Rest Step

You can't control the grade or the footway of a mountain. But you can control the way you approach them. The key to hiking comfortably is finding a pace that you can sustain all day — even going uphill.

Yes, there is such a thing! You don't have to gasp for air, or lurch from tree to tree, or count 50 steps and then stop to catch your breath. There is an easy way up. It's called the rest step, and once you master the basics, you'll find that you can walk uphill for hours.

The rest step is a rhythmic combination of breathing, walking, and resting. It's slow going, but there's nothing wrong with slow. Forward motion is your goal, and as long as you're moving constantly, comfortably forward you'll get where you're going.

Here's how the rest step works. Try it on a stairway to get the idea. 1) Your right leg moves forward and up, with weight still on your left (downhill) leg. 2) As your weight is fully transferred to your right (uphill) leg, lock your right knee, momentarily transferring weight from your muscles to your skeleton. While the right knee is locked, forward motion is briefly interrupted. Your left leg dangles behind. The toe of your left boot can just touch the ground for balance, if needed, but it isn't bearing any weight. 3) The left leg moves forward and up

to repeat the sequence, this time with the left knee locking as weight is transferred to the left leg. The right leg dangles behind.

Endurance — comfortable, sustained endurance — is what it's about. "Sustained endurance" may sound like a redundancy but endurance nowadays is a word too often associated with gonzo types who "push the edge of the envelope," "go to the limit," and "survive extremes." You know the type.

Tell your faster hiking partner to go on without you and wait at the top.

Don't worry if people pass you. Don't be intimidated if those descending tell you that you're in for a tough climb: Their downhill perspective is different from your uphill one, and everyone has a different definition of difficult. Above all, find a pace you can sustain and stick with it.

The secret of the rest step is that temporary halt in forward motion and with your stepping. I sometimes find myself humming a waltz to the three-part rhythm of the rest step: Step-lock-pause; step-lock-pause; breathe-two-three; breath-two-three. Experiment with what keeps you moving forward. On some climbs, you might pause for a rest with every step; on others, you might stop once every three steps, or five, or seven. (Using

The key to hiking comfortably is finding a pace that you can sustain all day — even going uphill.

the transfer of weight from muscle system to skeletal system. It's akin to the rest between beats that gives the heart its endurance. Your muscles get a chance to rest; you get a chance to catch your breath. On gentle slopes, the rest step may be only a split second long. On steeper slopes, you may want to coordinate your breathing odd numbers to count paces means you'll be resting both legs equally.) Once you get used to this new technique, you'll probably find that you need to stop less frequently to sit down and recuperate.

Thinking about Climbing

Climbing comfortably is a matter of

practice and attitude as much as it is of strength and fitness. Sure, fitness helps. But even a fit person is going to be a miserable hiker if all he thinks about is getting somewhere (that is, the top) other than where he is (that is, the bottom). The point of a hike is to enjoy vertical world. Look for the changing plant life, the lichen and mosses and especially the alpine krummholz (or "crooked trees") that eke out a precarious existence on wind-tossed ridges. Stop for views. Or blueberries. Don't worry about where the top of the

The boardwalks that traverse wetlands are there primarily to protect bog plants from hikers' boots. They also are a reminder to slow down.

it. That may seem an unreachable goal on your first 3,000-foot ascent, but after a while, you'll know how to ration your energy and — equally important — you'll have confidence in your ability to keep going. Your body will actually learn how to climb. But in the meantime, there's no need to psych yourself out. Take time to look around and appreciate the terrain of your new mountain is: All you have to do is keep going and you'll get there.

As one hiker said, "Is the point of a piece of music to get to the end?"

Descending

Walking downhill is, for many hikers, more demanding than walking uphill. This is particularly true on very steep slopes, especially if you have bad (or complaining) knees. Going downhill too fast and jumping over obstacles — especially if you are carrying a pack — can actually damage your knees. You're also more susceptible to ankle sprains on tough downhill terrain because gravity is pulling you down faster than you want to go.

The best downhill trick I know is to use a walking stick or a ski pole — or better yet, two. Taking a big step down puts strain on your knees, but with two sticks, you can plant the poles ahead of you and take some of the weight of the descent in your arms. It's a real knee-saver.

CROSSING RIVERS

Fording rivers and streams causes a lot of unnecessary worry among hikers. Most fords on most trails are short and shallow; those that aren't are often spanned by bridges. If you're going to more remote areas or off-trail, you may have to negotiate your way across something a little deeper and faster flowing.

Rock hopping is an option if you're crossing small creeks with big rocks, but if the water is more than shin deep, chances are that there won't be enough rocks, or the rocks will be covered with slippery mosses. So first things first: Accept the fact that you're going to get your feet wet. And maybe your boots, too.

WHAT TO WEAR. If you have to ford, you'll need something on your feet. Crossing barefoot is a bad idea. Even a placid, sandy streambed can harbor a

DID YOU KNOW
That many trails in the supposedly gentle mountains of the East are actually much more difficult than the high-elevation trails of the Rocky Mountains and the Pacific Coast ranges? How is it possible that a modest bump of 3,000 feet can be more difficult than a 13,000-foot peak?

Many of the western trails were built with stock animals in mind, so they switchback gently up the mountains on good footway. In the East, many trails were built before the idea of switchbacking was understood. Today, switch-backing is a luxury: The land available to an eastern hiking trail may be only a narrow cor-ridor, so the trail is forced to go straight up and straight down. More than one Coloradan has had to swallow his pride on an Appalachian mountain.

hidden rock or two, and a sprained ankle or a bad cut on your foot is much more serious on the trail than at home. Amphibious sport sandals give adequate protection — most of the time — and they dry out easily. Sneakers take much longer to dry, but they give even better protection. Some

On heavily used trails in the East, mud will as likely slow you down as steep climbs and descents.

people prefer to wear their boots if the water is deep and they can't see the bottom. If the crossing is very rocky, this is probably the safest way — except in very cold weather, when wet boots are downright painful. If you do cross in your boots, take off your socks first so at least something will be dry when you reach the other side.

PICKING A ROUTE. Pick the widest area; a narrow channel is generally much deeper. If the current is relatively fast, head downstream and across; if that's not possible, angle upstream. Going straight across leaves you most vulnerable to the current. Unfasten your pack's waist belt so that if you do fall in, you can extricate yourself quickly. And use a ski pole or walking stick to help you balance. Better yet, use two.

6 6 Some of those mountains down south—I start climbing them and after a while I wonder if I'm ever going to get to the top. But then I make it, and I think, Wow! I did this! I can still do this! 9 9

— Verna Soule,
age 70,
Michigan Center, Michigan,
long-distance hiker, trail volunteer, and great-grandmother

G E A R
What to Wear

ore-Tex, Synchilla, Capilene, Thermax, Hollofil, Lite Loft, Ultrex, polypropylene, and Thermolactyl. When you start looking at outdoor clothing, you might think you've taken a wrong turn and ended up in a graduate chemistry class.

There's no doubt that the good old days were simpler. The old-time mountain men took to the woods without a thought of whether their fibers were hydrophilic or hydrophobic. Their shirts were made of wool (and so were their underwear, hats, pants, and sweaters), not petrochemicals, Teflon, or recycled soda bottles. Even Himalayan mountaineers wore wool and tweed.

But if the good old days were simpler, they were also wetter, heavier, colder, harder — and a lot less fun. You, on the other hand, will be drier and warmer; your pack will be lighter and your mileage easier — all thanks to the technology of fabrics and fibers you can't even pronounce. The trade-off is this: At first, you might be a little confused.

It doesn't help matters that everything looks so attractive. Outdoor equipment has shed its old image of functional drab for trendy colors and sophisticated designs. No lumberjack plaids here! It is easy to be seduced when confronted with a cacophonous array of sleek, trendy gear shouting BUY ME!

But before you buy any piece of

equipment, remember: As a backpacker, you are a throwback to another era, one in which "need" was still sandwiched somewhere in the equation between "want" and "have." Over and over again, as you look through the clothes and the tents and the sleeping bags and the stoves and all their attendant accessories — the color-coordinated bags and pouches and kits and sets, the polypropylene, the Capilene, the pile and the fleece — ask yourself:

"Do I really *need* this?"

"Can I do without it?"

"Is it worth the weight?"

"Is there anything else I could use instead?"

Because if there is a single eternal, inviolable law of backpacking, it is this: If you buy it, you are going to have to carry it.

Technotalk notwithstanding, you don't need a Ph.D. in organic chemistry to buy backpacking gear. To choose the right gear, you simply have to understand what function each piece of equipment must perform. You may occasionally need to understand some basic distinctions between fabrics and between materials. But remember: Gear is a means to an end. And that end is the safe enjoyment of hiking and backpacking.

Finally, there is no single right answer, no one way to dress or walk or pack a pack. The more you talk to other backpackers, the more you will realize that everyone is different; one person's necessity may be another

Having the right clothing at the right moment means comfort for you and your loved ones. Gore-Tex or other breathable, waterproof fabric is the best answer to rain.

The right gear is a means to an end: the safe enjoyment of the outdoors.

from here to there has always been a matter for comparison and often-heated debate. People like to talk about their transportation: I wouldn't be at all surprised to learn that the Romans compared their chariots ("Hey, Tiberius, look at this baby! Only used on Sundays to get to the Colosseum...").

Modest though they are, feet are the backpacker's wheels, his hooves, his chariot, his wings. It's our feet that do our drudge work, step after step after step. It's our feet that take us where we want to go, and the backpacker who doesn't show respect for his feet is in for a rough journey indeed. Nothing can make a hiker more miserable than ill-fitting boots. And nothing so clearly marks the neophyte as a foot bandaged from heel to toe in moleskin, or the tentative, painful gait of a person whose feet have come up lame.

Finding the right pair of boots is easily the most important decision a backpacker makes. But it is easier said than done.

person's luxury. Furthermore, your opinions about gear and clothing will change with experience, with time, and with new technology. While the number of choices and the divergence of opinion might seem confusing at the start, take heart: It also means that there are many solutions to the challenge of traveling comfortably through the wilderness. Many of them will be right for you.

BOOTS

Automobile, train, plane, horseflesh, hansom, or carriage; whatever the century or the technology, the way we get

Carrying a fully loaded pack over tough, rocky terrain calls for sturdy, midweight hiking boots.

Lighter Is Better

As in all else in backpacking, the rule "the lighter the better" applies to boots. The old saying has it that a pound on your feet is equal to five on your back, and while you might quibble about the exact proportions, you can't take issue with the basic principle: A heavier boot takes more energy to lift.

How much more energy? Multiply the pounds per boot by the number of steps taken in the average hiking day (10 miles would be roughly 20,000 steps) and the issue of weight takes on a whole new meaning.

But wait! Don't cross boots off your list and run off to buy sneakers or sport sandals. While it's true that a few iconoclasts insist on hiking long distances shod only in sneakers or sandals, the overwhelming majority of backpackers find that they need the support of a proper hiking boot. The woods are an unfriendly place for unprotected feet. You need the traction of a decent sole, you need support for your ankles and arches, and you need something to absorb the impact of roots and rocks. For a short hike on easy terrain (especially dry, easy terrain), by all means, wear your running shoes. But if you're going into the backcountry for any length of time (and more important, any distance), boots ought to be your first major purchase.

Types of Boots

All-purpose hiking boots generally fall into three categories, which can be conveniently differentiated by weight. But note that not even the manufacturers agree about exactly when a lightweight boot becomes hefty enough to move into the midweight category, or when a midweight boot becomes a heavyweight boot. Think of the lightweight/heavyweight issue as a continuum; the weight breakpoints given below are approximations.

HEAVYWEIGHTS (More than 4 Pounds for the Pair). They're the waffle-stomping clodhoppers of yesteryear, which are still on the market to the delight of their stubbornly loyal devotees. These boots can be purchased ready-made, or they can be custom-made by specialty bootmakers. The heavyweights have several advantages. First, they last virtually forever, which is a reassuring thing in the back-country, where a defective boot is far less welcome than a flat tire (you're not carrying a spare). Second, they offer unparalleled protection on rough or rocky terrain. And third, if you opt for custom-made boots, you can rest assured that you have the best fit possible.

But their disadvantages outweigh their advantages, the most obvious of

DID YOU KNOW
The word *mile* derives from the Latin word *mille*, meaning "thousand," and refers to the fact that the Romans counted a thousand double paces to the mile. This is still a fairly good measure of steps to the mile, at least on flat ground.

which is that these boots are simply too heavy. Concomitant with their weight is the fact that they are notoriously difficult to break in: I've known hikers who had to walk more than 200 trail miles before their boots and their feet finally came to a truce. (No exaggeration, I promise.) Finally, consider the environmental impact: Studies have shown that the heavier the boot, the more it crushes vegetation and

The terrain you plan to hike should define which style of boot you purchase. From left: a heavyweight (more than 4 pounds); a midweight (2³/₄–4 pounds); and a lightweight (less than 2³/₄ pounds).

contributes to trail erosion.

The bottom line: Heavyweights are more boot than most of us, and especially the beginner, will ever need.

LIGHTWEIGHTS (Less than 2³/₄ Pounds for the Pair). Lightweights just keep getting better and better. Generally made of a combination of fabric and leather, with or without a waterproof liner (generally Gore-Tex, which is both waterproof and breathable), lightweight boots combine the support of a hiking boot with the comfort of a running shoe. The boots break in much more quickly than their overweight cousins, and they are less likely to cause blisters. (But view with suspicion any claim by a manufacturer or retailer that the boots don't require breaking in. Even if they don't, your feet do.)

The right boots (properly broken in) let your feet take you where you want to go *without* blisters.

This category contains the most variety and requires the most caution, because not all lightweight boots stand up to rugged terrain. Lightweight boots can cost as little as $35 and as much as $200. Your choice depends on where you'll be hiking and what you expect the boot to do. I hiked 1,000 miles of southwestern desert on a pair of $75 Nike boots that weighed about 2 pounds for the pair. I got no blisters, my feet stayed cool, and the boots were light, comfortable, and — somewhat to my surprise — didn't fall apart under what most manufacturers would call prolonged abuse. Such boots are perfect for places like the High Sierra in California or Utah's canyon country where the trail is smooth and the weather is dry. They'd be a disaster in

Vermont in the spring, when frequent heavy rains turn woodland trails into rivers of mud. (Among other things, wet boots take forever to dry.) However, if you are hiking in dry places, or if you are going out only for a weekend and plan to bail out if the weather is bad, or if you are mainly interested in dayhiking, inexpensive lightweight boots are certainly a viable choice.

If you plan to do more extensive trips and don't want to be limited by your footwear, consider a high-quality lightweight boot with a Gore-Tex liner. More expensive than their non-waterproof cousins, these boots have become increasingly popular among hikers of all levels of experience. A pair of Vasque Skywalker IIs can last 1,000 miles or more, even under heavy use on tough terrain. A couple of disadvantages of lightweight boots: Most models cannot be resoled, and they can't be used with crampons, little icepick-like wedges that strap onto the soles of your boots for extended walking on snow and ice. If you need a lot of ankle support, or are hiking off-trail on scree or boulder fields, you may find them a little flimsy.

MIDWEIGHTS ($2^3/_4$–4 Pounds for the Pair). Midweights, of course, are the compromise, combining characteristics of the old wafflestompers and the new lightweights. For many backpackers, it's the perfect compromise. Midweights are generally all-leather, resoleable, and waterproof, but without quite as much heft as their heavyweight predecessors. On the wet and rocky terrain found in the East, I prefer a midweight boot like Merrell's Wilderness ($3^1/_2$ pounds for the pair), which offers superior support without taking forever to break in. Merrell's Wilderness boots can also be worn with crampons for those of you planning on snow-and-ice hiking. In the West, I prefer lightweights, unless I expect to be hiking in snow. But if you must choose only one pair of boots, midweights are the safest bet; they stand up to all conditions.

Ensuring a Good Fit

"How do they feel?" the sales clerk asks, once I've laced up the boot I've selected to try on. "Like cement blocks," I'm tempted to reply.

"Walk around and try them out," the clerk suggests. But 10 minutes in the store, while decidedly better than no minutes in the store, isn't the same as 10 minutes on the trail, much less 10 miles. A boot may be on its best behavior during its trial run through the store's level, carpeted aisles, or

even when put through its paces at home. It's not until 10 miles into the backcountry that the infernal things start to cause trouble.

Some outfitters will actually let you exchange a pair of boots that don't fit, even after they've been worn on the trail. Note, however, that the exchange should take place in relatively short order: after 50 miles, maybe, but certainly not 500. Outfitters' policies vary widely, so ask before you buy.

There are a few things you can do in the store to ensure a good fit. Start by wearing the socks you intend to use when hiking: a pair of liners against

CARING FOR BOOTS

Leather needs care. Like your own skin, it reacts to environmental stress (sun, heat, water, snow, wide swings of humidity and dryness) by drying out and cracking.

Conditioning your boots will lengthen their life. Sample products include silicone water guard, Biwell waterproofing conditioner, liquid Aquaseal, Sno-Seal, saddle soap, mink oil, and neat's-foot oil.

Follow the manufacturer's instructions for care, particularly if they recommend a specific conditioner or waterproofing compound. I know of one company that refused to honor a guarantee on a boot that was treated with a snow-sealing product. Read the instructions!

Even if thoroughly treated and lined with Gore-Tex, no boot is completely waterproof in a downpour, so if it rains for days and days, you'll probably end up with wet feet. Gaiters or rain pants help keep water from leaking in.

Never dry boots by a fire. Never, ever. At best, you will end up with damaged leather. At worst, you will end up with boots burnt to a crisp.

How long your boot soles last depends on how much weight you carry and how rough the terrain is. My experience is that soles generally last somewhere around 1,000 miles. It's best to have the manufacturer do the resoling, although if you're stuck with a boot-gone-bad in an out-of-the-way place, you may have to rely on a local cobbler.

your skin and a pair of midweight or heavy wool or wool/synthetic blend socks (even in summer) over those. Make sure the liners are Thermax or polypropylene, or some other yet-to-be-invented high-tech wicking fabric, which will draw the sweat away from your skin and into the wool socks, leaving your feet pretty dry. Do NOT purchase COTTON liners, which will absorb your sweat and give you blisters. In boot socks, look for a snug fit and smooth toe seams (more blister prevention).

When the boots are unlaced, you should have just enough room so that if you scrunch your toes toward the front, you can squeeze a finger between your heel and the back of the boot. When the boot is laced, there should be little or no heel slippage, but you should be able to wiggle your toes freely. Some stores have a step-and-ramp contraption for trying on boots. Go up the stairs to check the flexibility and down the ramp to make sure your toes don't jam against the front of the boot. Kick the toe box of the boots hard against an obstacle other than the sales clerk's shin. Your toes should not feel the impact. Finally, make sure the boots are wide enough. Many stores carry only medium widths even if wide sizes are available from the manufacturer. A good store will special-order boots for you to try on. (A hint for women with large or wide feet: Try men's boots.) Whatever you do, DON'T compromise on fit!

Camp Shoes

Consider taking along a pair of camp shoes. Some people consider these luxuries, but not me — comfort alone justifies carrying the extra 1 1/2 pounds. At the end of the day, my feet want to be released from prison, and I'm willing to bet yours will, too. Some hikers use sneakers in camp, but by far the most popular choices are sport sandals like those made by Teva and Apo.

Sport sandals can come to the rescue if boot problems or blisters arise, and they are terrific for fording streams, because they dry almost immediately. I don't think much of using them as substitute hiking shoes: I worry about roots, rocks, and

twisting an ankle, and the sandals appear too flimsy to support me and my load. But in an emergency, they definitely come in handy, as I found when my boot soles suddenly and completely delaminated on one of New England's toughest backpacking trails: the ascent of South Kinsman in the White Mountains. The hike is more of a rock scramble than a walk, frequently requiring the hiker to use arms as well as legs. My Apos, much to my surprise, held up for 10 of the most rigorous miles on the Appalachian Trail, and got me safely to a road. I've also used Tevas to scramble 1,000 feet up and down some trailless scree.

CLOTHING

Clothing is the tool you use to regulate your warmth and stay dry. Simple. You need enough of the right kind.

Sport sandals make great camp shoes and are ideal for fording streams. They can also be a life-saver if your boots give out mid-trek.

You don't need to memorize a long list of fabrics that sound like they are made of complex proteins or NASA-designed polymers: By the time you do, they'll be out-of-date. Fabrics change so quickly that by the time I get around to replacing a piece of clothing, it's no longer made, which isn't a problem because yesterday's miracle fibers are often superseded by something lighter and better. But you do need to understand what your clothing must do for you.

The Basic Outfit

For most three-season hikers, the basic outfit consists of a pair of shorts and a T-shirt, a hat, a bandanna, socks, and liners. You might want to try out the shorts before you go because your pack will hold them close to your body and restrict movement. Most hikers end up choosing shorts designed for hiking that have an underwear layer attached. Some hikers prefer modified bicycle shorts (without the seat padding); these prevent painful chafing, a common problem in hot or humid weather. Most hikers do not hike in long pants because in cool weather they generate enough body heat to stay warm, and in cold weather they find that tights or long johns are warmer and more versatile, especially if made of a fabric like Capilene that wicks moisture away from the skin.

In camp, you'll probably want a couple of extra layers, depending on the season and the climate. As night temperatures drop, most hikers put on polypropylene or Capilene long johns and a long-sleeved shirt of the same fabric, and then add layers as needed. On warm nights, I prefer a very lightweight long-sleeved cotton shirt and loose-fitting long nylon pants, which I usually purchase at a department store. Not everything has to be high-tech.

Three-season outfit: loose-fitting shorts and T-shirt. Staying cool can be as important as staying warm.

The Law of Layering

There are precious few rules to backpacking: Layering is one of them. The bottom line: Never bring one heavy item of clothing when two lighter layers can be combined to do the same job.

Layering kicks in when the wind does — or cold or rain. It's the only way to cope with wilderness weather's violent temper and ferocious mood swings. Layering helps you regulate your body heat so that you stay warm without overheating and cool without becoming chilly. It also keeps you warmer than one thick layer because air is trapped (and warmed) in between each layer.

For hikers, the benefits of layering are more numerous than the layers themselves. One heavy layer (a heavy down jacket with an attached waterproof shell, for example) is useful only in truly frigid conditions, and even then, only at night: Most hikers generate so much heat while backpacking that they aren't comfortable walking in a down jacket. But three lighter layers (a light down parka, a separate waterproof shell, and a wool shirt) can be used individually or in combination to help you adjust to changing conditions. By combining various elements of the three layers, you can remain comfortable in temperatures ranging from 60 degrees Fahrenheit to well below freezing.

Dressing from the Inside Out

The bottom layer is the wicking layer; it is made out of a fabric that will pull sweat and condensation away from your skin. Polypropylene was long the standard wicker, despite two draw-

backs: It retains body odor and it melts at relatively low temperatures so it can't be machine-dried. Recently, polypropylene has been supplanted by Capilene, which doesn't retain as much odor and can be put in a clothes dryer. Thermax and Coolmax are other popular wickers.

Wickers come in different thicknesses from silk weight to expedition weight. But remember the basic rule of layering: Two layers are better than one. Even in long underwear, it's wise to use two lighter layers instead of a heavy, expedition layer (unless, of course, you are assaulting Mount Everest). On a recent winter trip, I found Patagonia's expedition-weight Capilene far too heavy for hiking in 20-degree temperatures. Using two lighter layers gave me versatility and allowed me to stay comfortable in a wider range of temperatures. I used a light layer during the day, a heavier one at night, and occasionally both together.

Staying Warm

Over your wicking layer, you'll want to add insulating layers: maybe another, heavier Capilene layer, a wool shirt or sweater, or a pile or fleece jacket. In winter, a down jacket is a good choice, but, following the layering principle, get a lightweight down jacket that is designed to go underneath your rainwear. Also note that down loses its insulating value when wet, so a synthetic fill is the better choice in wet climates. I have a Moonstone synthetic "down" jacket that is almost as lightweight and compressible as down, and it has served me well for several years. Dan, however, prefers a down jacket — although he's careful not to wear it while cooking in the rain. (The same down-versus-synthetic argument goes for sleeping bags.)

Hat Tricks

Your hat is your personal thermostat: Feel cold, add a hat. Feel too hot, take it off. Keeping your head warm is the most important thing you can do to stay warm on a cold day: You lose more heat through your head than through any other part of your body. A balaclava protects your face and neck as well as your head; a hat on top of that will really keep in the heat.

You're unlikely to need two layers of headgear unless you're hiking in winter or at high elevations. But you should always carry one warm hat, no matter what the weatherman says. Look for wool (perhaps lined with polypropylene) or fabrics like Polartec or Synchilla. All are warm and stay that way even when wet. Some hats even have a layer of Gore-Tex sandwiched in between the inner and outer layers.

In hot weather, a lightweight hat protects your head from too much sun. Which kind of head protection to use is entirely a matter of personal preference: I use an inexpensive ultra-light synthetic Australian-style brimmed hat, because I find that the brim discourages bugs. But you'll also see baseball caps, wool caps, felt hats, and bandannas tied in various outlandish ways. Light colors are cooler in the hot sun.

Finally, some hikers like rain hats. Personally, I haven't found them worth the extra weight, especially since there's a perfectly good hood on my rain jacket.

A Word about Cotton

NO. All right, four words about cotton: Leave it at home.

This goes for sweat suits, union suits, blue jeans, and socks. As far as I'm concerned, it even goes for T-shirts, although some veteran backpackers think cotton is ideal for desert hiking. I admit I'm in the minority here. (However, it's a growing minority, as more and more hikers discover the benefits of quick-drying synthetics that don't hold clammy sweat against your skin. REI (Recreational Equipment Incorporated) makes a polyester close-mesh shirt that lasts forever and dries in half an hour on a sunny day. Another option is silk-weight Capilene. Silk itself doesn't stand up well to the rigors and stresses of backpacking. It is, however, warm and an effective wicker, so some people use it for camp wear and sleeping.)

I can think of only two exceptions to the no-cotton rule: First, your bandanna, which can serve a host of functions from emergency bandage to tent mop. Second, a cotton long-sleeved shirt, which is what I carry for camp wear in the summer. But this is a luxury item and not part of my layering system.

The problem with cotton is that when it gets wet, it loses 100 percent of its insulation. Wet clothes wick heat away from your skin — you are better off going naked in a cold rain than wearing wet cotton! Cotton takes longer to dry than synthetics. Cotton socks soak up sweat and then rub, causing blisters. And in cold weather, when a perspiration-soaked sweatshirt freezes into a potential body bag, the word "sweatshirt" takes on new meaning. Instead, look for fabrics that wick away moisture (like Capilene), or fabrics that retain their insulating capacity when wet (like wool, or synthetic pile or fleece). Read every single fabric label.

Rain Gear

The perfect rainwear may be the

The microscopic holes in the Gore-Tex laminate allow tiny perspiration droplets to escape, yet are so small they keep raindrops out.

Polyester or nylon shell

Gore-Tex laminate

Lining

hiker's Holy Grail. Certainly, I've not found it, although the quest may be ending. As synthetic fibers and fabrics improve, manufacturers are coming closer and closer. Even the newest, most expensive fabrics can't entirely overpower Mother Nature when she is in a really foul mood. But if rain gear can't keep you completely dry, it can usually keep you fairly warm and comfortable until you get where you are going.

GORE-TEX. By far the most commonly used fabric for foul-weather gear among serious hikers, Gore-Tex, technically, isn't a fabric at all. Rather, it is a thin laminate that is bonded to one of a variety of tough outer fabrics, usually polyester or nylon. The laminate has microscopic holes: about a billion of them per square inch. Because these holes are smaller than water droplets, the laminate is waterproof. Because these same holes are big enough to let water vapor escape, Gore-Tex is breathable. Sound too good to be true? Some backpackers complain that Gore-

Tex is neither waterproof nor breathable: that sweat and dirt make the laminate less efficient, and that they find themselves drenched with sweat. I've

Cool, wet, windy conditions will drain away your body's warmth unless you dress in several thin layers topped by a breathable, waterproof shell.

had the same problems, but I also remember what we wore before Gore-Tex: coated nylon that was about as breathable as your average plastic bag. I'm a lot warmer, drier, and happier in my Gore-Tex.

The disadvantage of Gore-Tex is its cost, which is high, even for a basic model. If you add extra features like under-arm venting zippers (which help immeasurably with the sweat problem), extra pockets, storm flaps over the zippers, or drawstring closures, you end up with an even higher bill.

OTHER WET-WEATHER CHOICES.
There are several Gore-Tex imitators on the market. When a salesperson tells you that something is "just like Gore-Tex," be sure that you know what you are buying. Sympatex, another breathable/waterproof membrane, is currently Gore-Tex's chief competitor. Other products use polyurethane or fluoropolymer coatings, over a variety of fabrics — nylon, taslan, taffeta, and polyester — and while they are to some extent breathable and waterproof, they tend to be more one than the other; some of them work well only in a narrow range of temperatures. Finally, some brands of rain gear rely on slits for their so-called breathability; they are, in fact, nothing at all like Gore-Tex, and they don't perform particularly well, especially in warm, wet weather. Quiz the salesperson and remember: Gore-Tex is highly engineered and expensive. There is no bargain version available at "a fraction of the price." A deal that looks too good to be true usually is.

On the inexpensive side of the spectrum is coated nylon. It doesn't breathe, but some hikers prefer it, usually because of cost.

Another choice is a poncho, which goes over you and your pack. This is an excellent option when you are hiking in warm wet conditions because

The Law of Layering

Layering in Spring, Summer, and Fall

Layering in Winter

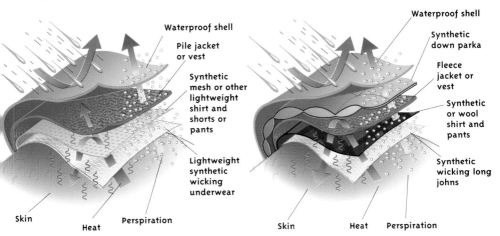

Layering in Spring, Summer, and Fall:
- Waterproof shell
- Pile jacket or vest
- Synthetic mesh or other lightweight shirt and shorts or pants
- Lightweight synthetic wicking underwear
- Skin
- Heat
- Perspiration

Layering in Winter:
- Waterproof shell
- Synthetic down parka
- Fleece jacket or vest
- Synthetic or wool shirt and pants
- Synthetic wicking long johns
- Skin
- Heat
- Perspiration

the skirtlike poncho provides ventilation. But at higher elevations, especially on exposed slopes and ridges, a poncho works less successfully because it flaps around in the wind and it doesn't hold in your body heat. A solution is to combine a poncho with a lightweight, windproof jacket. The poncho is waterproof and breathable; the wind jacket offers a little extra water protection and keeps body heat in. This would be my choice if I didn't use Gore-Tex.

RAIN PANTS. You'll probably want a pair of rain pants in addition to a rain jacket, especially if you're going anywhere where hypothermia could be a problem. In warmer weather, I rarely wear rain pants, but at higher elevations or in cooler temperatures, they keep me dry and, more important, they keep me warm. Rain pants are not necessary if your first few hikes are

summertime walks through lowland forests. They are necessities above treeline.

Whatever decision you make, try the jacket and pants in the store to make sure they are roomy enough to go over a couple of layers of other clothes. Put a pack on over the jacket to make sure you will have adequate mobility around the arms and hood once you're strapped in. Drape the poncho over you and your pack to be sure it covers both.

Dressing for the Highs and Lows

Find out what the average lows and highs are for the time of year you are hiking and dress for the range in between. If you're hiking close to home, this information can be found in your local television or newspaper weather report. The Appalachian Trail

Layering is the only safe way to cope with the weather's violent temper and ferocious mood swings.

Conference provides weather data collected by weather stations near the trail. If you're traveling to another part of the country for your backpacking trip, call a local ranger station, park supervisor's office, BLM office, or airport. Ask what the weather has been like, as well as how cold (or how hot) it can get at that time of year. Remember that record temperatures are frequently broken, and take enough emergency gear so that you would be comfortable if that happened.

Finally, consider altitude. A valley forecast is not valid for a mountaintop, even if it's only a couple of miles away. On average, you lose 3 to 5 degrees for every 1,000 feet you gain in elevation, and that doesn't count the additional effects of wind and rain. You can get hypothermia in August. You can awaken in a desert in June to find ice floating in your water bottle. It snows in Georgia. Always carry one more layer of clothing than you think you need.

GEAR
What to Carry

You may have seen the bumper sticker that declares "He who dies with the most toys wins." That bumper sticker does not belong to a backpacker. A backpacker's bumper sticker would read "He who dies with the *right* toys wins."

Backpackers have a love-hate relationship with gear. They know that with the right sleeping bag, you can doze comfortably when it is 30 below zero; with a good tent, you can stay dry in a downpour. A reliable stove promises that you will always have a hot meal. Good gear can make the difference between comfort and discomfort; between safety and danger. That's the love part.

The hate part is just as simple.

Every piece of gear adds weight to your backpack. It only takes several ounces here and a few pounds there for communing with nature to turn into a battle against gravity. (And it's no accident that the word *gravity* shares its roots with *grave*.) Experienced backpackers know that gear is important. They also know that almost as important as what to put in your backpack is what to leave out.

ASSEMBLING YOUR KIT: BEG, BORROW, RENT, OR BUY

Good backpacking gear is expensive and there is a reason for that: Equipment that can keep you dry in a

There is something liberating about hoisting a pack and knowing that you can go anywhere with what you have on your back.

need to be able to depend on your gear. As far as the expense is concerned, think of it this way: The initial outlay is on the steep side, especially if you're going for the good stuff, but over time (and not very much time, either) your investment will pay off. A backpacking vacation can take you to some of the most dramatic places in the world for little more than the cost of getting there.

Fortunately, you don't have to buy everything all at once. Nor should you, especially if you are just getting started. You don't know what your needs are. You don't know what style of backpacking you prefer, or what terrain, or what weather conditions. And most important, you don't know how to distinguish between real backpacking gear and the toys. Buying your gear before you've been out in the woods is like buying a car before you have a driver's license. It's best to get a feel for the road — or trail — first.

At the same time, you can't venture into the woods completely unequipped. What you can do is beg, borrow, or rent. Don't buy until you've spent a little time getting to know the sport. If you go on an organized camping trip with a local club, chances are that you can double up with someone who already has a tent and a stove. Get an equipment list from the leader, and figure out what you can share or borrow, what you might already have, what you'll need to rent or purchase. If you do rent (many items, including tents, sleeping bags, mattress pads, backpacks, and

downpour, warm in the cold, and comfortable while you're walking, all without weighing an ounce more than necessary, requires sophisticated design and top-quality materials. You stoves, can be rented from outfitters for a reasonable fee), make sure that you tell the store clerk you are going backpacking and want the lightest gear available. Otherwise, you could end up with a tent that sleeps two people — and weighs 9 pounds. (How do you know that 9 pounds is too heavy for a two-person backpacking tent, or that 5 pounds is about right? Check the outdoor magazines and equipment catalogs from outfitters. Both include weight when discussing outdoor gear.)

When It's Time to Buy

Once you've been on a couple of trips and have an idea of the sort of hiking you'd like to do, start browsing at your local outfitters. Some salespeople have great outdoors experience, but it's not uncommon to run into a clerk who has learned all he knows about gear from a couple of employee training sessions. If at all possible, go to a store with a good reputation, even if it means traveling an hour. I often make a 45-minute drive to Campmor, a retailer and national mail-order supplier of

---

GETTING GOING WITHOUT GOING BROKE

As you become more involved in hiking and backpacking, you'll probably want to collect special gear for your new sport. But in the meantime, there are a few things you can use that are probably lying around your house.

● Cook kit: You've probably got an old 1-quart pot in some corner of your kitchen. An aluminum pie plate will do for a lid.

● You can eat out of your pot, but sometimes it's convenient to have a bowl, too. A plastic bowl will do — any kind. Plastic take-out food containers, Tupperware bowls, or margarine tubs are good choices.

● Empty plastic soda bottles make serviceable water bottles, but they crack easily, so it's best to take two. One-liter bottles are a good size.

● An empty plastic gallon milk jug tied to the back of your backpack can be used instead of a water bag.

● Store your gear in garbage bags. Clear ones will let you find your gear more easily. Bring extras because they tear easily.

● But don't use garbage bags as rain gear! Hypothermia is too serious a risk to cut this corner. At the very least, take a poncho.

● Check the bulletin boards at the gear shops; sometimes hikers post notices of used gear for sale.

● Look at your old clothes. Wool is nature's miracle fabric. Silk long underwear is as warm as ever. If you do have to buy long johns, polypropylene is cheap, now that newer fabrics have become popular.

outdoor gear, even though there are several excellent outfitters much closer to my home. Why? Because

Campmor's staff is made up of people I'd be just as likely to meet on the trail as in a store. Better outfitters make an

GETTING THE BIGGEST BANG FOR YOUR BUCK

● Most of the top-end manufacturers have excellent reputations for customer service and standing behind their products, and many guarantee their products for life. Companies I've personally dealt with that have gone above and beyond the call of duty include Northface (sleeping bags, tents, and packs); Marmot (foul-weather gear); Patagonia (clothing); L. L. Bean (full line of clothing and gear); Dana Design, Gregory, and Kelty (backpacks); and Merrell and Vasque (boots). Brand-name products are more expensive, but I find the service worth the extra cost.

● Guarantees from retailers double your protection if a piece of equipment fails. REI (Recreational Equipment Incorporated), EMS (Eastern Mountain Sports), and L. L. Bean all have stellar reputations for customer service and for honoring guarantees on anything they sell. Their policies boil down to "satisfaction guaranteed, period." If you don't live near one of these stores, don't despair: You can shop by mail order. Be aware that not all retailers have such generous policies. Some honor guarantees only for a year, after which they send you back to the manufacturer. Ask before you buy.

● A good store encourages you to try on gear, learn about it, and feel it out. When I bought my Dana Design backpack, a sales clerk at a local outfitter filled it with 35 pounds of climbing rope, fitted it to my back, and let me walk around the store for an hour. Another quality outfitter insisted that I try out a sleeping bag by lying down in it. Yet another showed me how to put up two tents I was looking at. In all three cases, the equipment I ended up buying was exactly right for my needs.

● If something doesn't fit or feel quite right, ask if the retailer can order something else for you to try. No matter how well stocked an outfitter is, it carries only a fraction of what is available. Don't be afraid to ask questions.

● How do you tell a good outfitter from a not-so-good one? Specialization is one way. Stores that concentrate on serious outdoor gear are more likely to carry good brands and offer a knowledgeable selection than are stores that also sell basketball hoops for driveways, swimming pool rafts, and car-camping supplies.

effort to hire experienced outdoors people and train them well. And the top stores stand by all the products they sell. That's an important bonus with outdoor gear, because you may need replacement or loaner equipment if you have a problem on the trail.

Finally, ask anyone you know who hikes for their recommendations about gear. Remember, though, that people often recommend what they have because (a) that's all they know and (b) they have an investment in their gear.

BACKPACKS

Closet, office, kitchen, bedroom: Your pack is your home. Small wonder that, grunt and groan though they might, backpackers grow attached to their load — indeed, downright affectionate. Call it whatever you like — the monster, the thing, the instrument of torture — the pack is almost an extension of the backpacker. There is something liberating about hoisting a pack and knowing that it contains everything you need, that you can go anywhere (or at least as far as you can walk) with what you have on your back.

I am not, in general, a high-tech person. I still own a phonograph. My computer is Jurassic. I buy a new car when my old one is no longer drivable, repairable, or safe. But as far as backpacks go, I am a convert to the high-tech faith.

The reason? Simple. My body knows, down to the deepest recesses of muscles and bones, the difference between a well-designed, sophisticated

External-Frame Pack: It offers good ventilation against your back, heavy load-hauling capacity, and savings—half the cost of internal-frame cousins. But a high center of gravity makes it a poor choice for tough terrain.

pack that fits exactly right and a pack that isn't and doesn't.

A good pack doesn't rub or hurt or drag. A good pack is sturdy. It can rub against trees and rocks without tearing, bounce against rocks, and be pressed into service as a makeshift chair. A good pack feels as if you're wearing it, not carrying it. A good pack can multiply your enjoyment of a trip.

Choosing a Pack

Like choosing a pair of boots,

choosing a pack is a personal decision. Along with lots of other people, the first pack I ever used was one of those cheap frame packs with an orange sack. The first pack I owned wasn't, technically, a pack at all — it was a backpack-suitcase hybrid. I wouldn't recommend it for the serious back-packer: It doesn't have enough room for more than a couple of days of mild-weather gear and food, and it doesn't have a sophisticated suspension system for balancing heavy loads. But when I was getting my feet wet, it did fine; and if you have one stuck in a closet somewhere, by all means use it for the odd weekend trip. These days, mine mostly sits in the attic, but three years ago I took it trekking in Nepal, choosing it over my "real" backpack because on that particular trip, I didn't need to carry much stuff.

Different packs work for different people. My next pack was a Gregory Cassin that for some reason never felt comfortable, even after several adjust-ments and 5,000 miles of hiking. Dan, however, loves his. After some 20,000 miles, Dan's pack stood out in sharp contrast to the brand-new packs of brand-new AT through-hikers, and it became briefly famous on the Appalachian Trail: Strangers would ask Dan if they could take a picture of his immortal, indestructible pack. When Dan's Cassin started looking what even he thought was a little ragged, he started using mine, and has since rehiked the AT with it.

Dana Design, Gregory, Lowe, Mountainsmith, and Osprey have excellent reputations both for their quality packs and for their customer service. Our Gregorys have endured all kinds of abuse and wear, but the only repairs required have been replacing worn-out webbing and worn-out zippers. Despite the fact that these problems are technically "normal wear and tear" and thus are not covered by warranty, Gregory has repaired them at no cost.

My current pack is a Dana Design Terraplane, which fits perfectly and has never, ever hurt me. I'm not sure what you would have to do to get me to use a different pack — probably carry it for me! Like Gregory, Dana Design has a reputation for excellent products and excellent customer service. Many users of Dana packs are, like I am, fiercely loyal and somewhat boring on the subject. As far as repairs go, I don't have any personal experience: After my Appalachian Trail through-hike my pack still functions as if it were brand new (although it doesn't exactly look it anymore).

The biggest pack-buying decision you'll have to make is whether to buy an internal-frame or external-frame pack. Everything follows from there.

External Frames

External-frame packs were once the state-of-the-art choice for serious backpackers. This is no longer the case, now that internal-frame packs have been engineered and designed to do almost everything but carry your load for you. Still, external frames have loyal fans. A friend of mine hikes with one of the old orange-sacked jobs — the kind I used at summer camp 25 years ago. I'm willing to bet she couldn't get $10 for it at a garage sale, but she wouldn't trade it for the world. Her reason is simple and valid: Nothing hurts, and the pack fits.

People like external frames for different reasons. Many hikers appreciate the convenience of being able to unzip the main compartment and get at any piece of gear

The venerable purist's choice, the external-frame pack rides best with weight high over the shoulders. It provides easy access and, for some, greatest comfort.

at any time. "You can't do that with an internal frame," a friend tells me, and he has a point: Internal frames are a little like top-loading duffel bags, and once they are packed, you can't easily rifle around inside to try to find something. I don't find that advantage compelling because my internal-frame pack has enough outside pockets to hold anything I'm likely to need during the day. And more and more internal-frame packs are being equipped with

zippers that allow access to the middle of the pack.

Some other advantages of external frames: They are less expensive than their internal-frame cousins. In the lower price ranges (around $80–$150), an external frame is a better buy than an internal frame. The problem with inexpensive internal frames is that they lack the sophisticated load-carrying designs that make their high-end cousins perform so well. External

The internal-frame pack carries weight low and close to your body, making it more stable than the external-frame pack for climbing or rock scrambling. Its low profile also provides better clearance.

frames are simpler by design (there are fewer adjustments; the weight rides high up and directly over your hips, and that's that), so a modestly priced external frame performs better than a similarly priced internal.

Many hikers find external frames cooler in hot weather because the frame holds the pack away from your body and allows moisture to evaporate. (This is definitely something to think about if you plan to hike a lot in hot or humid weather.) Another advantage is that externals tend to weigh less than internal-frame models. Finally, external frames fit some people better than internal-frame models — and that's what it comes down to.

Internal Frames

When internal-frame packs first hit the market some 20 years ago, they were derided as toys. External-frame owners turned up their noses at the new packs on the block, insulting everything from the way the load was distributed to the idea that a pack with no visible frame could even be carried for more than a mile or two.

But over the years, internal frames have won more and more converts, aided, no doubt, by the fact that their design has become more and more sophisticated. Now they are the rule, rather than the exception, among long-distance backpackers, who are obsessed with anything that can make their journeys more comfortable.

Good internal-frame packs have

ADJUSTING YOUR PACK

To get the most out of your pack, you need to make sure it fits perfectly and you need to know what all of those straps and buckles and adjustments are for.

- Before you put on your pack, make sure all straps are loosened.
- The hip belt should be just above your hip bones. Tighten the hip belt first.
- Next, tighten the hip-belt stabilizer straps.
- Now tighten the shoulder straps so that they are snug but not constricting.
- Pull the load-adjuster straps tight: This transfers weight to your hips, which is where it should be.
- Finally, clasp and tighten the sternum strap. This can be minutely adjusted to relieve pressure on your shoulders.

External-Frame Pack

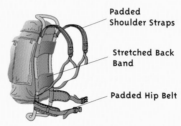

Padded Shoulder Straps

Stretched Back Band

Padded Hip Belt

Internal-Frame Pack

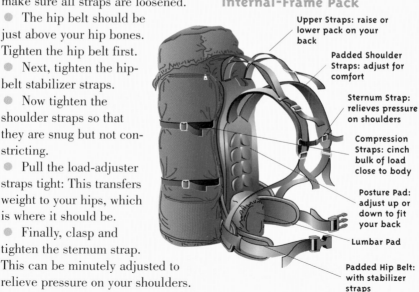

Upper Straps: raise or lower pack on your back

Padded Shoulder Straps: adjust for comfort

Sternum Strap: relieves pressure on shoulders

Compression Straps: cinch bulk of load close to body

Posture Pad: adjust up or down to fit your back

Lumbar Pad

Padded Hip Belt: with stabilizer straps

several advantages that are so important that, all things being equal (and comfort being more equal than other factors), I would choose a good high-

ABOUT PACKS

● Bigger is not better. You want a pack that carries what you need — and not much more. According to the manufacturer, my 5,800-cubic-inch Dana Design Terraplane is designed to carry a load in the 50- to 60-pound range, and can manage 80–100 pounds. I, however, can no more carry 100 pounds than I can go to the moon, so I can think of no reason to ever buy a pack with even more capacity. (But just in case I go completely nuts, Dana offers the Astralplane, with 7,000 cubic inches of space.) A big pack might be necessary for major expeditions, or for long winter trips to brutal climates. For most of us, a big pack merely offers a temptation to take too much stuff along. Packs are designed to ride comfortably when full: A half-empty big pack doesn't ride as well as a full small pack. If you've got a smaller pack and find that you need more space, side pouches are available from many manufacturers, so you can usually add on.

● Find a reputable outfitter. In most cases, the pack will need to be specially fitted to your back. Pack frames and hip belts come in different sizes so they can be adjusted to both the length and curvature of

your back. In internal frames, the stays are actually bent to provide a custom fit. These measurements must be done correctly by a well-trained person for the pack to ride comfortably.

● The suspension system of a highly engineered backpack does add weight, but don't worry too much about how heavy the pack is when empty. You might be initially taken aback when you find that an expensive internal-frame pack weighs 6 or 7 pounds, compared with the 3 or 4 pounds a cheaper internal-frame might weigh, but the additional weight earns its way. This may run counter to common sense, but the benefit of carrying a properly balanced load outweighs the added poundage.

● Be wary of packs with too many bells and whistles and straps dangling all over the place. In backpacking, good design is concerned with function, not form. Overly complicated packs have more things that can tear and break. And they are needlessly confusing: I once ran into someone who was having a problem with a feature of his pack. Since I had just figured out how to operate a similar feature on my pack, I showed him. "It must have been on page 160 of the instruction manual," he commented.

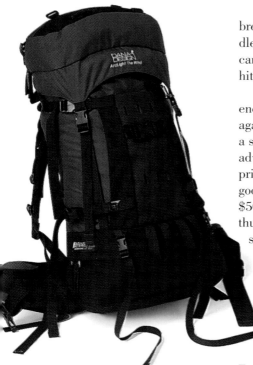

Internal-Frame Pack: Many find its weight distribution more comfortable. A flexible plastic frame sheet adds support, yet has enough "give" to match your moves.

breakable parts (again, baggage handlers). They also fit more easily into car trunks when you're driving or hitchhiking to town to resupply.

The only disadvantage I've encountered is that they are sweatier against your back. For me, that seems a small price to pay for all their advantages. Oh, and speaking about prices to pay, one more thing: The good ones are expensive — up to $500. A highly subjective rule of thumb shared with me by a backpack salesman: If you're spending less than $150, you're probably better off with an external frame. More than $250, get an internal frame. In between, your choice will be a matter of personal preference.

end internal-frame pack, sight unseen, over a similarly priced external pack. Internal-frame packs are better for balance (the load rides down low, close to your back), for winter (they let in less snow when they are all closed up), for off-trail (they are less likely to catch on brush and branches), and for rock scrambling (the weight rides closer to your own center of gravity). As far as traveling is concerned, they are less vulnerable to the tender ministrations of airline baggage handlers. They fit more easily into duffel bags (which can be used to protect them from said baggage handlers!). They have fewer

Daypacks

For dayhikes, of course, all this talk about suspension systems and load balancing is overkill. You do need to carry something on most dayhikes — especially and always above treeline. But anything that rides comfortably and is big enough to hold your extra clothes, rain gear, water, lunch, and emergency supplies is fine. Daypacks are a good choice for adverse or possibly adverse conditions because they have enough room for everything you'll need. Get one with a waist belt; it'll keep the load from bouncing around. OTHER CHOICES: So-called fanny packs ride comfortably on your hips, but don't have much room. Some backpacks have a convenient feature in which the top compartment can be removed and used separately as a

PACKING A BACKPACK

There is some divergence of opinion on how to pack a backpack so that it rides most comfortably. Two of the variables are what kind of pack and where you propose to hike. (Off-trail and on boulders, you'll want the weight as low down as possible; on easy trail, you might be more comfortable stashing some of the heavier items up top.) Check with the person who fits your pack for suggestions on what, if any, adjustments to make. How you pack makes a difference!

FOR EXTERNAL-FRAME PACKS:
Heavyweight items go as high up and as close to your back as possible. This positions the weight over your hips, where it belongs; otherwise, the weight will pull against your shoulders. (This weight distribution makes external frames ride high, which makes them difficult to balance on very uneven terrain.) Your sleeping bag goes on the bottom. Midweight items go — guess where? — in the middle.

FOR INTERNAL-FRAME PACKS:
The load is actually part of the pack's suspension system. The general principle is the same as that of an external-frame pack: Heavy items go on top and close to your back; your sleeping bag goes at the bottom. For off-trail scrambling, a lower center of gravity is better: Pack heavy items in the middle, close to your back.

● Keep items you might need during the day handy: rainwear, lunch, water, pack cover, maps, first aid items, extra layers of warm clothes, toilet paper, toilet trowel.

● Store your fuel bottle upright. A separate outside compartment is a good place for the fuel container — in the unlikely event of a spill, it won't get all over your gear.

● Make sure that hard-edged items like stoves and pots don't poke at your back.

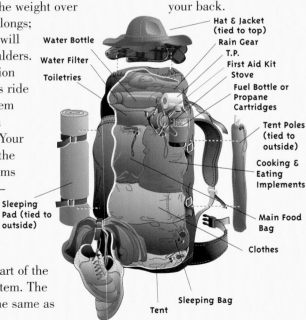

Water Bottle
Water Filter
Toiletries
Sleeping Pad (tied to outside)

Hat & Jacket (tied to top)
Rain Gear
T.P.
First Aid Kit
Stove
Fuel Bottle or Propane Cartridges
Tent Poles (tied to outside)
Cooking & Eating Implements
Main Food Bag
Clothes
Sleeping Bag
Tent

fanny pack. Another option is a compression stuff sack (see below): Lowe makes one with straps running vertically along the sack; the straps can be slung around your shoulders and you can carry the sack like a daypack.

Backpack Accessories

RAIN COVERS. First off and right away, you'll need a rain cover, because packs are not waterproof. There aren't too many choices to worry about here. Other than making sure the cover fits my fully loaded pack, I look for a basic model with an adjustable elastic cord (instead of Velcro closures or snaps). When it's raining, I want to be able to put the rain cover on in seconds with no fuss. (Some people use garbage bags, but I wouldn't advise this if you're going out for more than a weekend: Garbage bags tear too easily.) Ponchos that go over you and your pack are another alternative, but they pose a problem at the end of the day when you have to make camp in the rain: Who (or what) stays dry: you or your pack? If you are carrying a ground cloth for your tent, you can wear the poncho and drape the cloth over your gear.

POUCHES. Many companies offer pouches that attach to the front of your pack's waist belt so you have your daily necessities (lip goop, bug spray, sunscreen, sunglasses, a snack or two) conveniently at your fingertips. The best I've seen is Dana Design's "ribs pack," which hangs not from the belt but from the bottom of the shoulder straps right against your ribs. They

DID YOU KNOW

The stuff sacks that come with your purchases of tents and sleeping bags may not be the best place to store these items. Use stuff sacks that are just slightly bigger than you think you need. A loosely packed sleeping bag or tent gives you more flexibility because it can be squished into different shapes when you try to fit it into your pack. And the extra space is good for your sleeping bag, because the down won't get as crushed.

offer two models: the "dry" one, which is simply a pouch, and the "wet" one, which has room for a 1-liter water bottle. No contest here: Get the wet one. You'll appreciate not having to stop every time you need a drink.

STUFF SACKS. You'll need an assortment of stuff sacks in different sizes and colors. Not only do stuff sacks make packing easier, they also make it more convenient to organize and retrieve your gear, especially if you color-code as you pack: snacks in an orange stuff sack, bug juice and toiletries in a small blue one, spare clothes in a red one, and so on. Use a compression sack to make bulky loads more packable. Waterproof stuff sacks are a good idea, especially for sleeping bags and clothing (starting out, you can use plastic grocery bags).

How Much Weight Can You Carry?

The stock answer: $1/4$ to $1/3$ of your body weight. But that doesn't take into account one important question: Whose body? Should a 5-foot-7-inch man who weighs 180 pounds carry more weight than a 5-foot-9-inch woman who weighs 145? Nonsense! The man in this example is already lugging around extra weight.

Good shelter means the right tent (or tarp) for the conditions and a sheltered location, like this spot at Waterpocket Fold, Utah.

Use the $1/4$-to-$1/3$ rule only as a guideline, and add a good dose of common sense. Most three-season backpackers carry packs that weigh between 30 and 50 pounds. You probably shouldn't carry more than 50 pounds unless you are very fit. You can carry loads that exceed $1/3$ of your body weight if you are in good shape, but even so, expect to be uncomfortable. If you're not fit, lean toward the $1/4$ figure to start. If you can't decrease your pack weight, you may have to decrease your mileage.

If you are a lot fitter than your hiking companion, you can probably afford to take on a little extra communal gear. The same is true if you and your hiking partner are in similar shape but one of you is a lot bigger. Whatever you do, you'll want to examine and reexamine every piece of gear that goes into your pack.

SHELTER

Shelter is one of those things you only truly appreciate when you need it. On a fair-weather trip, your tent may migrate to the deepest recesses of your pack while you sleep under the stars and occasionally wonder why you brought the darn thing along to begin with. But the minute you get caught in an unexpected storm, you'll remember. I don't know of a feeling as comforting, soothing, and secure as being huddled in a tent that I know doesn't leak in a storm. That a couple of thin layers of nylon fabric can protect me from a maelstrom of wind and hail and rain and snow seems nothing short of a miracle.

You have an almost unlimited number of choices when it comes to sheltering yourself from the elements. Tents come in a wide variety of shapes and functions: three-season, four-season, two-person, five-person, A-frame, hoop, dome, freestanding — the list goes on. And on. Nor are you limited to tents: You can also protect yourself with tarps, rain flys, and all manner of bivvy sacks. Finally, you may plan to sleep out under the stars or in one of the lean-tos, cabins, or other shelters that are fixtures on certain trails.

With all the choices available to

backpackers, it is interesting that most (although by no means all) veteran backpackers end up making very similar decisions about their shelter. Tents like the Northface Starlight and the Sierra Designs Clip Flashlight weigh little enough (about 4 pounds) to be carried by one person, but can sleep two (albeit in close quarters). They don't take much space, so you can pitch them almost anywhere. Solo hikers sometimes use smaller versions that are something between a one-person tent and a bivvy sack (Eureka Gossamer: 2 pounds, 14 ounces).

Bivvy sacks (the word comes from "bivouac") are a choice for the hardy, although most hikers complain about condensation. My take on bivvy sacks (and tarps, too, for that matter) is that in a real storm, I want a "real" shelter. But others, especially solo hikers, find the weight advantage compelling. Bivvys are especially useful for solo hikers who plan to sleep out (as in a desert) or in shelters, but who want to carry something in case it rains or in case a lean-to is full when they get there.

Choosing the Right Tent

It comes down to asking yourself lots of questions:

WHO IS GOING TO USE THIS SHELTER? Just you? You and a spouse? A friend? A family? Two 6-foot-4 rugby-playing hiking partners will need more room than a couple of smaller folks. A family with small children might require the type of tent that looks like it could double as a condominium. I bought my first Northface Tadpole (the precursor of the Starlight) when I was hiking predominantly alone because I could carry it by myself, but also use it with a partner. Soon, Dan moved in. If you're going solo, be ruthless about weight: You don't have a partner with whom to share the load.

WHERE ARE YOU HIKING? In a desert you can afford to go light: A tarp is a good choice. Or get a tent, like the Starlight, that can be used with just the rain fly and poles. If you leave the inside part of the tent at home and sleep under the rain fly, you'll save almost 2 pounds. If you're going to be hiking at higher elevations, choose a tent, not a tarp, because it offers better protection against blowing winds and rain.

WHAT IS THE DOMINANT WEATHER PATTERN? If you plan to hike in places where the weather tends toward quick-and-noisy thunderstorms that blow in and out, tent selection is less critical than it is in places where day-in-day-out rain is the norm. In cold weather, the temperature inside the tent will be about 10 degrees warmer than outside, an advantage. In hot weather, that temperature variance is even greater — and decidedly unwelcome. A tarp is a cooler choice.

WHEN ARE YOU HIKING? In summer, a tent with walls made out of mosquito netting lets in a breeze and lets out your sweat. But in winter, the same tent will let in spindrift, or swirling snow. Your three-season tent may function in the winter — depending on how it handles spindrift and snow accumulation, but if you're doing serious cold-weather hiking, a winter tent may be worth the cost. During bug season, you'll definitely appreciate a well-screened tent, not an open-sided tarp or a bivvy sack.

HOW OFTEN AND UNDER WHAT CONDITIONS DO YOU EXPECT TO USE THE TENT? As with every other kind of backpacking gear, you have to trade off between weight and convenience. Is a bigger, roomier, more comfortable tent worth the weight? If you're going to hike a trail with lean-tos, such as are found on the Appalachian Trail, Vermont's Long Trail, and in New York State's Adirondack Mountains, you may never even need your tent, so you certainly won't want to lug around the extra weight of a larger model. (Note: Even if you plan to use lean-tos, you should always carry some kind of shelter in case the lean-to is full.) In severe winter conditions, when you'll be spending long nights in your tent, cooking from the tent (never in it), and eating in the tent (at least sometimes), you may want something that lets you move around more freely. Dan and I always grouse about the weight of our winter tent (a Northface VE-25, 10 pounds), but in really foul conditions, we never regret having it at the end of the day.

If there is a possibility that you'll

be stuck in the tent for an extended period due to storms, a larger tent is worth the extra weight. Caught in an out-of-season blizzard, I once spent three nights in my Northface Tadpole. There was plenty of room for me to fidget and switch positions because I was alone. Sharing that small, cramped tent for three days would have been unadulterated misery.

What to Look for in a Tent

QUALITY. Don't skimp! Your tent is your defense against the elements, and you may need to be well defended. Tents that cost $30 in your local Save-A-Lot Super-Discount Camping Equipment Center will not do the job. I have yet to meet one person after a rain-drenched foul-weather backcountry night who thought a cheap tent was a

L.L. Bean Freestanding Ultralight (rain fly not shown). Three-season; sleeps 2; weight, 4 lbs., 4 oz.

good bargain. A properly erected tarp performs better, and costs even less.

SIZE. You need a flat spot to put down a tent. There are more small flat spots than big flat spots; ergo, there are more places to put a small tent than a big tent. A small tent (less than 35 square feet of floor space) also works

The North Face VE-25 (with rain fly). Four-season, mountaineering; sleeps 4; weight, 10 lbs., 1 oz.

better if you plan to camp in heavily used areas like the White Mountains of New Hampshire, where you are required to set up your tent on wooden platforms constructed by the Forest Service. But small tents require strong interpersonal relations between tent users, especially in prolonged bad weather.

WEIGHT. For a lightweight two-person backpacking tent, 4–5 pounds is about the norm. There are plenty of tents available in this weight range. Prices run from $150 to $200. For backpacking (as opposed to sleeping overnight in a car campground), you should have a specific reason to get a tent that weighs more. If, however, you plan to walk a very short distance or car-camp, you can afford a more spacious (and heavier) model.

SEAWORTHINESS. Make sure you see the tent fully pitched before you pull out your charge card. Does the rain fly

adequately protect the tent interior — even if the wind is blowing the rain in sideways? (This should be obvious, but you'll be surprised to see how many tents are protected with skimpy little rain flys.) A tent bottom that comes up a few inches before the walls start (called a bathtub design) is more water resistant than one that has seams at ground level. If the tent does have seams at ground level, they should be folded over each other and double-stitched. Also consider wind. Tents with three crisscrossing poles handle wind better than tents with two poles. Look for a tent that squats low to the ground.

FREESTANDING TENTS. The great advantage of a freestanding tent is that you can pitch it virtually anywhere, including gravel, sand, cement, wood platforms, and snow. Tents that need to be staked down (the traditional pup tent is an example) require more fuss, and they can't be put up if there isn't a

Clips (above) are replacing sleeves (below) to make tent pitching easier. Sleeves, however, still provide greatest strength.

ABOUT TENTS

● Before you go on your trip, practice putting up the tent. It'll make life easier if you have to pitch it in the rain or dark.

● You'll need to seam-seal the tent before you use it. This is a simple process of coating the seams with a waterproof substance provided by the manufacturer. It takes about an hour, but it adds essential protection against a stormy night. (See page 72.)

● Keep the tent in a convenient place in your pack where you can get to it without taking everything else out first. The reason for this becomes evident in a downpour.

● Use a ground cloth under the tent to protect the tent bottom from roots and rocks. Make sure the ground cloth is completely tucked in underneath the edges of the tent. If it sticks out, it will collect water, which will then leak into the tent, which will collect in your sleeping bag, which will make you miserable.

● Never cook in the tent, even in the rain. If the weather is really bad, you can stick your arms out of the tent and cook just outside. If you must cook "indoors," use the vestibule. Candles are hazardous, too: If your tent has a loop hanging from the poles, you can hang a candle lantern there. Otherwise, you're safer with a flashlight.

● Shake a wet tent before packing it away: A completely wet tent weighs more than a partly wet tent. If possible, air it out during the day, perhaps at lunch, so that it's dry when you put it up.

● Don't fold the tent when you put it away: Stuff it. If you fold a tent in the same creases every day, the folds will eventually weaken the coating and fabric.

● Avoid leaving the tent up in direct sunlight, because sunlight weakens the tent fabric and the waterproofing.

● Don't wear your boots or shoes inside the tent: The mud and dirt will eventually abrade the fabric of the tent floor.

● Never store a tent without airing it dry. Do this even if you thought the tent was dry when you stuffed it away on the last morning of your trip. You may not have noticed condensation or dampness, which can lead to mildew. And mildew can turn your tent into a rotten, shredded, stinking glob of unidentifiable muck.

place for the stakes. Other advantages: If your first spot doesn't work out, you can move the tent without taking it down. And cleaning a freestanding tent is easy. All you have to do is pick it up and shake it out. Freestanding tents don't have to be staked, but always do so anyway. Should a strong wind come

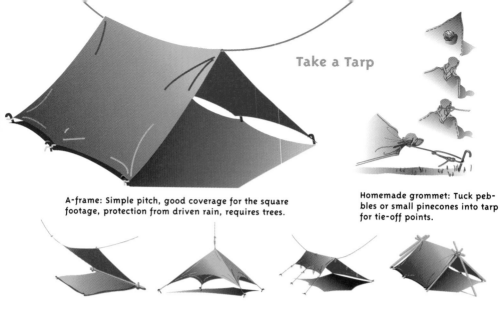

Take a Tarp

A-frame: Simple pitch, good coverage for the square footage, protection from driven rain, requires trees.

Homemade grommet: Tuck pebbles or small pinecones into tarp for tie-off points.

Modified lean-to: Good if wind direction is predictable, protection from damp ground, requires trees.

Peaked canopy: Good ventilation, protection from rain falling straight, can't handle high wind, requires trees.

Lean-to: Simple pitch, if near fire captures radiant heat, good coverage for the square footage, requires trees.

Modified A-frame: Uses sticks (or hiking sticks) for support when no trees are available.

up, you'll appreciate the added support. When the wind is blowing hard, even a tent full of gear can become airborne. EASE OF USE. Having solved the problem of providing portable lightweight shelter, tent manufacturers have turned their engineering and design departments loose on the question of ease of use. Northface's "no-hitch-pitch" (NHP) system is one approach. NHP tents are designed so that the poles stay attached to the tent when the tent is taken down; when you put the tent back up, the poles are already in place. Personally, I don't find that the advantage outweighs the drawbacks: Taking down the tent is more complicated, and you have to

pack and carry the tent body and the poles all together, which makes both packing and weight sharing more difficult. A better innovation is the "clip" system; you simply put the tent poles in the tent grommets, then snap them into clips that are sewn to the tent body. Also look for tents with equal-length poles: You'll appreciate not having to fuss over whether the right pole is in the right sleeve if you have to put up your tent in the dark.

About Seam-Sealing

Seams are the Achilles' heel of waterproof fabrics because the little holes made by the needle and thread are big enough to let in water. A lot more water than you would think, judging from the size of those tiny little holes. The solution is seam-sealing.

Factory seam-sealing is the longest-lasting and most effective option. It's not always available, and when it is, it's expensive. Labels will tell you if the product has been seam-sealed.

If your tent was not factory seam-sealed, you'll have to do it yourself. The tent will probably come with sealant and instructions, and if not, these are readily available from your outfitter. The sealant is a liquid that is applied to the seams from the outside. At the minimum, you'll have to seal all seams on the rain fly and the seams at or near the floor of the tent. Two coats are required for maximum waterproofing.

To those who think the whole process sounds over-fussy, like something your fifth-grade teacher would make you do, be warned: One rainy night in an unsealed tent will prove otherwise.

STOVES

The old-fashioned mountain men wouldn't have known what to do with a backpacking stove. They were experts on fires, and they could make them in the pouring rain. (They also stripped boughs to make beds, dug trenches, and buried their tin cans. But more on that in Chapter 6.)

Today's ethic is different. Unrestricted fire-building by too many backpackers is environmentally unsound (for a discussion of fires, see Chapter 6). Backpacking stoves are the answer. For-

MUST HAVES

There are 10 essentials that no hiker should be without. Before you head out to the trail, check your pack to be sure it contains the following items:

1. Map
2. Compass
3. Water
4. Extra food
5. Extra clothing
6. Firestarter
7. Matches
8. Army knife
9. First aid kit
10. Flashlight

Above treeline, in the desert, or in snow, the list grows to 12:

11. Sunscreen
12. Sunglasses

If you don't have sunglasses, you run the risk of temporary snow blindness and permanent eye damage, which can occur when the retinas are sunburned. I use glacier glasses (about $50), which filter out UV light.

tunately, they are also a lot less trouble to cook on than any fire ever was.

Don't be intimidated by backpacking stoves. I put off buying one for the longest time because I'd get to the stove chapter in books like this and become hopelessly confused. I'm a little timid around machines and gadgets, and the dire warnings convinced me that I'd do something wrong and the stove would blow up. I've since spent a great deal of time with stoves, and I've become well acquainted with several models. Here's the good news: There is no reason, none at all, to be intimidated by a backpacking stove. Stoves are among the most reliable and simplest pieces of equipment to operate, if you learn how to use them first and clean them occasionally. I carried a stove repair kit the entire length of the Appalachian Trail and never even opened it. If the maintenance instructions confuse you, as they might, ask a more experienced or mechanically adept hiker to show you how to do it.

Stoves fall into three general categories.

Refillable Stoves

These stoves run on liquid gas, most often white gas, which is a highly refined gasoline available at sporting goods and hardware stores. (Coleman fuel is the most common brand.) Recently, advances in design have led to the development of multi-fuel stoves, so that many stoves that previously ran only on white gas now run on a variety of fuels (unleaded gasoline from a gas station, kerosene, diesel fuel, or even dry-cleaning fluid). Like your car, the better the fuel, the better a stove will run. Additive-laden gas from a service station will sooner or later clog a stove, even a multi-fuel model.

Finding Coleman fuel (or other white gas) can be a bit of a nuisance when you're on an extended trip. You can generally carry enough fuel for at least a week, so refueling is really only a problem for long-distance hikers. Fuel use varies widely from person to person and trip to trip: It depends on what you're cooking, how often you cook, what kind of stove you use, how cold the weather is, the altitude, and whether you occasionally cook on fires.

MSR Whisperlite refillable stove with fuel bottle attached (left) and Bleuet propane/butane cartridge stove (right).

Generally, Dan and I carry a 33-ounce fuel bottle for a week, which we find generous for our needs. Smaller sizes of bottles are available; you'll have to experiment to decide how much fuel to carry.

If you do have to refuel, you're likely to find that you need only a pint or two, and the fuel is sold by the gallon. (Although in some heavily used recreation areas, stores do sell fuel by the pint.) Often, other hikers who are leaving the trail will help you out: They've been in, or can imagine being in, the same situation and will give you some of their leftover fuel. Another trick: Ask around at a car campground. If you're stuck buying a gallon of fuel, do a good deed and ask the store owner if he will keep the unused amount on hand for future hikers.

Tank stoves either plug directly into the fuel bottle or have a small tank of their own that holds enough for a couple of meals. The operation is fairly simple, with a few variations from stove to stove. In general, the principle is: Pump the stove to pressurize the contents of the fuel bottle or tank. Then prime the stove by preheating the fuel cup with a little gas or priming paste. (Note: If you are using kerosene in a multi-fuel stove, you should know that kerosene is difficult to light with a match, so you might have to use priming paste to get started. If you are pouring gas from a fuel bottle to a priming cup, you will need a special spout, available where you buy your stove. An eyedropper works, too. If you forget the spout,

improvise: I once used a Q-tip soaked in white gas.) Once the flame starts going down and the fuel cup is hot, open the valve that lets the gas through and, voilà!, you're ready to cook. Once in a while you may have to pump the stove to keep it pressurized.

Lighting the stove for dinner, Glacier National Park. Stay a safe distance; the gas you light to prime the stove can flare up.

Stove owners can be passionately loyal to their stoves, and I find that I am no exception. I adhere to the "If it ain't broke don't fix it" school of gear, so for what it's worth, I'll tell you that my multi-fuel stove, an MSR XGK II, has hiked the Continental Divide and the Appalachian Trail, and has worked on dry-cleaning fluid in Africa (at 15,700 feet) and on kerosene in Nepal (at 16,000 feet). It's a little on the noisy side (some hikers less charitably call it the blast furnace), and it has only two speeds — explosion and dead — so simmering is a tedious, fuel-wasting process of turning the stove on and off. But if you can live with a little noise and no simmer, it's just about perfect. Even more popular in the backcountry is the MSR Whisperlite, which now comes as a multi-fuel. As its name suggests, it doesn't make as much racket, and it is actually a little more fuel efficient than the XGK. But it doesn't simmer, either. The new Peak 1 Apex II is a little heavier than the Whisperlite, but it simmers.

Cartridge Stoves

These are stoves that use prefilled,

ABOUT STOVES

● Read the instructions and practice at home. Learn how to take the stove apart and put it back together. If you are timid about mechanical objects that involve fire, ask the salesperson to demonstrate the stove for you and to show you how to clean it.

● Carry a repair kit and instructions.

● You can't take fuel with you on an airplane, so you'll need to think about how you're going to fill up before you hit the trail. We usually make a quick detour to a town and find fuel at a hardware store before we head to the trail. As a last resort, users of multi-fuel stoves can fill them up at a gas station.

● When cooking on a backpacking stove, use the smallest pot practical. These stoves are small, and even the best are a little unstable, especially under a big, heavy pot. You don't want to be picking your dinner out of the dirt.

● If you have long hair, tie it back before lighting your stove. The gas you light to prime the stove can flare up unexpectedly.

● Be careful if you are cooking near your tent or while in your sleeping bag: You don't want to burn a hole in your gear.

● The purer your fuel, the better your stove will run. If your old fuel sits around between trips residues will build up, which will clog your stove. You can pre-filter fuel through a fine wire mesh that is available at outfitters. This is especially important if your fuel has been sitting around for a couple of months, or if it is of dubious quality. MSR stoves come with small filters that can be attached to the fuel intake tube.

● Use pot lids, windscreens, and heat reflectors: They dramatically increase the stove's efficiency.

● Don't fill your gas tank completely full: To properly pressurize, the tank should be no more than 80 percent full.

● In very cold weather, sleep with your fuel bottle. While fuel won't freeze (at least not in temperatures backpackers are likely to encounter), a stove runs more efficiently on warm fuel.

LET THERE BE LIGHT

FLASHLIGHTS. There are several brands of miniature flashlights available. Maglites are the most popular. They weigh just a few ounces, and some models come with a headband that enables them to function as a headlamp. You should always have some sort of flashlight in case of emergencies.

HEADLAMPS. Here's an even better idea: A headlamp frees up your hands and allows you to direct your light where you need it. It's more comfortable for reading in bed and more convenient for night hiking.

CANDLES. Some experienced hikers prefer candles to flashlights. We take them along as emergency backup and firestarters, and we occasionally use them on still nights in shelters. Some people set them in food cans and use them in tents, but Dan and I consider any open flame in a tent an invitation to disaster.

CANDLE LANTERNS. Some tents have fabric loops from which to hang candle lanterns. Lanterns cast a warm, glowing light, and you don't have to worry about running down the batteries. Candle lanterns are especially useful in shelters, because they shelter the flame from the wind, and in winter, when the sun goes down early in the evening.

disposable gas cartridges containing butane or propane (or, in some cases, a combination of the two). Propane burns better in the cold, but it requires heavy containers and is hence not often seen in the backcountry. Butane is more common, but it does not work as well as white gas in cold weather, or at extremely high altitudes (above 15,000 feet), which is when you most need your stove to be foolproof. Cartridge stoves are initially seductive: Even after a long and monogamous relationship with my MSR, I was tempted to try one out, infatuated with the quick-'n'-easy, all-you-have-to-do-is-light-the-match factor. But my trial run took me square

into the March 1993 "Blizzard of the Century," and I didn't rest easily knowing that I couldn't tell how much fuel I had left, that the stove didn't work well when the mercury plummeted to near zero, and that, near the end of the trip, I started hearing a hissing that sounded suspiciously like gas escaping from the cartridge.

On the positive side, butane cartridges are common in the United States. If you need to resupply in Outer-Nowhere, chances are the local 7-Eleven sells them, especially if you are close to a popular camping area, national forest, or the like. (Note: You do have to pack out the empty cartridges.)

A damp bag, whether down- or synthetic-filled, is an uncomfortable bag.

at all. Finally, if you leave the battery in the stove, it can be switched on inadvertently, so be sure to take it out when not in use. And carry extras. In very cold weather, keep batteries close to your body, because they can freeze up. Personally, I wouldn't rely on a battery-powered stove for a trip into subfreezing weather.

Zzip Stoves

In a category all its own, there is the so-called Zzip stove, which burns wood as well as anything else that is flammable. It operates with a small battery that runs a fan that circulates air through the stove. Users boast of cooking on pine cones, birch bark, cardboard, and wet twigs. They also boast about the light weight of the stove unit and the fact that they don't have to carry a fuel bottle or worry about refilling it.

There are a few problems with the Zzip that may make you think twice about using it as your primary stove. In very strict no-fire zones, they may not be permitted. If you use a Zzip stove, you'll have to keep a small stash of dry tinder to start it up; once it gets going, it runs on just about anything that burns, including wet wood. If you plan to camp above treeline, however, this stove is probably not the answer, especially if you are up in the arctic-alpine zone where there may be no vegetation

SLEEPING BAGS

Remember the bag you took to summer camp? The one with the cotton stuffing and the duck pattern on the inside? If you've still got it, leave it home. For backpacking, you need a bag that gives you good insulation for its weight, and that packs into a reasonably small bundle. The old flannel ducks, may they rest in peace, do neither.

The first decision you'll need to make is whether to buy a bag stuffed with down or stuffed with a synthetic fill. There are very good arguments in favor of each.

GOOSE DOWN BAGS. Despite all the technological advances in recent years, goose down remains the best insulator, ounce for ounce, available. It's also more convenient, because down compresses into a smaller space, which makes it easier to pack. But down has a vital flaw: It loses virtually all of its insulating capacity when wet. Even if you zealously keep your sleeping bag in a waterproof compartment lined with an extra garbage bag, ambient moisture will start to make it feel a little soggy if you hike with rain and humidity day after day. If you are careless, you could end up with a heavy, useless piece of expensive equipment just when you need it most.

SYNTHETIC BAGS. Made with such trademarked insulating fills as Lite Loft or Polarguard, synthetic bags have become progressively lighter and more compressible. Most important, synthetic fills retain the ability to insulate even when wet, making them an excellent choice for really foul weather. Years ago, serious backpackers swore by down, and left the heavier, bulkier synthetics to novices. But in recent years synthetics have improved so dramatically that the backpacking community is split. Take, for instance, two bags made by REI, both rated to 0 degrees. The down bag (the "Downtime 0") is 3 ounces lighter and $25 more expensive than the synthetic bag (the "Nod Pod 0"). The advantages of synthetics may well be worth the extra 3 ounces (that's about the weight of two candy bars). The gap is narrowing fast. One disadvantage still to be conquered: Synthetic fill tends to break down and lose its loft much faster than down.

A rule of thumb is to use down bags in dry cold, such as is most com-

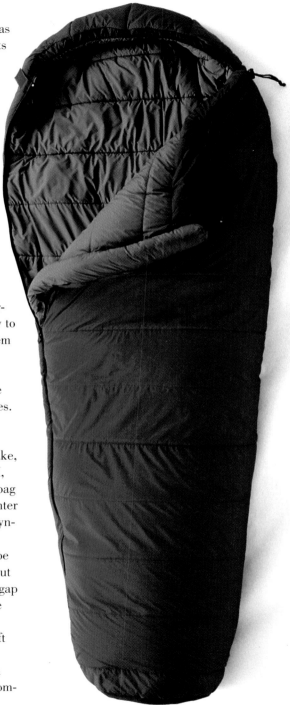

Mummy bags (top) are the warmest, but some find tight-fitting ones too constricting and, in many conditions, too warm. Semi-rectangular bags (bottom) are one answer so long as winter camping is not contemplated.

monly found in the West; try synthetic bags in the all-day rain and wet conditions sometimes found in eastern hiking. Dan and I have seven sleeping bags, all of them down, and we've never had a serious problem — even on the Appalachian Trail in the wet spring months of March and April. But on a few occasions, when our bags became a little clammy and clumpy, we've been happy to see the sun! Given the vast improvements in synthetics, our next bag may well break the pattern.

What to Look for in a Sleeping Bag

TEMPERATURE RATING. Temperature rating is a somewhat misleading measurement, because it varies from manufacturer to manufacturer — and from hiker to hiker. Some hikers just naturally sleep warmer than others. Additional variables include how you sleep (wearing lots of layers or in the buff) and where (in a tent, in a trail shelter, or out in the open).

There is no industry-wide standard for temperature rating — a Northface 20-degree bag may be warmer or colder than an EMS 20-degree bag. However, manufacturers are consistent within their own line of products. Buy a bag rated to 10 degrees below the temperatures you expect to encounter. Many hikers use three-season bags rated at 20 degrees,

CARING FOR SLEEPING BAGS

● Wash your bag only when it's so dirty you can no longer stand it. Each time you wash a bag, it loses a little of its loft.

● To keep your bag cleaner between washings, try a lightweight sleeping bag liner — either silk or nylon; not cotton.

● Wash sleeping bags according to the manufacturer's instructions. Usually, this means going to a Laundromat, because front-loading machines are gentler.

● You can also hand-wash bags in a bathtub. Always handle a wet sleeping bag as if it's made of eggshells, because the weight of the water can tear the baffles, which will render all the "draft tubes," "differential cuts," and "shingle constructions" useless.

● Dry your bag on the air-dry cycle with no heat. This can take a couple of hours, a long haul at the Laundromat. If you have a dryer at home, transport the sleeping bag in a large plastic garbage bag.

● If you hang the bag up to dry, make sure it has plenty of support so the baffles don't tear. Several parallel clotheslines will work.

● Shake out and fluff up your bag before you use it to increase the loft and make it warmer.

● Don't store your bag in the sack it comes in! Instead, leave it out or store it in a big pillowcase. Too much compression of the down will break down the loft.

---

and these seem to keep most people comfortable most of the time. In winter conditions, you may need a bag rated to zero or even lower. One of ours claims a minus-20 rating.

Don't be seduced by low numbers, unless you really do plan to sleep out in the dead of winter. A 0-degree bag is virtually useless in the summer, especially if you plan to sleep under the stars or in lean-tos, when you'll want to pull the bag over you to keep off the bugs. Plus, a warmer bag is a heavier, bulkier bag. Remember layering? It works here, too: You can increase the temperature rating of a lighter bag by adding a vapor barrier liner, a bivvy sack, and extra layers of clothes.

SHAPES. Mummy bags, which look just like their name suggests, are the warmest and most popular. The logic behind this design is that a sleeping bag keeps you warm by trapping warm air heated by your body. A mummy bag's tight fit means that there is less air for your body to heat up. There is some variance among mummy bags, from very close fitting to fairly loose. Loose, of course, is more comfortable, but it's heavier and not as warm. Those who find mummy bags too claustrophobic can opt for semi-rectangular

Moonrise from the 14,494-foot summit of Mount Whitney, California. On such a site, a freestanding tent is a necessity. Even so, such tents must be anchored; note the rocks piled to the right of the door.

bags, which are looser still.

SIZE. Get inside the bag — yes, in the store — to make sure it fits. Roll around in it. Are your feet pushing against the bottom? Is there enough room around your chest and shoulders? Can you turn around in it? Can you reach the toggles and zippers? Look for extra room around your feet, especially if you're buying a winter bag: Winter hikers often sleep with their boots and anything else that might freeze overnight.

FOR COUPLES. Romance in the backcountry? Why not? Consider getting his-and-her bags: the same brand for each of you, one with a right-hand zipper and one with a left-hand zipper so that they can convert into a giant bag big enough for both of you. Warning: There is a trade-off between romance and comfort! You'll feel it every time your partner turns over. You may also be a little colder because you can't pull the bag closed around your neck.

FABRIC SHELL. There are all kinds of shells ranging from plain old nylon to Gore-Tex to "wind-, water-, and UV-light-resistant Super Microfiber" (whatever that means). When I bought my last bag, the salesman insisted on pouring a cup of water on it (with me in it) to demonstrate how repellent the fabric was. I'm not convinced the neat gimmick was all that reassuring, since I'm not so much worried about a sudden spill from my water bottle as I am about the insidious day-after-day humidity and rain of an eastern spring, or condensation and sweat, or moisture leaking into a tent floor. Still, considering how vulnerable down is to water, anything helps.

LINING. Some sleeping bags are lined

DEPARTMENT OF THE KITCHEN SINK

A recent trip to my local outfitter demonstrated that even after spending money on the big-ticket items (tent, boots, sleeping bag, rainwear, stove, and pack) the addicted shopper need not despair: There are plenty of other gadgets to buy. Like a camping espresso maker. Or a battery-powered portable fan. There were spice kits and cook sets and a contraption that enables you to bake fresh bread in the woods. After an hour of roaming around the store, I was convinced that it would be entirely possible to fill my pack with 100 pounds of lightweight gear.

Many veteran hikers have a couple of pieces of odd-ball equipment that they can't go without. A gadget that turns a Therm-a-Rest into a chair. A square of closed-cell padding (Ensolite) to sit on during breaks. A hammock. An inflatable pillow.

For me, it's a pair of ski poles that I use as walking sticks. Yes, two of them. Mine are adjustable, with springs that act as shock absorbers. The benefits: Two poles let you use your arms cross-country-ski style to help you up hills. Going downhill, the poles help with balance and footing, and — most important — they take weight and strain off your knees. Crossing streams, they provide balance. If you get tired of using them, they can be collapsed and strapped to your pack.

Baffling Basics

This cutaway view of a down-filled bag shows how a system of baffles keeps the down from shifting. Square-box baffles (detail, right) provide maximum loft and keep the down from shifting.

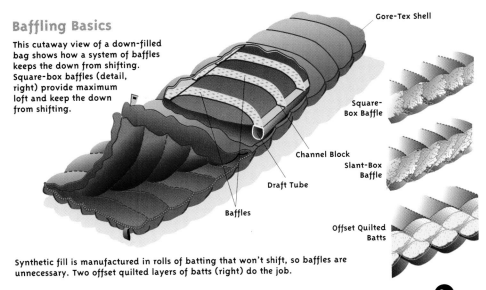

Gore-Tex Shell

Square-Box Baffle

Channel Block

Slant-Box Baffle

Draft Tube

Baffles

Offset Quilted Batts

Synthetic fill is manufactured in rolls of batting that won't shift, so baffles are unnecessary. Two offset quilted layers of batts (right) do the job.

WHAT TO TAKE, WHAT TO LEAVE HOME

Some hikers suggest dividing equipment into three piles: the things you know you'll need, the things you might need, and the luxuries. Then, you throw out the second two piles! My problem with this method is that it doesn't take into account emergencies, or the consequences of not having safety equipment.

Use the following matrix to help you think about gear. The chart helps you determine what you should take by weighing how often you'll use an item against the consequences of not having it if you need it. I've put a few sample items in for illustration.

Note that each trip will be different, and different pieces of equipment will migrate from one category to another. For a June trip into the desert, rain pants would go in a different box than they will in April in New England.

I take everything in the shaded columns. Things in the half-shaded columns can be taken depending on the length of the trip and the pack weight, but usually they get left at home. The unshaded box is for illustration only: I'd never even consider taking something that falls into this category.

		CONSEQUENCES OF NOT HAVING IT		
		Safety hazard or basic need could not be met	Would miss it, but safety would not be affected	Minor inconvenience, if any
FREQUENCY OF USE	Every day	Water bottle, stove	Journal, camp shoes	Book
	Some days	Tent/shelter	Camp clothes	Extra clean clothes
	Infrequently	First aid kit, extra warm clothes, hat, rain gear	Shampoo	Games, rain pants in summer desert

with synthetics that try to imitate the feel of cotton, so that you don't have that slippery, sweaty feel against your skin. This is more important in warmer temperatures. When it's really cold, you'll be wearing too many clothes to feel the fabric.

BAFFLES. As with any other gear, you can get mired in endless technotalk about the innards of sleeping bags. Sleeping bags need baffles to separate the stuffing (or fill) so it doesn't all migrate to the same place. Merely sewing together tubes containing the fill doesn't do the trick because there's no insulation at the seams. Baffles (see illustration) solve the problem.

EXTRA PADDING. Sleeping bags should have an insulated panel along the length of the zipper (called a draft tube), otherwise you'll lose heat even if the zipper is shut. Other things to look for are a hood (very important), a system of draw-string closures around the neck and head (also important), and a storm collar around the neck (for cold weather only).

FOOT ZIPPER. A zipper at the bottom of the bag (most

The complete campsite: a clean, well-lighted (and ventilated) tent; a well-stocked kitchen nearby; and a few well-chosen creature comforts.

common in winter bags) helps regulate the temperature in the bag. It also allows you easy access to anything you might have stashed down at the bottom.

Pads, Pillows, and Liners

SLEEPING PAD. You'll need a sleeping pad of some kind, not only for comfort, but also because body heat is lost

through contact with cold ground. The inexpensive alternative is some sort of closed-cell foam pad like a Ridge Rest. More comfortable, and also more expensive, are self-inflating foam-filled air mattresses. Therm-A-Rest is by far the most popular air mattress out there, and it's a lot sturdier and less prone to punctures than you might expect. Keep air mattresses away from open flames, and just in case, take along a repair kit. (A note for couples: A strap is available to hook two pads together.) Pads come in different lengths: For summer, a three-quarter length will do, but in cold weather, a full length is a must. At home, store the sleeping pad deflated and out of its sack to prevent mildew.

PILLOWS. A few sybarites bring light-weight, usually inflatable pillows with them; the rest of us make do with stuff sacks filled with whatever clothing we're not wearing (which can make for a pretty flimsy pillow on a cold night). A T-shirt can be used as a pillowcase if you are fussy. Or check out the new stuff sacks that are lined with a thin layer of fleece.

LINERS. A thin nylon or silk liner can keep your sleeping bag clean and add to its longevity. It's also more comfort-able than sleeping against the clammy sleeping bag fabric. Another kind of liner is the vapor barrier liner, which goes into your sleeping bag in cold weather and traps body heat close to you. It's worth a good 10 degrees of extra warmth, although some people object to the clammy feel.

GOING ULTRA-LIGHT

Going ultra-light is the backpacker's response to the problem of ounces adding up to pounds. You may at first be tempted when you see someone vir-tually running along the trail with something that looks no bigger than a day pack. A dedicated ultra-light

backpacker would have a field day with the gear I carry: I'd have to give up my camp shoes and my cotton camp shirt and my spices and my book. I'd have to justify carrying two plastic bowls. ("Why can't you and Dan share the pot and eat out of that?" an ultra-light backpacker once demanded. I had a good answer: If we did, we'd stab each other's fingers trying to get to the food!)

With enough work (including cut-ting the handle off my toothbrush, the tags off my clothes, getting rid of any stuff sacks I didn't absolutely need, and drilling holes in my spoon), I might well get my pack weight down to 20 pounds or even less. But the fact is, I want my camp shoes and cotton shirt. I don't want to ration bug lotion or give up my Therm-A-Rest! I want extra matches and a cigarette lighter so that even if my pack falls into a river (it has happened) I can start my stove.

You, however, may have a different opinion, and I invite you to slice at your gear and chortle at all the weight you don't have to carry. But do yourself a favor and wait until you've been out a few times. Among other things, ultra-light hikers have (or believe they have) the confidence, experience, and phys-ical conditioning to compensate for any mistakes or misjudgments they might have made in packing. A friend of mine who hikes on the Appalachian Trail without a tent says that if the shelter he is aiming for is full, he'll just go on to the next one — or the one after that. But he can cover 40 miles in a day! I can't. And I don't want to.

F O O D

5

The secret of losing weight has long been known to backpackers: Hike all day for several days on end and eat only what you can carry. Before long, you'll discover that backpacking is one of the best ways to lose weight and improve fitness ever invented.

The reason is simple. Back-packers burn off more calories than they can comfortably carry — as many as 4,000 calories every day, and sometimes even more. When hikers aren't talking about their gear, they're talking about food: what to eat, when to eat, what they wish they'd brought, what they'll eat when they're done with their hike, what they'll bring on their next hike.

Nowhere is our relationship with food as clear as it is after a couple of days in the backcountry: Food is fuel.

WHAT TO EAT

Backpacking cuisine used to be limited to a combination of canned foods, which are heavy, and freeze-dried concoctions, which in their early incarnations tasted like reconstituted cardboard. By comparison, today's backpacker has almost unlimited choices. What you eat on the trail depends on how much time and effort you want to spend cooking, how much weight you are willing or able to carry, and — of course — your imagination.

There are as many ways to plan food as there are hikers. Some people don't eat breakfast until they've walked a couple of miles; most can't start without their coffee. Some stop for long lunches; others pop a short snack every hour or two. There are a few iconoclasts who eschew cooking altogether and subsist on granola, cheese, peanut butter, and candy bars. At the other end of the spectrum are the handful of serious cooks who make backcountry cuisine an art form. But by far the majority of hikers wind up somewhere in the middle, using a fairly standard repertoire of prepared meals and ingredients — despite the vast number of options available.

For the most part, quick and easy reigns. Certainly, it makes sense on your first few trips to keep complications to a minimum. You're probably going to be tired at the end of the day, and you'll have enough to deal with learning the eccentricities of stoves and water filters. Every once in a while I read an article extolling the virtues of fine food on the trail. Somehow, I've never been tempted to spend the time and effort to copy the complicated-sounding recipes — and I've never seen anyone else do it either. There may be a few gourmet cooks out there feasting happily on pasta with andouille and fried sage, to take one example from a recent backpacking recipe book. But most of the rest of us opt for economy of effort. After all, just about anything tastes good after a hard day of hiking!

Start simple, and look to other hikers for ideas. Do not, however, stare into their food pot like a hungry puppy. Be forewarned. Hikers will share advice, stories, and more advice. They will help you set up your tent, get your balky stove to light, and untangle your bear-bagging rope. They will not, as a general rule, share their food.

Even if you miscalculate, you probably won't go hungry: Most hikers err on the side of too much, not too little. Some people feel their stomachs growling the minute they are out of sight of the road; others find that it takes a few days for their appetites to kick in. Experience is the best teacher: It'll take a little while before you can pack so accurately that you return to the road with only your emergency stash intact.

As always, however, there are rules of thumb to follow or ignore. Two pounds of food per person per day will keep your stomach at bay; you can cut down on your pack weight by sticking to ultra-light foods such as packaged oat-meal, freeze-dried dinners, and Lipton side dishes. If you take cans, your food bag will be heavier. In winter, figure $2^{1}/_{2}$ pounds per person per day — your body needs more calo-ries to stay warm.

Hikers share a breakfast of hot oatmeal at dawn on Max Patch Mountain along the Appalachian Trail in North Carolina.

On a short hike, the question of what to eat needn't be complicated. If you're going out for a week or so, your best strategy is to take foods you like. On a longer expedition, you'll need to think more about variety and nutrition. Some hikers carry vita-mins to compensate for any imbalances.

WILL IT WORK IN THE WOODS?

There are a few issues to consider about food before you hit the grocery store. DOES IT NEED REFRIGERATION? You'd be surprised to learn how many foods that we commonly refrigerate can sur-vive a few days, or even longer, in your

pack. Cheese (hard, aged cheeses like cheddar and Parmesan are best), pep-peroni and salami (a hunk of the real thing, not packaged, pre-sliced lunch meat), boiled eggs, and yogurt all travel well. In moderate to cool tem-peratures, of course, they last longer. Conversely, leave home foods that spoil easily. Unless it contains preservatives, bread goes moldy quickly, especially in wet weather, so bring crackers instead. Mustard lasts well. Mayonnaise can make you sick if it is exposed to warm temperatures; leave it home.

HOW MANY CALORIES DOES IT PROVIDE? You don't have to become a calorie counter, but do remember that more calories means more fuel. Think of yourself as an automobile: In the backcountry, you need high-octane. This is your opportunity to splurge on

Freeze-dried cheddar cheese and tortilla dinner. Be sure to pack out all packaging that cannot be safely burned.

high-calorie and even high-fat foods. ARE YOUR MEALS BALANCED? The longer your hike, the more important it is to think about nutrition. Over a weekend, you can well afford to have Lipton's linguine Alfredo the first night and Lipton's fettuccine Parmesan the second, a couple of instant-oatmeal breakfasts, and a nonstop supply of

Snickers bars to fill the holes. But if you're going to be out for more than a couple of days, bring along some variety. Your body needs it, and so do your taste buds.

HOW COMPLICATED IS THE PREPARATION? This is more important to high-mileage hikers — they're likely to be exhausted at the end of the day. But it's also important in inclement weather: You don't want to be crouched over your stove sautéing this and parboiling that in a downpour. Even die-hard gourmets should throw in a just-add-water meal.

HOW LONG DO YOUR MEALS TAKE TO PREPARE? This isn't only a convenience issue; it's a fuel issue. The longer the cooking time, the more fuel used by your stove. Plan accordingly.

DID YOU PACK ENOUGH SNACKS? Hikers are constantly burning fuel, so they need to constantly replenish it. Eating small amounts often helps maintain the body's glucose level, as well as body heat and energy. Some people are prone to hypoglycemia, a precipitous drop in blood sugar that

SHOPPING LIST

STAPLES:

Dried milk, sugar, honey, Parmesan cheese (makes everything taste better). Spices (suggestions: salt, pepper, Louisiana hot sauce, dried garlic, oregano, onion flakes, lemon-pepper mix, soy sauce; pack them in tiny bags or plastic containers available from outdoor shops). Packets of clarified butter (they don't need refrigeration). Sun-dried tomatoes and dried mushrooms. For fresh flavor and variety, an onion, several carrots, and a clove of garlic last well.

can bring on a headache followed by dizziness and nausea. A quick fix of brown sugar or a candy bar can solve the problem, but it's better to avoid it by snacking at regular intervals.

ABOUT DINNER

By far the most looked-forward-to, satisfying meal is dinner. It's the biggest meal, the most filling, and usually the tastiest. It's also — because there are so many choices — the most confusing to plan.

FREEZE-DRIED DINNERS. For the "just-add-water" crowd,

This Swiss-made Sigg Fire Jet stove melted pots and pots of snow for water on a winter trip through Waterpocket Fold, southern Utah.

freeze-dried dinners offer the most variety and the least fuss. You'll find a selection at your local outfitter. When freeze-dried foods first hit the market they were roundly derided. The meat tasted like shoe leather, and the various flavors were differentiated only by the hype on the packaging. Today's offerings are far better; some of them are downright delicious. Freeze-dried meals offer several important advantages: They last virtually forever. They are quick and easy to prepare (look for dinners designated "no-cook," which means all you have to do is add boiling water). And they offer a wide range of choices, from spicy Mexican dishes to more traditional beef Stroganoff or chicken and rice. There are even main-dish vegetarian meals. The different spices and herbs go a long way toward satisfying your craving for something new.

But there are a few disadvantages as well. Freeze-dried meals are expensive, and some of them actually require considerable cooking time and fuss. Read the instructions before you buy and consider low-cost alternatives: Pasta-and-cheese dishes, spaghetti, and rice and beans are available far more cheaply at your supermarket.

A warning about recommended serving sizes: They're too small. The normal-sized pouch — the one that says "feeds two" is really more like dinner for ONE hiker. The large packets ("4 8-oz servings") serve two.

Finally, check out the packaging. Aluminum is convenient for in-the-pouch cooking, but it's not burnable — you'll have to pack it out. Some companies use plastic instead. Another option: you can repackage the meal in Ziploc bags.

Burning plastic packaging and Ziploc bags is controversial among backpackers concerned with minimizing their impact. First, minimum-impact campers avoid having fires. And second, burning plastic releases toxins into the atmosphere. But many backpackers argue that this is taking the minimum-impact ethic too far, that the release of toxins from a couple of Ziploc bags is negligible (certainly less than the toxins released by driving a car to the trailhead). They also point

SHOPPING LIST

SNACKS

Depending on how many miles you cover, you'll need two to six snacks per person per day. Most hikers find that it's important to keep eating small amounts throughout the day to keep their energy and blood sugar up. Some suggestions:

Nuts (check out your local food co-op). GORP (the ubiquitous "good old raisins 'n' peanuts" plus whatever else you add: fruit chunks, coconut, M&Ms, chocolate chips). Beef jerky (also try chicken or turkey jerky; if you have a dehydrator, you can make your own). Granola bars, Snickers, Kudos, Fibars, fruit leather: Trade with your hiking partners. Power bars and pemmican bars (expensive but great for an energy boost; they're available at your local outfitter). Fresh fruits like apples and oranges last well but are heavy. If you can carry the extra weight, they make a delicious treat.

Instant soups are among veteran hikers' favorite dinners. Easy to pack, easy to fix, easy to eat, warming, and nutritious, they're hard to beat.

out that burning food containers means that fewer animals will be attracted to a campsite. You'll need to make your own decision. In this chapter, I have suggested using and burning Ziploc bags because it's an improvement over the unfortunate widespread practice of leaving charred chunks of aluminum in firepits. See Chapter 6 for a discussion of minimum-impact ethics and garbage.

DRY YOUR OWN. What about those who want their woods-cooked meals to taste home-cooked? You probably know that you can home-dry fruit leather, fruits, and vegetables. But did you know that you can dry homemade sauces, chilis, soups, and stews? Just pour them into a dehydrator tray, turn the machine on, and a day or so later,

S H O P P I N G   L I S T

BEVERAGES

Coffee and tea. Powdered beverages like Kool-Aid and Crystal Light. Electrolyte-replacement beverages like Gatorade are excellent, particularly in hot weather, but the mixes are surprisingly heavy. Crystal Light is excellent for camouflaging the taste of chemically purified water. Hot chocolate is a nighttime favorite. Another choice: hot liquid Jell-O.

Fixing a quick lunch — on the summit of Mitchell Peak in Wyoming's Wind River Range.

you'll have home-dried dinners that you can package in Ziploc bags and take on the trail. Home-dried meals offer the best flavor and the most variety — but also the most pre-hike fuss. You'll need a dehydrator. You'll also need plenty of time.

SUPERMARKET STAPLES. Last but far

SHOPPING LIST

BREAKFAST

Coffee (coffee bags are best — they give you a precise measure, they don't spill, and they taste more like the real thing than instant) and tea (bags, of course). Cocoa. Instant cereal (oatmeal, farina, Cream of Wheat, and so on; take two packets per hiker per day). Boxed cereal (granola, muesli, and the like are a little heavier than instant, but add variety; add some powdered milk, and hot or cold water; figure on 2–3 ounces per hiker per day). Ramen noodle soup (the Japanese eat soup for breakfast; some hikers do, too). English muffins and bagels (will you want to toast them? and how?). Pop Tarts. Some people attempt real breakfasts of pancakes or eggs and bacon, but these hikers aren't generally planning to hike very far. Such breakfasts take a lot of time. Freeze-dried versions are available. In either case, do a trial run before you go out for more than a day or two. You might decide that a fancy breakfast isn't worth the effort.

from least, there's your supermarket, which offers a surprising number of choices that will work just fine on the trail — at affordable prices.

One popular choice is prepared foods. Lipton's side dishes are by far the king of the outdoor kitchen. Most are variations on the old macaroni-and-cheese favorite, although the kinds of cheeses and pastas vary. Also available are some good rice dishes, although hungry hikers find them a little less filling. Either rice or pasta dinners can be doctored with leftover lunch cheese, Parmesan, freeze-dried vegetables, small cans of meat or tuna, and spices. As for macaroni and cheese? It's still out there, and it's as

Dining on macaroni and cheese to fend off the cold and rain, Dolly Sods Wilderness, West Virginia.

easy as ever.

QUANTITIES: One Lipton side-dish packet (the kind that says "Makes 4 4-oz servings") is dinner for one hiker. A small box (about 7½ ounces) of Kraft macaroni and cheese is plenty

SHOPPING LIST

LUNCH

Cheese lasts outdoors for a longer time than you would expect. So does salami. Crackers don't go moldy; bread can. (Crackers keep better if stored in their original boxes.) Some hikers take English muffins or bagels. Mustard lasts (get packets from fast food places). Peanut butter is a favorite. Some hikers swear by sardines. Alternatives: Just-add-water mixes for refried beans, hummus, and tabbouleh are popular with the health-food crowd (they're light to carry, but low in fat). Pita bread lasts a couple of days; much more than that, and you're likely to see green spots. Chips stay more intact than you might expect, at least for a day or two.

for one hiker, but works for two if you throw in extra cheese and a can of tuna fish or chicken.

Finally, some hikers prefer to concoct meals from scratch. Pasta, instant potatoes, and rice all work well in the woods. You can add a small can or pouch of freeze-dried vegetables or meat. Packaged gravies spice things up. You might want to try new recipes at home to check out quantities and to be sure they are as easy to prepare — and tasty — as you imagined.

PACKING

If you have ever doubted that our society is wasteful, try this: Buy your backpacking food for a week's trip. Remove all the excess packaging and put the food into Ziploc bags. Now look at the pile of discarded packaging: Chances are that it's about the size of your food bag!

Try shopping at your local food co-op, where you can buy exactly as much as you need of each ingredient, without all the wasteful packaging. You'll find a good selection of nuts, dried fruits, pastas, grains, and cereals, as well as dehydrated foods like Nature's Burger, falafel, or hummus, which can be easily prepared in the woods. (But a warning: Most hikers find that these meals are not as filling as the more traditional pasta or potato combinations.)

If you do buy food in multiple layers of wrappings and boxes, get rid of the excess. Repackaging your food makes it easier to fit everything into your backpack. Ziploc bags work best. (Anything that is squishy, oily, or liquid needs to be double-bagged.) Sandwich-size bags are fine for most purposes, but you'll need a couple of larger bags, too.

A hint: Most hikers find it worth the extra effort to measure out their meals in advance. Planning meal by meal is less complicated than loading up on staples, and it avoids the

SHOPPING LIST

SOUPS

Most hikers start dinner with instant soup. In fact, some consider soup the best part of dinner, especially on a cold day. It's easy to make, easy to clean up, and it helps fill the empty spot at the bottom of your stomach. Ramen noodles are a big favorite. I ate them for 200 days in a row on the Appalachian Trail and — this is not an exaggeration — never got sick of them. Salt replenishment is important, and packaged soups are high in sodium. Knorr and Lipton offer a wide selection; make sure you buy the no-cook, just-add-water selections. Miso soup (available at your local health-food store or co-op) is another good choice.

problem of opening your food bag on the last day to find out that you've got plenty of spaghetti sauce — and no spaghetti.

Repackaging Tips

- Staples and flavorings can be kept in their own individual bags: Parmesan cheese in one, dried milk in another, and so on.
- Put the main ingredients for each meal together. Make sure that you don't forget any flavoring packets. You can also cut out any instructions and keep them in the bag with the meal.
- A few of your purchases won't need to be repacked: Instant soups, Ramen noodles, hot chocolate, and such can stay in their original packets.
- Whenever possible, remove aluminum foil. It's tempting to throw aluminum-lined packages in fires, but aluminum doesn't burn. You'll need to pack it out. Best not to have it at all.

On short hikes you can indulge in gourmet dining. A hiker at Banff National Park, Alberta, Canada, fixes a salad and champagne lunch.

- Choose freeze-dried dinners that come in burnable pouches — or repackage them to avoid the extra garbage.

EXTENDED TRIPS

Most hikers can carry 5 to 7 days' worth of food (10–15 pounds) without too much discomfort; food for 8 to 10 days (15–20 pounds) is a grunt, and more than that is very tough. Here are a couple of things you can do to lessen the burden.

LIGHTEN YOUR LOAD. When Dan and I go out, we think of our food in terms of weight. If our hike is fewer than 5 days, we take whatever we want. If we'll be out for more than 5 days but fewer than 10, we take whatever we want for the first 5 days. For the remainder, we pack ultra-light foods like Lipton side dishes and freeze-dried meals. (Home-dehydrated foods may not fall into this category because they retain more moisture than commercially freeze-dried foods.) If we're going out for 10 or more days, we take all lightweight foods.

BREAK UP YOUR JOURNEY. Some people leave caches of food for themselves in the woods. (This means additional planning, and driving, and making sure your cache is animal-proof.) Or you can use the so-called food drop, where you mail a box of supplies to yourself in care of "general delivery" at a post office near your route of travel. This is particularly convenient in the East, where trails are never very far from towns. Again, this requires a little extra planning: You'll need to figure out where to send your box; how much food to take with you and how much food to mail; and how you're going to get from the trail to the post office.

SHOPPING LIST

DINNER

Freeze-dried meals, Lipton side dishes, macaroni and cheese, home-dehydrated meals. Or concoct your own on the spot by using what I call the Chinese-menu approach: A carbohydrate from Column A + a meat and/or vegetable from Column B + a sauce or flavoring from Column C, and you've got yourself a meal. (But pay attention — not everything goes with everything.)

BASE (A)	PROTEIN AND VEGGIES (B)	FLAVORING (C)
Instant potatoes	Small cans of:	Tomato paste
Rice	tuna	Tomato sauce mix
Pasta ($^1/_4$–$^1/_3$ pound/person; angel hair cooks quickest)	turkey	Gravy mix
	chicken	Onion or mushroom
Stovetop stuffing mix	TVP*	soup mix
Couscous		Parmesan cheese

* Textured vegetable protein for the uninitiated: can be used to make veggie burgers or to add bulk to one-pot dinners.

PLANNING

With all the choices, planning meals for a couple of people for a few days can be daunting. Here's how we do it:

IF YOU'RE GOING OUT FOR:	TAKE:
1–5 days	Whatever you like best
6–9 days	5 of your favorite meals and the rest lightweight* meals
10 or more days	All light-weight†

*No cans. Lightweight meals include Lipton dinners and freeze-dried foods. Home-dried foods retain more moisture; they may or may not be lightweight.

†Some of these lightweight meals should be no-cook, freeze-dried meals to save on fuel.

Experiment and have fun with your meals. It's a good bet that whatever you cook on the trail will taste delicious. But don't be surprised if you end your hike and feel an irresistible urge to head for the nearest restaurant. After a few days in the backcountry, chances are that you'll feel an overwhelming affection for the words "Open" and "All You Can Eat."

NO-TRACE
CAMPING

You reach the campsite at 5
P.M. Ten miles was a little much for
the first day out, but you've managed
to do it, and you're feeling a little
proud of yourself. Also a little tired.
As you approach the site, you see two
tents up already. You also see that the
camping area looks different from the
surrounding woods. The earth is
trammeled into a network of trails,
and there isn't much ground cover: no
shrubs or flowers or grasses, and no
downed wood either. It's all been
burned for firewood, you realize, as
you look down and see a series of
charred rock fire rings, most of which
are doing double duty as garbage
pits. Nor does the wood scavenging
stop at ground level: Sharp white
scars mark where sticks and
branches have been torn from trees.
From inside one of the tents, you can
hear a radio playing.

When you approach a little
closer, you hear someone say, "Darn!
We've got company." You scope out
the area, looking for a place to pitch
your tent. You don't want to disturb
the current occupants, but you don't
see many choices. The two tents that
are already up occupy the flattest flat
spots. The other hikers look at you
warily, obviously wishing you would
go somewhere else. You wish you
could go somewhere else, too, but
you can't: This is a park that has a
"camping in designated sites only"
rule, and the next designated site is 3

miles away. Finally, you find a spot back in the woods a little. As you're putting up your tent, you hear some new arrivals enter the area, and when you turn around, you see a group of eight teenage boys and three leaders. "Darn! More company!" you mutter as you look warily at the group, hoping

they will go somewhere else — or at least let you get a good night's sleep.

Ah, wilderness!

What's a hiker to do?

WHY MINIMUM IMPACT?

In bygone years, woodsmen could chop wood, dig trenches, burn fires, and bury trash with nary a thought to their impact on the wilderness. The wilderness was bigger back then, the users fewer. In fact, in the early years of this century, the Appalachian Mountain Club, which maintains a vast network of trails in the northeastern forests and mountains, found that its trails were suffering not from overuse but underuse. There wasn't enough foot traffic to keep them from growing over.

That's not the case anymore.

Today, backcountry recreation is big business, and it's not limited to hikers. Backcountry use among everyone has skyrocketed: Mountain bikers, ATV riders, fishermen, hunters, skiers, snowmobilers, rock climbers, boaters, and a host of others are all competing with one another for a share of a wilderness pie that is itself shrinking with each passing year.

You may have seen the results of overuse. In some oft-visited areas, trails are so deeply eroded that tree roots form a spiderweb structure a foot or more above the ground. Fire rings, garbage, and bare, lifeless patches of earth are common — but they are only the most obvious signs of impact. There are many others that are less immediately evident: water pollution;

> 66 This place has everything — every essential, every conceivable extra. It has the level ground, the good grass, the wood, the easy access to water, that make a camp comfortable. It has the shelter and shade, the wide views, the openness and breeziness, that raise comfort to luxuriousness. There are no mosquitoes on that clifftop; there are trees shaped to the back where a man can sit and read; the ground is the coarse granular kind that produces no dust and that, in the remote possibility of rain, would not produce mud either. Every tree has stubs of branches at the proper height for hanging things; there are enough downed logs for benches and cooking tables. And this air, at ten thousand feet, hits the bottom of the lungs like ether. 99
>
> — Wallace Stegner,
> *Where the Bluebird Sings
> to the Lemonade Springs*

the absence of a certain plant; a decreased birthrate in a population of endangered species. Sometimes, we don't even know what the natural environment is supposed to look like. In Shenandoah National Park, for instance, visitors are apt to use words like "pristine" and "untouched" to describe a landscape that is in fact neither: The forests in the park were both logged and farmed until well into

A popular shelter on the Appalachian Trail in Shenandoah National Park. What better argument for the low-impact ethic than scenes like this? One remedy: Hike off-season.

this century. It takes a bit of time in the backcountry to be able to see the differences between a natural, unimpacted landscape and one that has been damaged or changed by humans.

Minimum-impact camping is a matter of sensitizing ourselves to the natural environment. It's a way of thinking about the backcountry, and about our place in it. It's a realization that while one person's activities may not be objectionable in and of themselves, a thousand — or a million — people doing the same thing is a different issue entirely. The minimum-impact camper realizes that the backcountry is fragile, and that those who venture into the wilderness need to take responsibility for leaving it the way they found it. What it comes down

Two antidotes to overcrowding: Hike off-season and go somewhere else, such as the Nordenskjöld Glacier near Pyramiden, Norway, at 650 miles from the Pole, the northernmost town on earth.

to is, in the end, quite simple. Remember kindergarten?

Pick up your toys.

Clean up your mess.

Leave things as you found them.

That's the essence of minimum-impact camping. And it's the new law of the wild.

AVOIDING THE CROWDS

Minimum impact begins before you even reach the trailhead; it begins when you choose where and when to hike. The backcountry is increasingly crowded, but the crowds tend to flock to the same areas and the same trails year after year. Considering that most people take to the woods to get away

from the congestion of everyday life, it seems astonishing that they don't take the trouble to find out where the crowds will be.

Go Somewhere Else

Take another trail. Stay at a different campsite. Choose the tough way, and remember a simple, inviolable rule: The farther you are from a road, the fewer the people. The backcountry experience is magical, and it's well worth the extra time and effort to find a place where an elk charges, splashing, into a river, or a loon sends its demented primeval cry echoing across a northcountry lake. A moose awkwardly lumbering into a pond for an evening snack is both comical and

TIPS FOR WALKING SOFTLY

As you grumble about how crowded the backcountry has become, remember that you're in there too, crowding it up for other hikers. The following tips will help you mini- mize your impact on your fellow wilderness travelers.

● Choose muted, "I'm-not-here" colors: browns and grays and dull greens, whenever possible. You'll blend in better with the environ- ment and be less obvious to other hikers. The one exception is hunting season, which demands a bright orange vest and hat.

● The size of your group makes a difference. Up to four or five people is fine, but if there are more of you, break into a couple of smaller groups. There's a benefit for you: Small groups are more likely to see wildlife.

● Stay on the trails. On moun- tainous terrain, switchbacks help ease the climbs and descents. They also help reduce trail erosion. Don't take shortcuts.

● Walking around the edges of boggy areas widens and erodes the trail, so whenever possible stick to the middle of the trail, even if it takes you through a mud puddle.

● The bane of the wilderness is a noisy group, whether it numbers two or twenty. Radios, if carried, should be listened to with earphones only. (Even a quiet radio is obtrusive.) Most hikers cherish their sense of isolation from the everyday world. If you must bring your cellular phone, be discreet.

majestic, but it's not something you'll see when you're camped at the back- country equivalent of Grand Central Terminal.

It's easy to get information about less crowded trails. In the national parks and forests, rangers are well aware of the problem of overcrowding: Tell them the kind of hike you want to take and ask their opinions. Or ask at your local outfitter.

Hike Off-Season

Even slightly off-season helps, espe- cially on very popular trails. Weekdays are better than weekends; above all, beware of common school holidays like Easter break. The weeks surrounding long weekends are also crowded.

Hiking off-season is a particularly good strategy when you want to hike a specific, popular trail. Take the Appalachian Trail in Great Smoky Mountains National Park, for example. Its ridgeline route is easily one of the most spectacular in the East, and it meets all the criteria for the perfect week-long hiking trip: length, road access, scenery, drama. Unfortunately, Great Smoky Mountains National Park is *the* most visited in the country, with more visitors than Yosemite, or Yellowstone, or the Grand Canyon. During peak hiking periods, the shelters on the Appalachian Trail are overcrowded, the litter is obscene, and the sanitary conditions are disgusting.

But there's no rule that says you have to hike during peak season. I hiked the Smokies in February and shared a shelter only twice with other hikers. (I did, however, have to carry winter gear and showshoes. For an off-season trip, you need to make sure you understand the weather conditions and are prepared, equipped, and skilled to deal with them.)

Does taking less popular trails or hiking off-season compromise your experience? If everyone else is going on a particular trail at a particular time, shouldn't you do the same? Does avoiding the crowds condemn you to the short end of the backcountry stick?

Mob reasoning may have a certain primal appeal, but don't let it fool you. The most popular season is not necessarily the best hiking season, even if you could magically make the crowds disappear. Say you want to hike in New Hampshire's White Mountains, which play host to an annual 6 million to 7 million visitors. You don't have to don snowshoes or crampons and head into the arctic conditions of a White Mountain January. But how about September, when the summer crowds are gone? Or October, when the spectacular New England foliage sets the mountains aflame? The weather is drier, the air crisp and cool; the mosquitoes, blackflies, and no-see-ums are gone — and so are the crowds. In other words, not only is off-season in the Whites less congested, it's also more pleasant — with the usual caveat: As with all hiking, be sure you are equipped for the weather. In alpine areas, fall hiking brings a risk of snow and colder temperatures. Remember the Boy Scout motto, and be prepared.

Hiking softly means respecting the natural world through which you're traveling. It also means you'll be more likely to glimpse that world.

THE MINIMUM-IMPACT CAMPSITE

● You need a flat spot the size of your tent, without too many roots and rocks protruding.

● Consider the ground cover. Forest duff is best: It's comfortable to sleep on, and you won't be crushing vegetation. Sand and gravel are good, too. Above treeline, look for barren ground to avoid damaging fragile alpine plants. Stay away from damp, vegetated areas — especially meadows. They may be pretty, but they're fragile, as well as wet, buggy, and not especially comfortable.

● In an established campsite, stay in the obvious tentsites. Otherwise, camp 100 (or even better, 200) feet away from the water supply. This helps prevent clustering and pollution.

● You'll have more privacy — and create less impact for others — if you're hidden in a clump of trees or behind some boulders. You don't want to be part of someone else's view.

● Watch for obvious hazards. In forests, look up! Dead branches are a real danger on stormy nights. In alpine areas, stay away from obvious rock and avalanche chutes.

● Burrowing in trees and rocks gives you protection from the wind. If possible, pitch your tent so the wind is at your back.

● Do not wash — yourself, your pots and pans, your clothes — directly in a water source. In particular, avoid introducing soap to a water source: It may be biodegradable, but that doesn't mean you want to drink it! Fill a pot or a water bag and rinse off away from the stream, lake, or spring.

● Wear camp shoes in camp. Tromping around a site in sneakers or sandals has less impact than tromping around in Vibram soles.

CHOOSING A CAMPSITE

Where to camp depends on where you are hiking. In very popular areas, there are bound to be established sites, noted in guidebooks, and even identified by trail signs. Such sites offer a nice flat spot, already cleared, for your tent, a water source nearby, and maybe even an outhouse. Often, there is a fire ring in the middle of the site, with a few big logs around it for comfortable seating. In heavily used areas, a resident ranger may patrol the area.

Camping at official sites like these is a good idea in a well-trammeled area. You'll notice that these sites show the usual impact of too much use: well-worn trails, stripped ground cover, no firewood (but plenty of fire rings). What's minimum impact about a site like this? Simply that the damage has already been done, and you're unlikely to cause further harm. Concentrating use in established sites is generally regarded as the lesser of two evils: It creates a great deal of impact in a small area, but the surrounding land is left alone.

On the opposite end of the spectrum is the pristine site, the campsite that didn't exist until you decided to call it home for the night. If you're traveling off-trail, or in a relatively remote area — or if you are trying to avoid the crowds — you'll probably end up creating your own campsite. Some people (I'm one of them) like the secluded, cozy feeling that comes with carving out a niche in the wilderness.

But remember the responsibility you take on when you do it. In the morning, you want to leave the area as pristine as you found it.

TO BURN OR NOT TO BURN

Time was when fire craft was the cornerstone of woodcraft. Scouts took to the wilderness armed with axes and saws and knowledge of which wood burned better, or quicker, or longer, or hotter. No more.

The advent of portable backpacking stoves has rendered some of these skills obsolete — or at least

MINIMUM-IMPACT FIRE

● Ask yourself, "What will the effect of this fire be?" Make fires only in areas that can sustain the impact. Forests are better than meadows. There's no place for fires above treeline, where timber is scarce and the vegetation is fragile.

● Fire rings serve a purpose in heavily used areas: They concentrate fires into one place. Always use existing fire rings, and avoid building new ones, especially in pristine sites.

● Fires make scars. It's best to make fires on mineral soil, or on gravel or sand. Otherwise, the National Outdoor Leadership School recommends making a pit

fire by digging a hole about 12 inches around and 8 inches deep. In the morning, the ashes are covered with soil, and the top layer of sod is replaced.

● Use only loose, downed wood. Do not break wood off trees — even if it's dead. Large logs serve a purpose in the ecosystem: Leave them alone. Go some distance away to find wood to avoid stripping the ground cover from the area right around your tent.

● Small fires have less impact than large fires, so resist the urge to have a sky-scarring bonfire.

● Make sure the fire is completely out before you leave it. It only takes a spark to start a forest fire.

A strategy for avoiding crowds: Hike in Death Valley. But pack *everything* out; in the desert anything you leave will last indefinitely, making the low-impact ethic more important than ever.

unnecessary. Even people who like the friendly warmth of a backcountry fire usually cook on stoves. Once you get the hang of them, stoves are quick and easy, and they do away with the risk of dropping a pot full of spaghetti into the ashes.

But while they may not be necessary, fires remain a part of the backcountry experience. Unfortunately, too many people are building too many of them. The scars are everywhere. In an eastern forest, it may be a series of streamside campsites, each with its own three-foot-high fire ring. Western lake basins are equally vulnerable: Some are literally dotted with fire rings — as many as a hundred, or even more. Worst of all is the backcountry

incineration site, with the remains of last night's log smoldering over a collection of half-burned cans and blackened aluminum foil.

Sometimes the problem is a matter of aesthetics. A lake surrounded by tired-looking, overused campsites and dirty, garbage-strewn fire rings hardly lives up to the wilderness image cherished by backpackers. Sometimes it's a matter of ecology: Small animals hide behind logs and downed wood; in certain fragile areas, an entire species can be threatened by indiscriminate firebuilding. And then there's Smokey the Bear. Each year, hundreds of thousands of backcountry acres are burned by forest fires; careless backpackers cause at least a few of them.

Still, there's no getting around the fact that people like campfires. Fires are a part of the wilderness experience: We enjoy their warmth, their companionship, their memories. Somehow the hypnotic flickering and the play of flames just seem right at the end of the day. Does minimum-impact camping mean you have to forgo a cherished part of the backcountry experience?

No. But it does mean you have to think before you light that match.

GARBAGE

"Pack it in, pack it out."

You'll see the sign everywhere: at trailheads, at designated campsites, and even, increasingly, at campgrounds accessible to automobiles.

It's probably the simplest, most obvious part of the minimum-impact canon, yet in many overused areas, it's also the most commonly ignored.

There are no garbage facilities in the backcountry, nor should there be. Garbage attracts animals, who then learn to associate humans with food. They also make a mess when they raid garbage cans and dig up buried trash.

The only way to handle trash is to burn it or carry it out. All of it.

HUMAN WASTE

There's no need to overcomplicate this simple subject.

If you are traveling in a group of more than 10 or 12 people, you'll need to dig a latrine. Diseases like giardiasis (see page 142) are commonly

Don't wash yourself, your pots and pans, or your clothes in any water source. Even Dunifield Creek on the Appalachian Trail in New Jersey is clean, but only because nearby campsites are carefully managed.

Woman's best friend: Molly and Smoky along the trail to Hilgard Basin, Lee Metcalf Wilderness, Gallatin National Forest, Montana.

● Minimize the garbage you take into the backcountry in the first place by repackaging your food in plastic bags or by choosing foods in burnable packaging. Some freeze-dried food manufacturers use aluminum for freshness. But others use plastic, which is burnable.

● Some hikers burn cans to get rid of food residue and smells. That's fine (especially in bear country) as long as they then pack out the remains. Nothing is uglier than a backcountry fire ring that has been used as an incineration site.

● Glass is heavy and it shatters. If it breaks, you won't want to pack it out. Leave it at home.

● Bring a few quart-size heavy-duty Ziploc bags for garbage.

● And while you're at it, it wouldn't hurt to leave the backcountry a little cleaner than when you found it....

spread by feces, and while it's true that cattle and beavers are often responsible, human waste can and does contaminate water sources. So before you choose a site, make sure you know where the water is — and then go the other way. It's important that your latrine be one that people in your group will actually use, so make it close enough for convenience — but far enough for privacy. Dig a hole about 10 inches wide and 10 inches deep. In the morning, you'll need to replace the dirt and the sod and cover the area to make it look natural.

Members of small groups can simply scatter in different directions to take care of their needs. You'll need a small plastic trowel with which to dig a 6-inch-deep hole. Fill it when you're done. Bacteria will do the rest.

Timing is, of course, an entirely individual issue. If you can, consider waiting until later in the day when you have hiked a couple of miles away from camp. When campsites are frequently used, the surrounding area is impacted by human waste. Bacterial counts in the soil can become high, and runoff from storms can spread disease into nearby water. Not to mention the fact that in a very highly used area there's always the unpleasant possibility of choosing a spot that has been previously used. Waiting until you've been on the trail awhile means that the impact is spread so widely that it's virtually negligible. In all cases, be sure to take care of personal matters well away from water.

Women will additionally have the problem of trash associated with menstrual periods. This material must be packed out or completely burned in a hot fire. See page 191 for more information on women and wilderness.

DOGS

Dogs are controversial in the backcountry. Some dogs scare some people. Dogs chase wildlife. And bark. They can get into confrontations with rattlesnakes, porcupines, and bears. They pollute water sources. They get into fights with other dogs. They can overheat on hot, exposed climbs; injure their feet on tough, rocky footway; develop hip and joint problems; and suffer from dehydration — or contract giardiasis. They are not permitted on trails in many national parks.

Dogs can also be fine companions, and they offer a measure of safety (if only psychological) to people traveling alone. For every person who wants to ban dogs in the backcountry, there is someone who wouldn't think about hiking without Rover. A wide selection of backpacks are available so that your pet can carry his food in comfort.

Taking care of canine companions in the backcountry is beyond the scope of this book, but before you take a dog into the wilderness, you should review some basic information. Remember: Your pet didn't ask to be included in your adventure, so the least you can do is ensure his health and safety.

A last word on dogs: Problem dogs usually have problem owners. If you are one of these, leave your dog at home.

BACKCOUNTRY
9 1 1

Wilderness first aid differs from the ordinary back-in-civilization variety in one critical way. In the everyday world of cities, towns, and roads, help is a phone call away. In the wilderness, help may be many hours away, and maybe even longer.

That's why the most important piece of first aid equipment you bring into the woods is knowledge. If you are going to spend any time in a place where there is no access to medical help, you need to have first aid training. Period. If you don't, take a course. (Your local American Red Cross chapter can tell you where and when.) Better yet, take a course in wilderness first aid.

It's merely common sense: You should know how to stop bleeding, splint limbs, treat burns, treat for shock, give mouth-to-mouth resuscitation, and perform CPR. In an ideal world, we would all know how to do all of those things. But in the back-country, it's not an ideal — it's a necessity. If you plan to lead a group into a remote wilderness area, you should also know how to plan an evacuation, how to build a litter, and how to stabilize a victim for transport. In addition, you'll need to have information from your participants pertaining to medical conditions, allergies, and prescription drugs.

The subject of first aid requires a book, not a chapter. (Many are available; see Sources and Resources for recommendations.) What I will do here is talk about the kinds of problems that are specific to medical emergencies in a wilderness setting. I'll also cover some other important issues pertaining to staying healthy on the trail.

ETHICS OF BACKCOUNTRY SAFETY AND RESCUE

I was nine years old the first time I visited Mount Washington. There are lots of superlatives to catch a child's attention on top of the tallest mountain in the Northeast: the arctic conditions, the 100-mile views, the worst weather in the world. What caught my attention was the display that listed the names of all the people who had died on Mount Washington.

That plaque still fascinates me, the more so because I can't quite believe that the list keeps getting longer. But it does.

Every year, people die in the backcountry, and most of these deaths are avoidable. The mountaineering and wilderness literature is filled with accounts of preventable accidents, yet every year people continue to make the same predictable mistakes — with the same predictable results. Anecdotes abound: Just about any experienced mountaineer can tell stories about climbs that had to be aborted in order to mount impromptu rescues. And search-and-rescue teams express justifiable anger when they are called upon to risk their lives for someone who violated basic rules of wilderness safety and common sense.

Recently, cellular phones have started to pop up in the wilderness, touted (among other things) as a solution to the problem of summoning backcountry rescue. An avidly debated aesthetic issue is at stake — at this point, cellular phones are shunned by most hikers — but that is not important here. What is important is this: Like any other technology, telephones are a tool; they are not a substitute for common sense, or skill, or proper equipment. Nor does having one give a backpacker the right to take risks he would not ordinarily take. For one thing, if you fall and smash your phone, or if the batteries freeze or run down, it's not going to do you any good. Second, although it is increasingly difficult to find a place where your phone will not work, it is still possible not to be electronically connected to the rest of the world. And third, every rescue puts rescuers at risk.

Shoulds and shouldn'ts become irrelevant when life is at stake. Climbers and hikers recognize a responsibility to help others, knowing that it may be their turn next to be rescued. The ethic of the backcountry demands that hikers help fellow hikers. But it also demands that each hiker be competent, appropriately equipped, and responsible. In other words, backpackers are first and foremost responsible for keeping themselves out of trouble. This means having the skills and equipment to cope with wilderness conditions and challenges. It also means understanding what those conditions and challenges are — and taking them seriously.

Is there a positive side to all of this

talk about accidents and risks and life-threatening challenges? Indeed there is: With a little forethought and responsibility, and with a firm respect for the terrain and environment in which you propose to hike, you can reduce the likelihood of a backcountry emergency to almost nil.

WEATHER AND SAFETY

Hikers quickly learn that the only certainty about weather is that they're going to have some. They learn that a rainy morning is going to be a rainy morning regardless of their opinions, expectations, or feelings on the subject.

They also learn that there is a different kind of beauty in foul weather: in the raindrops that hang, glittering, from spring ferns; in a curtain of high-country fog that blows in and out, now obscuring the views, now revealing them. "No rain, no pain, no Maine," Appalachian Trail through-hikers chant as they slog through the bogs of Vermont under overcast skies.

It takes a while to come to terms with weather. In the matter of our everyday environment, we're used to having control: air conditioning, fans, central heating — even dehumidifiers. We give up all that when we enter the woods. What we gain in return is an appreciation for the natural environment — and an understanding of how to coexist with it.

Our relationship with weather progresses. First, we learn to survive it; then to tolerate it. After we master the basics of staying comfortable, we begin

> 66 Generally speaking, a howling wilderness does not howl; it is the imagination of the traveler that does the howling. 99
>
> — Henry David Thoreau
> *The Maine Woods*

to accept rain and fog and snow and cold and heat as just another part of our environment, another challenge we can willingly meet. We revel in the knowledge that we can be comfortable in temperatures and conditions that drive most people indoors. And finally, we learn to enjoy the weather. Or, at the very least, we enjoy ourselves in it.

Sometimes, of course, the weather is just plain foul, and all the positive attitude in the world isn't going to compensate for the fact that your three-day-old wet socks smell about as bad as toxic waste, that your once warm and fluffy sleeping bag is now filled with soggy clumps of waterlogged down, and that your allegedly breathable/waterproof rain gear seems determined to be neither. It's hard to keep up a positive attitude after you've planned weeks ahead for a three-day wilderness weekend, and just as you hit the trail, a wet front does, too. Sometimes, a graceful surrender is in order.

But for the most part, it's not necessary to throw in the towel and head for the nearest motel. Backpackers can learn

HYPOTHERMIA

Hypothermia is the inability of the body
to keep itself warm, generally because
of prolonged exposure to cold weather.

So quick, a quiz: Who is most at
risk for hypothermia?
1) A hiker on an exposed, windy slope.
It's August, the temperature is 45
degrees, and there's a slight drizzle.
2) A skier on a forested cross-country
trail. It's January and the temperature
is 20 degrees. A light snow is falling
steadily.

If you picked the second one,
you're not alone. You are, however,
wrong.

This simple and common miscon-
ception — that hypothermia is a
danger only in wintertime — is
responsible for scores of backcountry
emergencies each year. Too often,
summertime hikers find themselves
unprepared to weather a spell of rain
and wind at altitude.

How can an August hiker be more
at risk than a January skier?

For one thing, the skier is unlikely
to be surprised by the cold temperatures. Even if he's just out for a day,
he's got a hat and a jacket and gloves
(and in this example, he has the added
protection from the wind of the surrounding trees). By contrast, an August
hiker is more likely to underestimate
the weather. I am always shocked to
see people walking above treeline clad
in nothing but shorts and a T-shirt, and
carrying no extra layers. Rainy 45-
degree days are not uncommon in the
alpine zone, even in midsummer, but
somehow, they continue to surprise

to make do in just about any combination
of conditions. And you can always take
comfort in the one certainty about
weather: If you stick around for a while,
it'll change.

When we talk about bad weather,
we're generally talking about a matter of
nuisance, not safety. You can spend your
entire hiking life without confronting anything more unpleasant than a few soggy
nights — unless you're unlucky or unprepared. Then one soggy night could stretch
into two soggy nights and then a third, followed by a cold snap that turns your
damp clothes into frozen ones. And all of
a sudden, an annoying situation becomes
miserable — and maybe even dangerous.

No one should ever die from environmental factors. Hypothermia, heat
stroke, and altitude sickness are all
usually preventable, even in foul conditions. The fact that people do die — not
often, but sometimes — is the reason
for this chapter.

An April snowstorm at Charlies Bunion on the AT in the Great Smoky Mountains, North Carolina–Tennessee border. Always carry clothing for the coldest possible conditions for the season and location of your outing.

newcomers to the highcountry. Even experienced hikers sometimes fall under the illusion that they can out-power or outrun the weather.

Second, snow doesn't make you as wet as rain. It's the combination of wet and cold, not just the cold, that is working against the hiker in this example.

And finally, the exposed, windy slope is a particularly nasty place to be caught. The hiker will probably be all right if he remembered his hat, gloves, rain gear, and an insulating layer. If not, he needs to get down to a more protected area quickly.

Hypothermia — not criminals, not snakes, not bears, not avalanches, not rockslides, not Lyme disease, not pol-luted water — is the most common, dangerous, and insidious threat in the outdoors. Every year, in mountain ranges from Georgia's southern Appalachians to New Hampshire's Presidentials, from the High Sierra to the Colorado Rockies, people venture into the highcountry without the proper equipment, or without knowing how and when to use the equipment they have. Far too often, hikers do not know — or do not believe — that in the backcountry, hypothermia-inducing conditions can creep up on them without warning, anywhere.

Hypothermia Prevention

THINK HYPOTHERMIA. The best defense against hypothermia is to rec-

Signs at treeline in the White Mountains of New Hampshire warn hikers that they are entering a zone where they could encounter the worst weather in the world. In 1934, the weather observatory at the summit of Mount Washington recorded a wind speed of 231 miles an hour — the highest land wind speed ever recorded.

ognize when you are vulnerable to it. This might sound obvious, but it isn't. Hiking generates body heat, so hikers can walk along comfortably without even realizing just how cold it is. In mild winter weather, I often hike wearing only a pair of Capilene tights, a polyester T-shirt, and either a light Polartec jacket or a windproof jacket (which, in my case, is also my Gore-Tex rain gear). But when I stop — even if only for five minutes — I have to put on extra clothes and a hat immediately. The combination of chilled sweat and low air temperature is a recipe for hypothermia.

Adjusting for cold should become almost second nature for you; if it does, you may never cross the threshold between being cold and being hypothermic. Covering and uncovering your head is the quickest, most effective way to control your body tempera-ture, so in cold weather, keep your hat handy. Not only does your rain gear shut out rain, it also protects you from wind and holds in your body heat. Make sure you snack often to keep your energy up. And above all, pay attention to your surroundings and to the way your body is reacting to them. Never forget that hypothermia robs you of your most important tool: your presence of mind. People have actually died lying next to a backpack full of warm clothes because they did not recognize their condition early enough. The time to stop hypothermia is before it starts.

STAY DRY. Wet weather multiplies the effects of cold weather, because moisture robs the body of heat. So staying dry becomes your most important concern. But even with the right equipment, staying dry is not as easy as it sounds. It's not just rain that makes you wet: Humidity, sweat, and temperature all contribute, especially if you are exerting yourself.

In cold, wet conditions, you'll need to constantly monitor yourself. The goal is to walk at a sustainable pace at a comfortable temperature. Forget about pushing yourself to the limit: Slow and steady is the key here. You want to work up some heat, but not so much that you drown in sweat, and you don't want to wear yourself out. If you have to stop for too many rest breaks, you'll quickly get cold.

STOP BEFORE THE PROBLEM STARTS. Hypothermia is sneaky. It creeps up on a victim a little at a time, offering plenty of chances to compound the problem with mistakes and misjudgments. The problem is exacerbated by peer pressure to keep up and be strong. No one wants to be a wimp, a wet blanket, the weakest member of a group. Hypothermia, however, is not a matter of strength or willpower. In fact, it's often the strongest members of a group who fall victim to it because they are more likely to try to ignore their symptoms and push on.

If anyone in your group is complaining of cold, stop: At this point, he may need nothing more than an extra layer of clothes followed by a stiff walk uphill. But if the problem persists, you need to act, immediately, before the situation degenerates. Give up your mileage goal and your intended campsite. Never encourage a hypothermia victim to "just hike a little while longer." Too often, hikers push on, thinking that they'll be okay if they just keep working up a sweat. In reality, they are getting colder and colder — and more and more exhausted — but they don't realize the danger because their exertion makes them feel warmer. When they stop, hypothermia can incapacitate them within minutes.

Hypothermia Symptoms

Unfortunately, the early symptoms of

A NOTE TO DAYHIKERS

People die from hypothermia because they don't have the right equipment for the conditions, or they don't know when to use it. Dayhikers are especially vulnerable when the weather turns bad. Backpackers have their houses on their backs. They can stop and get warm with their tents and sleeping bags and clothes and stoves. Dayhikers don't have that option. And in mountainous terrain, storms often strike without warning.

If you are hiking above treeline or anyplace where the weather can quickly get cold and rough, always take a daypack and carry emergency gear in it: rainwear, a hat, gloves, extra layers, a water bottle, snacks, and a basic first aid kit. Take this gear even if the weather is warm and sunny, even if the forecast is for continued good weather, even if your more experienced friend insists it's not necessary. If this seems excessive to you, remember that every year people die because they do not heed this advice. The reports of search-and-rescue workers are a series of variations on a droningly repetitive theme: What they have in common are an unprepared hiker and a mountain that changed its mood. No one should ever venture into the wilderness without first asking: What are the worst conditions I could encounter? Am I prepared for them?

hypothermia can mask themselves as everyday chilliness. Shivering and goose bumps, for instance, are actually two of the body's normal heat-regulating strategies — they don't necessarily indicate hypothermia. But prolonged shivering should never be ignored — it is a sign that your body is working overtime to maintain its temperature.

If your body is unable to maintain its temperature, it falls into the early stages of hypothermia. Shivering becomes quite violent, and the victim may make sudden contorted or convulsive movements. As the body temperature drops, the victim may complain of feeling cold or tired, and he may seem slow or sluggish. At this stage, the victim may not be thinking clearly. A classic occurrence in early hypothermia is misplacing or dropping a hat or glove — which, of course, further exacerbates the problem.

As the body's temperature continues to drop, the symptoms increase in severity. What was previously noticed as poor coordination becomes stumbling or staggering. Speech is thick and slurred. The victim may be irrational and may resist help, possibly violently. At this stage, the victim may not even be aware that he is in danger; instead of feeling consciously cold, he may simply feel drowsy. Shivering stops, replaced by a muscular rigidity. The skin is blue and pupils are dilated. Vision failure is common.

True winter camping requires special gear and special skills, but in early spring and late autumn or at high elevations, winter conditions can seemingly come out of nowhere.

Once the body temperature drops below about 92 degrees, the victim cannot warm himself by internal means. Without intervention, his temperature, blood pressure, and pulse will continue to drop, leading to the loss of reflexes and consciousness, an erratic heartbeat, and, finally, coma and death.

HYPOTHERMIA TREATMENT

1 Assemble your group and assess the situation. If you are in a frequently used area, ask other hikers for help.

2 Get the victim in as protected an area as possible. Put up a tent or a tarp, find a windbreak, or cover the victim with a space blanket. Put down a mattress pad for insulation.

3 Make sure the victim has a hat and, if possible, a hood or balaclava to cover the neck. If dry socks are available, cover the feet, too.

4 A severely hypothermic person cannot warm himself: He needs an external source of heat. But forget about the old body-to-body method. Recent research has shown that when a person becomes hypothermic, blood pools in the muscles, where it becomes acidic. Body-to-body contact warms the pooled, acidic blood too quickly and sends it back to the heart, where the resulting shock can lead to cardiac arrest. Instead, concentrate on stopping heat loss. Remove wet clothes and put the victim in warm, dry clothes. Then put him in a sleeping bag.

5 Winter hikers should carry heat paks (those plastic bags that can be activated to create several hours of heat). Place these in the victim's armpits and groin. This method is safer than body-to-body contact

because it warms only the blood that has been circulating in major vessels.

6 If someone else is available, have him heat up some water. If the victim is conscious, a warm drink or soup will help. If he is unconscious or semi-conscious, do not attempt to make him drink. A hot-water bottle can be put in the sleeping bag with the victim.

7 Do NOT give the victim alcohol. Alcohol is a vasodilator, and dilated blood vessels lose heat. Also avoid drinks with caffeine.

8 Do not allow the victim to fall asleep.

9 Any handling of a severely hypothermic person should be extremely gentle. In the late stages of hypothermia, the heart muscle is actually chilled and any shock or jolting could cause it to arrest.

10 Leaving a victim alone is the absolute last resort. If you must leave to get help, be sure his condition is stabilized and that he is protected from the elements.

11 Once a victim's condition is stabilized and his temperature has returned to normal, he MUST either hike out or be evacuated so that he can receive a full medical evaluation. The victim should NOT be allowed to continue the hike, even if he feels up to it.

MAKING CAMP AND STAYING DRY

● Use Waterproof Stuff Sacks for Your Clothes and Sleeping Bag. You'll also find several uses for extra garbage bags (temporary storage of wet rain gear; a waterproof lining for your pack; extra protection for food hung in a tree). Also carry extra Ziploc bags to keep smaller items like matches, flashlights, cameras, and papers dry.

● Have Easy Access to Your Tent. Your job will be easier if you can get your tent out of your pack without having to unpack everything else first. You need to be able to get to your tent without exposing everything else to the weather.

● Protect Your Gear. While you're setting up camp, be sure to keep everything else dry. Keep your rain cover securely on your pack. If necessary, drape your poncho or space blanket over any gear that needs protection.

● Pitch the Tent. Put the tent poles together first, then get the body of your tent out of your pack. Some people can get their tents up under their rain flys without getting the tent wet. This is a trick best practiced at home, and it doesn't work with all tents. The tent I use most often goes up in less than two minutes. A bandanna mops up the little water that sneaks in.

● Get Warm. Once your tent is up, in go your air mattress, sleeping bag, and warm clothes. If I'm not cold, I usually finish making camp before crawling into the tent and changing clothes. But if I'm cold, I take a break and warm up as soon as my tent is pitched and my gear is protected.

● Keep the Rain Out. Try not to bring in too much moisture when you go in and out of the tent — this is especially important if you have a down sleeping bag, because it completely loses its insulating capacity when wet. You might want to leave your bag in its waterproof stuff sack until you're all set up. Leave your wet rain gear rolled up in a corner or in the tent vestibule.

FROSTBITE

Unlike hypothermia, which can occur at temperatures up to 50 degrees (and, on rare occasions, even higher), frostbite requires temperatures well below freezing, so the three-season hiker is usually not at risk. But when the mercury drops below freezing, you need to be concerned with keeping your extremities — face, toes, and fingers — warm and dry. Avoid contact with cold objects (especially with metal fuel canisters), and avoid contact with liquids like water or, worse, fuel (which remains liquid no matter how cold it is). Pay attention to how your feet and hands feel. If they are numb with cold, warm them up with dry socks and mittens. If they are turning whitish and waxy, you have frostnip, and you need to take care of it before it gets any worse. If your cheeks are cold, cover them with warm hands. Hands can be warmed by putting them in your armpits. Your feet will need the help of a trailmate's stomach.

Anything worse than frostnip requires evacuation. Deep frostbite is characterized by tissue that is white and waxy, and the underlying tissue is hard — that is, frozen. You should never try to thaw the injury in the backcountry: Improper thawing can lead to infection and amputation. Deep frostbite should not be thawed until the hiker is in a place where the injury will not refreeze. Finally, forget about the old "rub-with-snow" method. Never rub a frostbitten area with anything: It can do permanent damage. As for rubbing with snow, it defies common sense, old wives' tales and woodsmen's lore notwithstanding.

SNOW AND ICE

You may have no intention of winter camping — ever. (Then again, these things tend to creep up on you, unexpected. That's how I ended up with a closetful of snowshoes, ice axes, crampons, and cross-country skis.) But even if you stay resolutely indoors until well after Groundhog Day, you may find yourself one day lured into higher, colder places.

Go high enough in any western

mountain range — even in July — and you'll find some stubborn old ice clinging to the shady side of a mountain. A little earlier in the season, and who knows? Your trail may disappear under a field of the white stuff; if the slope is steep enough, you could actually encounter avalanche hazards.

And then, there are the surprises. In the White Mountains of New Hampshire or in the Colorado Rockies it can and often does snow any day of the year. On one memorable Memorial Day morning, I awakened in the high desert of central New Mexico to see an inch of snow blanketing the cactus — and my sleeping bag! (I was camping "under the stars," or so I thought.)

Be sure you know what weather to expect. Call the local Forest Service office and ask about weather conditions. Make sure you take into account the effect of elevation. New Mexico might be a warm, arid state, but climb a 10,000-foot mountain and you'll be hiking in conditions equivalent to

?

DID YOU KNOW

The color orange and the number three are used as internationally understood symbols for distress. Three whistle blasts, three orange tarps lined up in a row, and three smoking fires are just some of the ways you can communicate that there is an emergency.

those found near Canada's Hudson Bay. At 5,000 feet in North Carolina, you need to dress for coastal Maine. And in the mountains of northern Georgia, January temperatures can drop well below zero.

Don't forget: If you're hiking in a place where it can snow any day of the year, you're hiking in a place where you are vulnerable to hypothermia. You're also vulnerable if you're pushing at the edges of three-season hiking: November in New England, say, or October in Wyoming's Wind River Mountains. Be sure you're prepared not only for the weather you expect, but for the weather you don't expect. If snow is at all possible, you should have all-leather boots, and you should have a pair of gaiters to keep the snow out of them.

Walking on Snow and Ice

In this section, I'll discuss the kind of snow travel the average hiker might face in three-season hiking. For true winter hiking, you'll need special equipment and experience that are beyond the scope of this book (see Sources and Resources for recommended winter-hiking texts).

Snow presents three problems to those traveling across it, and they all have to do with gravity: sinking into it; sliding down it; and having it slide down on you — as in an avalanche. SINKING IN. The first problem is resolved either with willpower, which can move a person forward, albeit slowly, or with snowshoes or skis. Snow that is deep enough to impede progress is uncommon outside of winter; in any event, the three-season hiker rarely carries snowshoes or skis, which leaves only his willpower in the event of a surprise storm. Post-holing is the term for slogging through deep snow, and it requires no special skill: just the ability to trudge on. Fortunately, most out-of-season snow soon melts off. If it doesn't, you've walked out of three-season hiking and into the winter. SLIDING DOWN. The second problem — sliding on snow and ice — is less easily dispensed with. At high altitudes, ice slopes linger well into the summer months. In situations where your snow travel is limited to a few ice slopes stretched along a mountain, you'll probably be able to get away without any added equipment. Sometimes, however, snow and ice present greater obstacles, even to the extent of stopping your progress entirely. You may have to backtrack to find a way around a cornice or a slope that descends too precipitously. As the saying goes: "Better to turn back 100 times too many than once too late." Or: "There are old mountaineers and there are bold mountaineers, but there are no old, bold mountaineers."

If your encounters with ice and snow involve more than a couple of slippery slopes, you need an ice ax and crampons. Crampons are metal spikes that attach to the bottoms of your boots and grip into the ice. Full-fledged crampons run the length of your boot and have points sticking out at the front for ice climbing (or "front-pointing"). There are also smaller, partial crampons, for those who just need a little extra traction. Crampons are easy to use — once they are fitted to your boot, and once you know how to put them on securely. Make sure you have tried this out at home first! If you have never used crampons, it would be wise to take a class to learn how to do so safely.

In situations where your snow travel is limited to a few ice slopes stretched along a mountain, you'll be able to get away without any added equipment, although a hiking stick may come in handy.

An ice ax, too, requires practice. Understand this: If you need to use an ice ax, you need to know how to use it, meaning you need to know self-arrest technique. Walking along holding an ice ax isn't going to do you any good when you slip, careen downhill, and find out that you don't really know how to make yourself stop. Self-arrest isn't difficult, but you do have to learn it, and in order to learn it, you have to do it, not read about it. Take a class. Wheedle a lesson from a more experienced friend. Practice a few times.

AVALANCHE DANGER. Finally, there is avalanche danger. Three-season hikers aren't likely to run into this problem; if they do, it will most likely be in springtime, in terrain where snow has accumulated over a long period of time.

Avalanche danger is highest when snow of various layers, densities, and temperatures lies on a steep slope, and when warm temperatures make the top layers susceptible to breaking away from the underlying snow. Backpackers need to be alert for two situations: walking under an ice slope, and walking across one. Neither should be done when conditions are ripe for an avalanche.

ALTITUDE

Once the backpacking bug bites, there's no telling where you'll want to go. For many, the answer is up. The high-country trails beckon with green glacial tarns and windswept rocky vistas, and what can you do but follow them?

You can walk to surprisingly high altitudes as a backpacker, even if you have no mountaineering experience. You need no technical skill — no jumars or fixed line or harnesses or carabiners — to hike to the top of Kilimanjaro (19,340), to climb Mount Kenya's Point Lenana (16,300), to cross 17,800-foot Thorong-La in Nepal. Closer to home, there are hundreds of peaks 12,000, 13,000, and 14,000 feet high that are accessible to backpackers. Western hiking trails frequently poke through the clouds: The Pacific Crest Trail crosses several 12,000- and 13,000-foot passes in California's High Sierra. The John Muir Trail starts on 14,494-foot Mount Whitney, the highest peak in California (and in the continental United States). The elevation of the Continental Divide Trail in Colorado averages more than 11,000 feet.

But when backpackers go high, they can run afoul of the disease of the highcountry.

Acute Mountain Sickness

Also known as altitude sickness, AMS is your body's response to the fact that as you go higher on a mountain, the density of the air decreases. With every breath, you take in less oxygen.

ABOUT AVALANCHES

● Know where you are at risk and go around risky areas. Avalanches tend to be found in the same places year after year. The chute will be steep and bare, usually with no trees. Avoid it!

● If you must cross an avalanche chute it's safest to do so just after there has been an avalanche, before more snow has had a chance either to fall or to begin to melt.

● Consider recent weather conditions. A series of cold nights followed by warm days is most dangerous.

● If you must cross an avalanche-prone slope, do it in the early morning, when it's still cold. This is not foolproof: On some mountains particularly prone to avalanches, you can lie awake at night listening to them fall. Avoidance is, as always, the best strategy. Late afternoon is most dangerous.

● There is special equipment available for hikers and skiers, including a device to measure the slope of a hill, ski poles that screw together to become avalanche probes, and a transmitter to mark your position in case you're caught in an avalanche. But if you need this kind of equipment, you need to have spent some time in the field with an instructor.

● Before going across an avalanche slope, unfasten your pack belt so you can extricate yourself from your pack if necessary.

● If you are using a transmitter, turn it on.

The good news is that at altitudes reachable by backpackers, AMS is almost entirely preventable.

It's difficult to predict at what altitude you will first feel the effects of thinner air. Some people can happily climb to 16,000 or 18,000 feet without so much as a headache; others feel light-headed when they drive to a 10,000-foot pass. Even at lower altitudes — say 8,000 or 9,000 feet — many backpackers feel a shortness of breath and are more easily fatigued, especially during the first few days of their trip. To further complicate matters, people do not always respond the same way from one trip to the next. You might go on several climbs to 15,000 feet with no adverse effects and then find yourself fatigued and nauseated at 13,000 feet.

Like hypothermia, altitude sickness seems to particularly prey on strong hikers, who are more likely to push through their symptoms, especially if other, weaker members of the group are not similarly affected. Unfortunately, altitude sickness does not affect the human ego.

Acclimatizing: The Key to Prevention

The speed of your ascent has as much to do with whether or not you get sick as the elevation you reach. Someone who lives at sea level in Seattle, drives

The first two rules in avalanche country are: Learn to recognize risky areas, and *avoid* them. Far better to take time going around a potential avalanche than to risk triggering it.

to 14,410-foot Mount Rainier, and climbs it too quickly is a likely candidate for AMS, even though 14,000 feet is an altitude that most people can reach with no problem if they are properly acclimated. On the other hand, someone who takes time to acclimate slowly might be able to climb to altitudes of 18,000 feet without any symptoms. People who live at sea level are especially vulnerable to higher elevations for the first few days of a trip. If you can, take a day or two to acclimate.

When you're climbing, take your time. Once above 10,000 feet, restrict your cumulative elevation gain to no more than 1,000 feet a day. (In other words, you should go to sleep at an elevation no higher than 1,000 feet more than the previous night.) If your route involves a continual ascent, you should plan to take a day off every few days. Heed the old mountaineering maxim: "Climb high, sleep low." By hiking 1,000 feet or so uphill on your day off, you can introduce your body to the rigors of higher elevations, and then let it recover overnight at the lower elevation.

The other key preventive is to drink often, even if you don't think you are thirsty. High-altitude air is dry, and many hikers experience painfully chapped lips and skin. (Lip balm, an ointment like Vaseline Intensive Care, and a moisturizing sunblock are helpful.) But more important, the dry air causes hikers to lose much more water through both perspiration and respiration than they normally would. Because the air is also cold, you may

be less aware of the need to drink. It is possible to become dehydrated without even knowing it. One easy way to tell if you are drinking enough: Be sure that you urinate frequently, and that your output is clear.

The drug Diamox, recommended by some physicians, can prevent AMS, but is *not* an effective treatment. Diamox has side effects, however — numbness, drowsiness, vomiting, and diarrhea among them — and may lead to a false sense of security. Doctors with experience at altitude tend to steer clear of using drugs as a prophylactic. And once you have symptoms, the only treatment is to go downhill.

Altitude Sickness Symptoms

The early symptoms of altitude sickness include general lethargy, a mild dull headache, and a loss of appetite — all symptoms that could indicate a lot of different problems. How do you know that your lack of appetite is due to the altitude? Doctors at the Himalayan Rescue Association, which runs seminars on the subject for trekkers in Nepal, say that the answer is easy: "When you hear hoofbeats, think horses, not zebras." In other words, assume the most probable explanation. If you are feeling bad at high elevations, blame it on the altitude.

If you have any symptoms of altitude sickness, stop climbing. If you catch the problem early, it may go away if you take time to acclimate. If you ignore your symptoms and push on, they will get worse: Your mild headache will start to pound, your loss of appetite will turn into nausea, and your lethargy will become poor coordination. You may also develop insomnia. If, after taking one day off, you do not feel better, go down 500–1,000 feet.

Otherwise the real trouble begins: The next cluster of symptoms — staggering, slurring words, and making no sense — means that you must go back down to the last elevation at which you felt well. Usually 1,000 feet or so will do the trick. Many hikers afflicted with altitude sickness find that after taking a couple of days to recover and acclimate, they can continue on and up.

Unfortunately, people's egos too often egg them on farther and higher, and the person afflicted with altitude sickness is the one least likely to recognize his condition. If you are the companion of someone in the later stages of altitude sickness, you'll need to firmly turn him downhill, regardless of what he says. He's no longer rational, and he can't make decisions for himself. Nor can he descend by himself: You'll have to go down with him, whether or not he wants you to. It's a little like taking car keys away from a drunk friend — you don't ask for permission.

If acute mountain sickness continues to be ignored, it can result in a cerebral or pulmonary edema: blood plasma in the brain or lungs. The symptoms of pulmonary edema include the symptoms for altitude sickness, along with a very rapid pulse (more than 120), bluish color, coughing, noisy or raspy breathing, and frothy pink sputum. Symptoms of cerebral edema include those for altitude sickness as well as increased confusion and possibly hallucinations or unconsciousness. In both cases, the victim must be immediately moved to a lower elevation (as low as possible, but at least to the last elevation where the victim was well) or he will die, sometimes within hours.

In the United States, the average elevation at which an edema occurs is only 12,000 feet, usually in the Pacific Northwest, where hikers who live at sea level have access to very high mountains. The tragedy is that mountain sickness at this elevation is almost entirely preventable.

HEAT

Heat is rarely life threatening, if only because most of us start to wilt in it and slow down as the temperature rises. Nonetheless, it is possible to push yourself into a stage of heat exhaustion, and possibly even heat stroke, if you insist on ignoring your body's pleas for respite.

A few commonsense precautions should keep you out of trouble — even if you insist on a strenuous workout in 100-degree temperatures. Dehydration is a major problem in hot weather, so drink often and plenty. Some hikers take along electrolyte-replacement drink mixes like Gatorade, which can be helpful on very hot and humid days when you are sweating out all your salts and need to replace them somehow. Other options are salt tablets

When hiking in extreme heat, dehydration is the greatest threat; drink plenty and often, *before* thirst sets in.

you feel drained and tired, you may have heat exhaustion. Symptoms include a feeling of light-headedness and possibly nausea or headache. Your pulse will be rapid and your skin clammy. Stopping for a drink and a good long rest will generally take care of the problem.

Far more serious is heat stroke, which occurs when your body's heat-regulating mechanisms simply shut down. A person with heat stroke will have a high fever and dry — not clammy — skin (the sweating mechanism is "broken"). A person with heat stroke needs to be cooled immediately. Immerse him in cool (not cold) water. If only very cold water is available, soak clothing in it and put the wet clothing against the victim's body. Finally, have him drink cool water.

and bouillon broth (or any packaged soup).

Try and keep your body as cool as possible. I soak my hat and bandanna in a cold stream and rechill them whenever I can. I also carry a bathing suit so I can take advantage of streams and lakes. A midafternoon siesta works for the animal kingdom, and it works for hikers, too. If you plan to be doing a great deal of hot-weather hiking, consider starting very, very early and walking till it becomes uncomfortably hot. Then take a long break before hiking again in the early evening. This works well in the desert, where there is a greater difference between day and night temperatures.

If these strategies don't work, and

INJURIES

In the backcountry, medical emergencies are generally caused by injuries, not illnesses. Apart from problems associated with altitude and temperature, falls are probably the most common cause of wilderness emergencies. There are, it seems, an unlimited number of ways to fall from a trail. You can slip on ice or mud or scree. You can trip while hiking at night. You can catch your foot on the guyline of your tent or lean just a little too far forward to take a picture. And here's one from my own arsenal: being pushed off the trail by a cow in Nepal.

Most falls bruise little more than the ego, but a bad fall can leave a hiker immobile: with a strain, sprain, or fracture, or with a badly bleeding wound. And falls can be particularly serious when they occur in tandem with other problems, such as hypothermia, heat exhaustion, or altitude sickness. Then, injury is compounded by environmental stress and the lack of judgment and coordination that can accompany all three of those problems.

Going for Help

First aid classes teach that your first response to an emergency is to call for help, and then stabilize the victim until help arrives. But what do you do in the backcountry, where help is far away? In any emergency, you'll have to stabilize the victim first — and then consider how to reach help or evacuate the victim.

If the victim is in a condition to walk out — or if he will probably be in a condition to walk out after a day or two of rest — he should. A hiker with a broken arm probably doesn't need to be evacuated; a person with a severely dislocated shoulder may be in so much pain that he can't walk. A sprain or a fracture can often be supported with a splint or a bandage or both, so someone with a leg injury may be able to walk — although slowly, and with a companion's assistance with carrying gear. But walking on some leg injuries can be dangerous, especially over tough terrain. Severe emergencies — especially head, neck, and back injuries — require evacuation.

If evacuation is necessary, you'll

When hiking in hot, humid weather, start out at dawn and take a break during the heat of the day, even stopping to swim when the chance presents itself.

need to start planning it as soon as the victim's condition is stabilized. Don't panic. Your group, if you have one, needs to take stock of your situation and discuss the options.

QUESTIONS EVERY RESCUER NEEDS TO CONSIDER. How far are you from a road? (You don't have to go out the way you came in — look at your map for other trails.) What is the terrain like? How long will it take to send a runner for help and bring rescuers back? Is there a backcountry ranger station? Are other people camped nearby? Is there a place to land a helicopter? Are you close to a wilderness ranch or a hunting camp? Can you leave the victim alone?

You may be able to perform your own evacuation, but this is much harder than it sounds, and it is only really practical with large groups that are within a reasonable distance of a road. You can improvise a litter from a wide range of materials: pack frames, ropes, pack bags, sleeping pads, sleeping bags, skis, walking sticks, and tree branches. But unless you've had a little experience, you'll find that this is easier said than done. So is carrying someone in a litter, especially over steep or rocky trails. It's not easy on the victim, either: The bouncing around and jolting can actually cause further damage. (According to the American Red Cross, "Perhaps more harm is done through improper transportation than through any other measure associated with emergency first aid.")

Other options may be available,

depending, of course, on where you are. Rescues can be undertaken with horses, all-terrain vehicles, snowmobiles, and pickup trucks. Your map will tell you where the nearest road and town are, and it may also include information about ranger stations and recreation facilities. Helicopters are also an option, although not always: They can't fly at night in the mountains or in bad weather at any hour, they are expensive, and they may take considerable time to arrange.

If you send a runner for help, be sure that he can clearly communicate your precise location on a map, the condition and injuries of the victim, supplies you have, supplies you need, and what has been done for the victim. If you must leave to summon help, first be sure that the victim's condition is as stable as you can make it: that fractures are immobilized and bleeding is stopped and bandaged. Before you leave the victim alone, be sure that he is sheltered (use a tent, a tarp, or a space blanket) and has enough warm clothes and sufficient food and water within reach. If you meet any other hikers, do not hesitate to corral them into helping you.

Shock

Shock is a general depression of the body's functions, and it can kill — even if the original injury (a broken leg, for example) was not itself severe enough to be fatal.

Always treat any injured victim for shock, whether or not he exhibits the symptoms: pale, cold, or clammy skin;

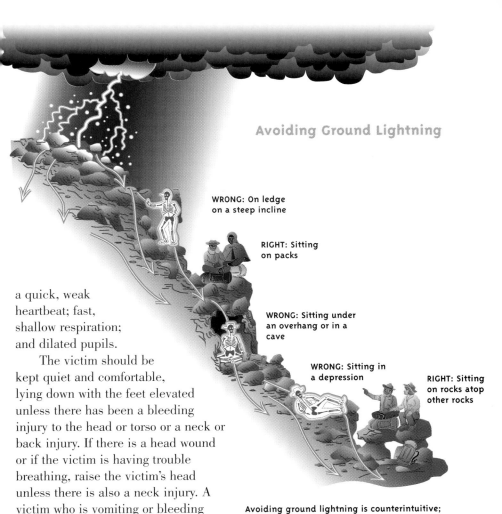

WRONG: On ledge on a steep incline

RIGHT: Sitting on packs

WRONG: Sitting under an overhang or in a cave

WRONG: Sitting in a depression

RIGHT: Sitting on rocks atop other rocks

a quick, weak heartbeat; fast, shallow respiration; and dilated pupils.

The victim should be kept quiet and comfortable, lying down with the feet elevated unless there has been a bleeding injury to the head or torso or a neck or back injury. If there is a head wound or if the victim is having trouble breathing, raise the victim's head unless there is also a neck injury. A victim who is vomiting or bleeding from the mouth should lie on his left side.

Loosen clothing and keep the victim's body temperature stabilized. Generally, this means keeping the victim warm, although in extremely hot weather you might need to shade the victim from the hot sun or apply damp cloths to his forehead. Give the victim small amounts of water or bouillon, unless he is unconscious.

Avoiding ground lightning is counterintuitive; seeking shelter can lead you to the most hazardous spots.

LIGHTNING

Lightning kills far more people in civilization than in the backcountry, but that fact affords precious little reassurance when you are stuck up on an alpine ridge as a storm rolls in. I know of very few things that are more starkly terrifying than the instant when the air smells of ozone and a crack of thunder splits the world at exactly the moment that lightning flashes.

A few precautions can minimize the danger of being hit.

Lightning looks for the shortest distance between cloud and ground — hence its attraction to the highest

THE FIRST AID KIT

The hiker's first aid kit differs from the standard kits in two ways. First, like everything else that goes into your pack, weight is a consideration: You don't want to carry around anything extraneous. Second, because backpackers are more prone to certain kinds of injuries and problems, there are a few extras that need to be added. I don't use pre-packaged first aid kits, because I find that I end up making too many changes. Ziploc bags let me organize the contents of my kit into items I use regularly and items I hope I never need to use. Just be sure, if you put your own kit together, that it is complete.

Contents of a Sample First Aid Kit

- Names and numbers of people to contact in an emergency
- Blister kit (mine has Second Skin, 1-inch-wide medicine tape, moleskin, and a needle)
- Antibiotic ointment (Neosporin or Bacitracin)
- Hydrogen peroxide or rubbing alcohol for disinfecting (a 2- or 3-ounce plastic bottle is plenty)
- Poison ivy preventives and medicine (if you are highly allergic)
- Painkillers
- Rubber gloves
- Medicine tape (1 inch wide — doubles for repair on gear)
- Tweezers and scissors (your army knife may have them)
- Hydrocortisone, calamine lotion, or equivalent for various afflictions due to bugs, poison ivy, heat rash
- Ace bandage
- Gauze (2-inch roll)
- Gauze pads: several 3-inch and 4-inch squares
- Band-Aids and butterfly closures
- Medicines: cold tablets, antihistamines, throat lozenges, Alka-Seltzer; if you're going on an extended trip, ask your doctor about prescribing a general antibiotic, and Flagyl too, if you're going to ignore the warnings in Chapter 8 and drink the water
- Personal prescription drugs, including drugs for bee stings, if you are allergic
- Extra moleskin
- Antidiarrheal
- Tincture of benzoin

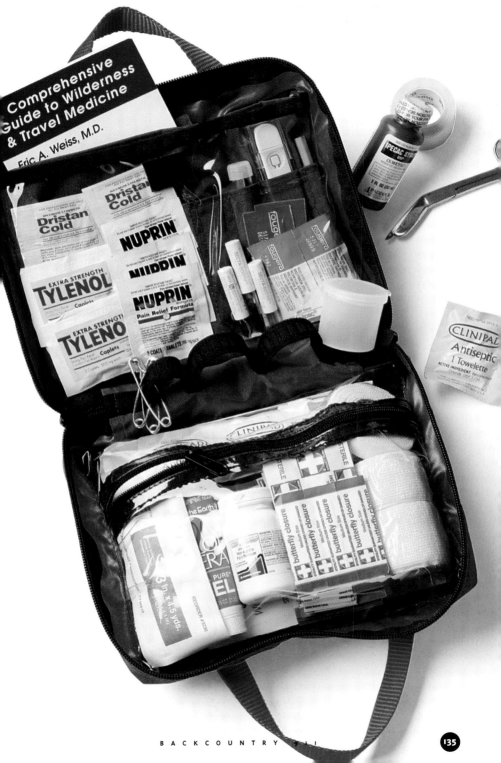

point. Get off peaks and ridges if possible. If you are, or can get, below treeline, huddle in a grove of medium-sized trees. Above treeline, look for a pinnacle rock that is taller than you and stand several yards away from it. (Standing directly next to it exposes you to risks from ground currents.)

Once lightning hits, it spreads out, traveling along the ground in the path of least resistance, so you want to stay out of that path. Avoid steep inclines, where the current travels more freely. Also avoid wet areas, because water is a good conductor. If you are stuck in the open above treeline, your best bet is to crouch on top of a rock (not the highest one in the area) that is somewhat elevated or otherwise detached from the rocks underneath it. Don't huddle in a slight depression, under the entrance of an overhanging rock, or in a small cave. Despite their illusion of protection, these are among the most dangerous places to wait out a storm because they attract ground currents.

The best position is to crouch low with your feet as close together as possible. Stand on something that insulates you from the ground, like a mattress pad or a coil of climbing rope. Stay away from metal objects — like

WHAT TO DO BEFORE HELP ARRIVES

Remember: First, do no harm!

● Do not move the victim until the extent of the injuries is known — particularly if the victim has a back, head, or neck injury.

● As with all first aid, the "big three" are breathing, circulation, and bleeding; the first two to be started, the last to be stopped.

● One person should be in charge of dealing with and handling the victim to minimize confusion and disorientation.

● Talk to the victim. Tell him what you're doing, and what is going on. He will be upset and may be incoherent; he needs to be reassured.

● Injuries due to falls — fractures, dislocations, and sprains — should be treated as fractures. Immobilize the injured area using materials on hand: a tree branch, a walking stick, or a ski pole, cushioned by a sleeping pad or clothing, and tied with a bandanna. Make sure that splints are not so tight that they cut off circulation.

● Take notes. Describe the victim's condition, what you have done, and what the response was. With each note, include the time. Take pulse and respiration numbers — even if they don't mean anything to you. The information may help rescuers.

● Always treat for shock, even if the victim is conscious and insists that he is all right.

A REVIEW OF
THE "BIG THREE"

MOUTH-TO-MOUTH
RESUSCITATION

① Position the victim's head by placing one hand under his chin and the other hand on his forehead and tilting his head back so that the chin juts out.

② Check for breathing: Listen for air, look to see if the chest rises and falls, or feel the victim's breath.

③ If the victim is not breathing, clear his airway of any blood, vomit, or loose teeth.

④ Pinch the victim's nose and cover his mouth with yours in a good seal. Give two full breaths.

⑤ Check again for breathing.

⑥ If the victim is still not breathing, give one breath every 5 seconds.

CARDIOPULMONARY
RESUSCITATION

Cardiopulmonary resuscitation can keep a victim's circulation and breathing going even though his heart has stopped. By pressing on the victim's breastbone with the heels of both hands, one on top of the other, the rescuer forces blood in and out of the heart. At the same time, the rescuer — or a helper — administers mouth-to-mouth resuscitation at the following ratio of heart presses to breaths:

	IF THE VICTIM IS:	
	AN ADULT	A CHILD
One rescuer:	2 breaths, then 15 presses	1 breath, then 5 presses
Two rescuers:	1 breath, then 5 presses	1 breath, then 5 presses

The American Red Cross stresses that CPR should be given only by people who are trained. Contact the Red Cross for programs in your area.

STOP BLEEDING

① Elevate the injury, unless it is on a fractured or broken limb.

② Always use direct pressure on the wound itself. (A clean bandanna is good, but if nothing else is available, use your hands.)

③ If necessary, use pressure points in addition to direct pressure. Pressure points are found at the inside of the upper arm near the armpit, and the upper thigh near the groin.

④ Bandage into place the cloths used to stop the bleeding.

⑤ Tourniquets should never be used.

⑥ Rubber gloves should be used to protect you from bloodborne diseases like AIDS. While HIV can't penetrate unbroken skin, you might have a cut or scratch you are unaware of.

your pack frame, ice ax, or ski poles.

If someone in your party is hit, you may have to treat them for shock or burns, or give mouth-to-mouth resuscitation or CPR.

> 66 Storms come announced by what old-timers call 'mare's tails' — long wisps that lash out from a snow cloud's body....
> A packer who used to trail his mules all the way from Wyoming to southern Arizona said, 'The first snowball that hits you is God's fault; the second one is yours.' 99
>
> — Gretel Erlich
> *The Solace of Open Spaces*

B U G S   A N D
B U G A B O O S

Excess, unwarranted, and in some cases ridiculous litigation has had a toll on the backcountry. Trail management agencies today practice defensive tactics, and nowhere is this more evident than in the way they handle the issue of water. No matter where you hike — whether at 12,000 feet in the Rockies or at sea level in Everglades National Park — you will be told the same thing: All unprotected backcountry water must be treated.

WATER

The problem is, that advice will keep you healthy only if you listen to it, and, from experience, I know that most hikers do not. I can duly warn you of a host of invisible bacteria, parasites, viruses, and the like; I can lecture you in the proper use of filters, chemicals, and boiling. But if you're like the average hiker, you will soon start wondering whether you really do have to treat every single drop of water. You'll notice that other hikers are drinking directly from some springs — but not from others. Moreover, you'll quickly learn that your brand-new water filter is neither as quick nor as easy as expected; that chemicals taste lousy; and that boiling water takes lots of time and fuel.

The issue is important. Hiking is a strenuous activity, and adequate

DID YOU KNOW

Desert plants need to be every bit as concerned as hikers with finding and conserving water. Some of their strategies seem very human (or is it we who are plantlike?):

COMPETITION:
The creosote crowds out its competitors by sending its roots out in a wide, shallow network and snatching up any water that falls as soon as it hits the ground.

SINGLE-MINDEDNESS:
Mesquite bores deep into the ground and keeps going until it finds what it is looking for, even if that means digging down 75 feet.

HOARDING:
Cacti grow fat and juicy every chance they get, and then live like misers off their savings. An adult saguaro cactus can hold several tons of water.

OPPORTUNISM:
The ocotillo grows leaves only when there is adequate rainfall. Otherwise, it's content to remain a bare stalk.

PATIENCE:
The agave plant can wait up to 50 years before producing a flower.

hydration is crucial for backcountry health — particularly in extreme conditions. Drinking frequently helps prevent altitude sickness, hypothermia, and hyperthermia, as well as the discomfort of an empty canteen miles from the next water source. Experienced backpackers know that the time to drink is before they are thirsty, and they automatically look for streams and springs when planning their hike.

Among hikers, water purification may be the issue that generates the most controversy. Some hikers treat every drop of water they drink; others treat none. Most, including me, fall somewhere in between. Some always use filters; others always use chemical treatments. Some are completely consistent; others never do the same thing twice in a row. Some hikers get sick. Many defend their pet theories with the conviction of an evangelical preacher.

These are the facts:
Some water is safe to drink.
Some water is not.

If you are not treating all of your water, you are taking a risk. Even if you know what you are doing. Even if you follow all the rules of thumb.

Caveat imbiber: Let the drinker beware.

What's in the Water?

There are — potentially, at least — all kinds of things in the water: bacteria and viruses; chemical and mineral pol-

lutants; fertilizers, insecticides, pesticides, and herbicides. But by far, the bugaboo of the backcountry is *Giardia*, and it's *Giardia* that people are usually thinking about when they wonder whether the water is safe to drink.

Giardia (the full name for the parasite is *Giardia lamblia*; the disease it causes is giardiasis) is a protozoan that spends part of its life cycle as a waterborne cyst and the rest in mammalian intestines. When it attaches to yours, you get sick. Giardiasis is not treatable with ordinary antibiotics; it requires a

THINK BEFORE YOU DRINK

● Where are you? In the West or the East? High up in a wilderness area or low down in a meadow? There are a few places that Dan and I consider so risky that we treat virtually all the water: These include heavily used trails in Massachusetts, Vermont, and Maine, as well as any unprotected springs in areas open to cattle grazing, which is common in the West. Conversely, there are a few places where we are willing to bet that the water is safe. In Colorado wilderness areas, we generally don't treat water if we're above treeline; below treeline, we treat almost everything because of beavers.

● What season is it? There are fewer campers and fewer animals about in the winter.

● What is the animal life? In a desert, water is scarce, so animals tend to congregate at the few sources that do exist. If you're seeing lots of animal tracks and scat — especially near a water source — you'll want to treat it. In the mountains, be sure you are above beaver dams.

● What is the land use? Could the water be contaminated by agricultural chemicals, by cattle, by mining tailings? Is there a development or a community upstream?

● Where is the water coming from? Can you actually see it? The safest water comes from underground springs. Seep springs can be safe in dry terrain, where the water percolates quickly through the soil. But in wet or swampy areas — Maine is a good example, with its forests of boggy sphagnum moss — the water gets to sit around and collect contaminants. Clear, flowing, cold water is better than standing, warmish, murky water, but beware: *Giardia* can thrive in a cold, fast stream. Snowmelt is generally safe, especially if you can see the snowbank.

● What do the local backcountry rangers do themselves? (They have to tell you to treat your water, but ask them where and how they get theirs. Be prepared for some divergence of opinion and go with the most cautious answer.)

special class of drugs to make it go away. (The most commonly prescribed is called Flagyl.) Even when treated, effects can linger for months.

Giardiasis is spread by the feces of dogs, cattle, beavers, and other mammals, including burrowing animals like voles and irresponsible animals like backpackers practicing poor sanitation habits around water sources. Symptoms strike a few days to a few weeks after contracting the disease, and include cramps, nausea, diarrhea, vomiting, and extreme fatigue. Giardiasis is not uncommon; if you drink backcountry water indiscriminately, you will probably get it sooner or later.

A SweetWater filter is put to the test in a sulfur/oil seep, San Rafael Swell, Utah. Some hikers swear by water filters, others swear at them.

Treating Your Water

BOILING. Boiling is the old-fashioned way to treat water, as long as you are worried only about biological contaminants and not minerals or chemicals. In the interest of avoiding litigation, some pamphlets put out by various land management agencies will advise you to boil water for 5, 10, or even 15 minutes. This is nonsense, not to mention impractical: You can't possibly carry enough fuel to boil all your drinking water for 15 minutes. At sea level, Dan and I generally bring our water to a rolling boil and declare victory over the microbes. At higher altitudes, where water boils at a lower temperature, we let it boil for 2 to 3 minutes.

In cool or cold weather, boiling water is a good choice. You need to keep hydrated to avoid hypothermia and altitude sickness, but in winter, water from a stream or spring is sometimes so cold that it's painful to drink. And when the temperature is below freezing, you need to take your water to bed with you so it doesn't freeze. With heated water you have water that is comfortable to drink, and at night you have the added benefit of a backcountry hot-water bottle.

Some people don't like the taste of boiled water. Try decanting it by pouring water from one water bottle to another. Or you can add flavored drinks or herbal teas.

CHEMICAL TREATMENT. The second method is chemical warfare. Tiny bottles containing 50 pills (Potable Aqua) are widely available at outfitters and general stores proximate to recreation areas. Most people find the taste of chemically treated water objection-

The safest water comes from springs, like this one along the Appalachian Trail near Hot Springs, North Carolina. Respect springs, making sure not to camp too near them and to do your part to keep them clean.

Katahdin Stream Falls, along the Appalachian Trail in Baxter State Park, Maine. Clear, flowing, cold water is better than standing water, but *Giardia* can thrive in a cold, fast stream.

able, but Potable Aqua now makes a pill containing ascorbic acid (vitamin C), and the additive removes the unpleasant taste. You should carry a chemical treatment even if you plan to boil or filter all of your water, just in case your stove falls apart, your filter cracks, or you can't get a fire started. Don't simply use a couple of drops of bleach, because it won't kill *Giardia.* Iodine — which is the active ingredient in Potable Aqua and is also available in liquid form — is effective against *Giardia,* but it doesn't remove mineral or chemical pollutants. Iodine is unsafe for pregnant women, and for those with untreated thyroid problems. The manufacturer of Potable Aqua specifies that it should be used only in emergencies, and not as an everyday water treatment. FILTERS. Finally, there are filters, rela-

tively new gadgets in the backpacker's arsenal. Filters are small contraptions, weighing from $3/4$ of a pound to $1 1/2$ pounds, made of some combination of steel, ceramic, and plastic. Water is pumped by hand through a thin intake hose, then into the filter assembly where it is purified, and it emerges through another hose. Filters remove a wide range of contaminants, both organic and inorganic; they don't leave an aftertaste; and they don't introduce a health risk of their own. If you use a filter designed for the backcountry, you do not need to boil your water. In recent years, there have been tremendous advances in design. Nonetheless, the industry still has a way to go before it comes up with the perfect filter. As of this writing, filters are among the most vilified kinds of back-

country gear, especially among long-
distance hikers, who use their equipment day after day after day. Some filters are reliable but unwieldy; others
are convenient but prone to cracking
or breaking. All clog up sooner or later
— and almost always sooner than the
field tests promise. Still, imperfect
though they may be, filters are indis-
pensable, especially in the West,
where hikers often must filter out
cattle droppings — or worse (I once
shared a water source with a dead
antelope — it was the only water
source for 10 miles in any direction).

Make sure that the filter you are
using is designed for backpacking, and
that it specifically states that it filters
Giardia. Four brands that are most
often seen include PUR, SweetWater,
First Need, and Katadyn.

SLITHERERS, CREEPERS, BITERS, AND STINGERS

The North American backcountry is,
as wildernesses go, fairly safe. Mosquitoes bite, but they won't transmit
malaria or yellow fever. You won't get
river blindness or schistosomiasis from
swimming in a stream. And as far as
dangerous animals go, I'd much rather
come face-to-face with a rattlesnake or
a bear than an anaconda or a tiger.

Still, we do have a few bugaboos
that you will want to recognize and,
presumably, avoid.

Ticks

Ticks have recently risen to the top of
the backpacker's worry list because of
the diseases they spread: including
Rocky Mountain spotted fever, which
is quite rare, and most notably, Lyme
disease, which is becoming more and
more common. The first is spread most

Top: The tiny deer tick (actual size at right) is the
greater potential threat to hikers because it car-
ries Lyme disease.
Bottom: The dog tick carries the far rarer Rocky
Mountain spotted fever.
In both instances, prevention is the best defense.

especially by the dog tick or the wood tick, though other ticks may carry the disease, and, despite its name, is found more frequently in the East than in the Rocky Mountains. Lyme disease, named after the town in Connecticut where it was first identified, is spread by the deer tick (and these ticks, contrary to their name, often contract the disease from birds). It is most common in the Northeast, particularly in Massachusetts, Connecticut, and New York, but its range is spreading, and cases have been reported in forty-five states. Both diseases are serious, but can be treated with antibiotics.

In both cases, prevention is the best defense. Ticks are most common in grassy areas, but they can be found in the woods as well. Going off-trail in high brush in the spring is a good way to make the acquaintance of large numbers of ticks. Bug repellents help. DEET is best (and it repels other nuisances as well), but some backpackers consider it a poison. Given the fact that a DEET spill actually melted my plastic watchband, I'd have to agree. If you prefer natural alternatives, citronella is good. Even if you use a repellent, be sure to check yourself at the end of the day — or better yet, a couple of times a day. If you have a hiking partner, check each other. Deer ticks are tiny, no more than the size of a pinhead or a speck of dirt. They like to burrow between clothing and skin. Check especially under your socks.

If you see a tick, don't panic. It takes several hours for ticks to transmit disease. If you find the tick before it's been there awhile, chances are that you'll be okay. Pull the tick off gently with tweezers, being careful not to leave the head embedded in your skin. Or try to entice it to come out with a dab of insect repellent or stove fuel.

Lyme disease is best treated early. One symptom — not all people get it — is a red circular rash around a pale center (the so-called bull's-eye rash). Other symptoms include fever, muscle pain, fatigue, and sweating. The later stages of the disease are very serious, and can include heart palpitations, chronic arthritis, and inflammation of the brain. If you have early symptoms of Lyme disease and you have been recently in the woods, be sure to bring up the subject with your doctor. A vaccine is currently being tested and may be available in 1996.

Insects

According to the Smithsonian Institution's Department of Entomology, an estimated 1 million species of insects have been identified worldwide. Some 10,000 new species are described each year, but it will be a while before taxonomists finish their job: It is thought that between 30 million and 50 million species remain to be identified! With so many insects around, it is inevitable that some of them are going to accompany you on your hike.

Some will inflict misery, the amount of misery generally depending on how many of them there are and the severity of your reaction. If you are particularly sensitive, you might want to consider avoiding especially bad times of year. Snowmelt in the high-country is mosquito season. June and early July in northern New England belong to the infamous blackflies. If you venture into the woods, be prepared for hand-to-bug combat, an activity that generally manifests itself as you slapping yourself while your quarry flies away well fed and free to bite again. Bug spray helps, but back-packers needs lots of it because it sweats off. Some hikers use mosquito netting around their faces. A hat with a wide brim helps by keeping flies out of your hair and away from your face. To wear around camp during bug season, I carry lightweight long pants and a long-sleeved cotton shirt (a white one; it repels insects). I count them respon-sible for maintaining my sanity.

Bees and wasps sting, but not unless you bother them first. They gen-erally cause a serious problem only for the highly allergic. You should know (and so should your hiking partners) if you fit into this category, and your first aid kit should contain the necessary medications. Ask your doctor about the new, easy-to-administer hypodermic cartridge for bee stings.

Spiders — which are, of course, not insects, but which belong in this discussion by virtue of function, if not form — can also pack a very nasty bite, particularly the black widow and brown recluse varieties, to which you don't have to be allergic to suffer greatly from.

Female black widows (the only ones you need worry about) have spherical, shiny black bodies with a red hourglass mark on the underside. Their bite is felt as a small pinprick, but in 2 or 3 hours there may be severe pain and cramping. The best treatment in the backcountry is to sit it out, possibly with the help of a painkiller. Brown recluse spiders have small, pale brown bodies with a darker, violin-shaped mark on the back. Their bite is painless, and symp-toms don't appear for several hours — or even days. The most common symptom is a skin ulcer that can become gangrenous. Fevers are also common. The best treatment is to get to a doctor; there isn't anything you can do in the field.

Spiders often hang out in out-houses; sometimes they check out a pair of conveniently located boots. Make a habit of shaking out your boots before inserting your feet. As far as the outhouse goes, you're on your own.

Snakes

Not many critters can lay claim to the widespread loathing and fear gener-ated by the snake. In rural towns across the country — particularly in the South and the Southwest — the snake is the subject of endless discus-sions and warnings and not a few dire predictions. It sometimes seems that every local I meet has just seen a snake "right up the trail apiece." The snake, of course, is always venomous — and usually big. Real big.

But to put it all in proportion: I hiked more than 7,000 miles before I ever saw a venomous snake, and those miles included the entire length of the state of New Mexico, which includes a bit of the Chihuahuan Desert as well as hundreds of miles of sagebrush and piñon; in other words, rattlesnake heaven. And I

The timber rattlesnake, found in the East, is every bit as venomous as its western cousins. Encounters with venomous snakes are rare, and learning to identify them is easy. Be aware when you are hiking through snake country, and keep a sharp lookout.

don't recall having had blinders on. To the contrary, the locals would have been gratified to see how seriously I took their stories and warnings: scouring the ground with my eyes; straining my ears for the telltale rattle. I've since been rattled at three times (don't worry, you'll recognize the sound when you hear it), and I've seen one copperhead snoozing deep among some rocks. I figure that works out to about one venomous snake per 2,000 miles.

Nonetheless, you do need to be able to identify venomous snakes, if only to keep yourself from panicking every time something long and reptilian slithers across the trail. In the contiguous United States, there are only four to worry about. The much-feared rattlesnake comes in about thirty species that live in a variety of environments. Local nature guides will tell you whether you need to worry about rattlers, and if so, which kind you're likely to encounter. One rule of thumb:

Rattlesnakes are not usually found in the highcountry near or above treeline. Rattlesnakes are pit vipers, characterized by flat, wide heads, elliptical pupils, and two infrared "pits" located on either side of the head between the nostrils and the eyes. These pits are heat-sensing organs that enable the snake to detect a temperature change of as small as several thousandths of a degree centigrade from up to a foot away (handy for detecting the movements of prey). Two other species of pit vipers you need to know are the cottonmouth and the copperhead.

The cottonmouth, also called the water moccasin, is a large, dark brownish snake — thick-bodied and up to 6 feet long — that lives in southern wetlands, and for the most part, it is found in or near water: swamps, rivers, and the like.

In the East, the copperhead is common and easily recognizable by the hourglass pattern of its reddish brown-and-gold coloring; as its name implies, it usually (but not always) has a copper-colored head.

The last venomous snake on our list is the brightly colored coral snake. Unlike the other three, it's not a pit viper, but it is easily recognized by its coloration of red, yellow (or yellowish-white), and black stripes. You can differentiate the coral snakes from other harmless, similarly striped snakes because only "red next to yellow will kill a fellow; red next to black, venom lacks." The coral snake, about 2 to 4 feet long, is resident in the southern United States, from South Carolina to Arizona.

Snakes are as interested in avoiding you as you are in avoiding them. If you're in snake country, do your part: Watch where you're walking or climbing, and be especially attentive on exposed rock ledges. Snakes are ectothermic, commonly termed "cold-blooded." On a cool day, they will be trying to get warm, often on sunny rock outcroppings. On a hot day, they'll be hiding in a crevice or lying in a patch of cool shade. But the everyday business of being a snake also includes some hanging-out-in-the-woods time: Of my four venomous snakes, three were coiled next to the trail in dense forest.

You can also reduce the risk by wearing gaiters (which are also good

SNAKEBITE TREATMENT

So you think you know how to treat a snakebite: Follow the directions on your snakebite kit, right? The ones that tell you to cut into the bite and suction out the venom, and maybe add a little ice or snow to slow down the spread of the poison.

Wrong! That's according to Maynard H. Cox of the North Florida Snakebite Treatment Center, who advises medical personnel worldwide on the treatment of snakebite.

The venom from a pit viper will seal itself off for 12 hours. Cutting into the skin allows the venom to spread more quickly — and it may damage tissue. Suctioning doesn't usually work. As for ice — assuming you could find it out in the boonies during snake season — it's more likely to cause frostbite than do any real good.

Instead, Cox suggests that the victim be treated for shock and kept quiet while a hiking partner goes for help. Remember that only about 50 percent of venomous snakes actually inject venom when they bite, and that the venom is not usually fatal. Still, the victim should receive treatment within 12 hours, because after 12 hours, the venom, if there is any, begins to spread. Treatment will probably include an antivenom, antibiotics, and a tetanus shot.

The northern copperhead. Only about 50 percent of venomous snakes inject venom when they bite. In the unlikely event that one does, see "Snakebite Treatment," left, for the latest advice.

protection from ticks, pebbles in your boots, water, mud, and snow). Some people wear long pants in snake country. If you see a venomous snake, stop. If you're close, move away. If it rattles at you, move beyond its range, immediately (this means quite a few yards). In thick woods where you may not immediately be able to see the snake, move backward several yards. When you've retreated and the snake has stopped rattling, look for it: It may be necessary to leave the trail to walk around it. Don't get closer for a better look, and don't stop to pick it up. These simple warnings may sound unnecessary, perhaps even idiotic. But people do get bitten. (See "Snakebite Treatment," left.)

POISONOUS PLANTS

"Leaves of three, let it be. Berries white, run from sight."

Poison ivy is not the most dramatic obstacle in the woods, but it is one of the most common. It's also one of the most commonly misunderstood.

Poison ivy and poison oak, along with their cousin, poison sumac, contain an oily substance called urushiol. About 70 to 85 percent of the population is allergic to urushiol. The rest are lucky — at least for now. Many people who think they are not allergic to poison ivy develop allergies later in life because of continued exposure. Some people claim they are allergic to one of the plants and not the others. However, the allergen is the same in all three plants. If you're allergic to one, you're allergic to all.

Poison ivy and poison oak are easily identified by their triads: The leaves, which are usually shiny, always grow in groups of three. The plants thrive in a variety of environments: on sunny rocky outcroppings, down along a riverbank, and anywhere in between.

Poison ivy — found throughout most of U.S. (Illustration shows both summer and autumn foliage.)

They are not, however, found above treeline, or in very cold climates. (In northern New England, for instance, poison ivy is found only at low elevations.) They can flourish as a climbing vine or as a shrub. Mature vines can be as thick as a forearm, and are easily identified by a thick mat of hairy roots. Young vines are not as densely "hairy," but if you look closely, you'll see the reddish-brown roots that the vine uses to attach itself to a tree trunk. Every part of the plant — leaves, stem, berries, roots, and vine — is poisonous at any time of year, including the midwinter. Guess how I know this!

Poison sumac (also called poison dogwood and poison elder) is a shrub that can grow to a height of about 12 feet. Its leaves, growing in groups of 7 to 11, resemble those of sumacs, but they are rounder. Poison sumac is found in the Great Lakes area and on the coastal plains of the Atlantic Ocean and Gulf of Mexico.

Top: Western poison oak — west of Rockies, a shrub or vine where oak trees are found below 5,000 feet. Middle: Poison oak — southeastern U.S., usually found on sandy soil. Bottom: Poison sumac — 5-to 10-foot tree, usually found in swampy areas. (Illustrations show both summer and autumn foliage.)

As usual, the best strategy is avoidance. Hikers who are very allergic seem to develop a sixth sense about poison ivy. It's not that they are neurotically searching out the underbrush for every sign of a shiny green triad; it's more that the plant seems to jump out at them. However, sometimes, it doesn't jump out fast enough. If you know you've made contact, washing with cold running water will help. A popular remedy is to wash with laundry soap immediately after exposure; personally, I haven't found this to be effective, but some people swear by it. A better choice is a special liquid soap called Tecnu, which is found in outdoor stores. It's most effective when used immediately after exposure, but you can also use it when the rash first breaks out.

If, despite your caution and washing, you nonetheless contract a bad case of poison ivy, go to a doctor. If you are very allergic, it can take several weeks for the rash to disappear by itself. Drugs prescribed by your doctor can dramatically shorten your misery.

THE
WILD
KINGDOM

One day, while walking in the High Sierra, I saved a life. I didn't do anything out of the ordinary. I was simply walking along, minding my own business, when I came upon a murder in progress.

I froze and watched the drama of predator and prey: Two sleek brown blurs engaged in a matter of life and death. The chipmunk zigged and the mink zagged, and with each turn, the mink came a little closer until he was virtually running in his quarry's shadow. In a final surge of desperation, the chipmunk squeaked a protest at the top of his tiny lungs and darted between my legs to safety on the other side. The mink skidded to a halt, cartoon style, and retreated to a pile of rocks. I still remember his expression: It looked like reproach.

For many hikers, not only does backpacking offer solitude, views, a sense of independence, and outdoor exercise, it is also an opportunity to see and hear wildlife. Can anyone forget the first time a hummingbird darted in front of his nose, hovered like a helicopter, and then zoomed off? Or the call of a loon echoing through the crisp northcountry air? Or the wild yapping of a pack of coyotes? Can anyone forget his first bear?

The marmot is one of several small mammals that may entertain you at your campsite.

FINDING WILDLIFE

Some animals are shier than others. They sense your presence long before you sense theirs, and by the time you become dimly aware of them, they are gone in a puff of dust or a sweep of wings. Antelope, pileated woodpeckers, loons, and coyotes are some of my favorite creatures, but I feel lucky indeed if I see one up close for more than a second or two. Other animals will allow us to come a little nearer before their flight instinct is triggered. Deer become quite nonchalant in national parks. Moose always look vaguely surprised to see a human in their path, and it usually takes them a few moments of seemingly slow-witted deliberation to decide what to do. Black bears — unfortunately — quickly lose their fear of humans once they've had a taste of a freeze-dried dinner or two.

Both animal and plant life are denser and more varied in places where two or more environments come together: a meadow and a marsh; a forest and a swamp; a river and a forest. These areas, which scientists call ecotones, or edges, play host to residents of both communities, and they support populations of their own unique species. Similarly, wildlife is more abundant near water, especially in arid environments where water is scarce. Beaver dams, streams running through meadows, and ponds are all good places to watch for animals.

Time of day is important, too. Most mammals are most active near dawn or dusk. That's when you're most likely to see them coming to a meadow to graze. The middle of the day tends to be nap time.

Seeing wildlife is partly a matter of chance, but it also depends on how sensitized you are to your surroundings. I remember photographing a black bear one afternoon in Kings Canyon National Park in California. The bear was on one side of the trail, I was on the other. The bear ignored me as he went about his business, which at that moment involved examining an oft-used campsite for leftover food. Just then, a hiker stomped by. Her two ski poles flashed, her eyes were set straight ahead — this hiker meant business. She didn't see me, nor did she see the bear; she kept marching, and in a few moments, she was gone.

The way you walk in the woods has a lot to do with what you see. A

As a rule, do not feed wild animals. But to every rule, there is an exception: Feeding birds is hardly courting disaster. Here a rosy finch takes a snack at the summit of Mount Whitney, at 14,494 feet, the highest peak in the lower 48 states.

DID YOU KNOW

If you don't see birds, try calling them. You don't need to have a bird-calling whistle, and you don't even have to know any special calls. One sound that attracts avians: Call "pish, pish, pish" several times. Another is loudly kissing the back of your hand.

fast-walking, heavy-breathing hiker is going to scare animals away. So is a group of jabbering teenagers — or, for that matter, a group of jabbering adults. Sometimes, this is a good thing. My first visit to grizzly bear country was a hike through Yellowstone National Park, and my nerves were frayed by rumors and warnings about a mauling that had occurred that same week on a trail just south of the park. Dan and I made so much noise — banging our walking sticks, talking loudly, stomping our feet — that we nervously joked that we would be the first people in history to cross the park without seeing any wild animals at all. Yellowstone's wildlife is used to humans: Despite our best efforts, we saw moose, elk, buffalo, and coyotes — but thankfully no grizzlies.

ABOUT BIRDS

Think of birdwatching and a stereotype jumps to mind: a bespectacled, vaguely professorial fellow with pen, paper, and guidebook in hand and binoculars at the ready, absently tripping through puddles and mud in search of the rarely spotted lesser red-bellied grub-catcher.

Backpackers become birdwatchers by osmosis if not intent. Of all our woodland companions, birds are the most noticeable, colorful, and noisy. Nature has gone wild with the design of birds: their colors and crests and calls, their adaptations that let them hunt, swim, wade, and fish, or fly more miles than many of us will ever even drive in a lifetime. There is something ghostly and magical in the way an owl lands on a tree branch, silently, with a single swoop of wings; something comical about the pileated woodpecker's outrageous crest and jungle cry; something delicate and graceful in the subdued colors and sleek lines of a great blue heron. And who can ignore the concert of an Appalachian spring, as the woods come alive with songbirds and the tiny peeps of baby birds?

There is a special, quiet pleasure in watching birds and learning to identify them. The vast number of species makes this seem a more daunting task than it is. Start out by learning a few of the common species in the area where you most frequently hike. After a while, you'll start adding on, as migrations bring new species to the neighborhood, or as you travel afar. A bird guide and binoculars will add to your enjoyment (or use the telephoto lens on your camera).

And who knows? You, too, may end up happily tramping through marshes and forests clutching a "life list" of birds you've seen, complete with details of when and where and how, hot in pursuit of some rarely seen migrant.

ANIMAL ETIQUETTE

Respecting Wildness

On a trip through Yellowstone, Dan and I had an opportunity to visit with some rangers, and learned — much to our surprise — that more people are injured by animals like moose and buffalo than by bears. Partly that is because there are far more moose and buffalo than there are grizzly bears, but it's also because people are more afraid of — and hence more cautious around — bears.

When watching wildlife, always remember that no matter how cute, stupid, slow, attractive, cuddly, harmless, or oblivious they may seem, wild animals are — above all — wild. If they are frightened, they will do what they need to do to get away from the threat. Usually, this means running away, but if an animal feels cornered, it may turn on you. Be especially aware during mating season: That ethereal bugling of the bull elk is performed for his benefit, not yours, and a pair of elk competing for a harem are not going to take kindly to interruptions. Large animals are usually aware of their size. If you encounter one on a trail, talk softly to it and give it a chance to leave. If necessary, give it

the right of way. After all, you're the visitor. And you're smaller.

Don't Feed the Animals!

There is certainly a temptation to make contact with members of other species, and the easiest way to make friends with wildlife is to offer them goodies. Resist the temptation — no matter how friendly or tame an animal appears to be. Animals that show no fear of humans may be rabid. And introducing animals to human food is ecologically unsound. First of all, it upsets their own cycle of nutrition and encourages dependency on an unnatural food source. Second, it trains animals to become beggars, pests, and thieves. And third, it encourages them to lose their fear of humans, which then increases the possibility that they will become a threat to you or to future hikers. In some cases — bears being only the most obvious example — human food can be the death sentence of an animal.

Animals Need Privacy, Too

Having just returned from hiking in New England, I'm thinking about loons, and how their calls — the signature of the northcountry — have been echoing across Maine's wilderness ponds for some 60 million years. Loons are among the oldest creatures on earth, but there are fewer of them than there used to be. You can lay some of the blame on development, and some of it on pollution and acid rain, but there's a share that belongs on the shoulders of boaters, fishermen,

> 66 Then comes an answer, distant from the origin of the first call, a repetition of the howl that brings to mind no image so comfortingly familiar as that of a wolf. And then, from the first area of endless dark night the first caller is heard again. Back and forth. You watch the darkness like a slow tennis game, and you begin to realize that this is conversation that you are hearing. How can a sound that has conveyed you past the stars to the edges of the universe mean nothing more than 'Come take your turn on the nest'? Or does it? 99

— Joan Dunning
The Loon: Voice of the Wilderness

vacationers — and yes, backpackers.

Loons need quiet, privacy, and a lot of space — a single nesting pair can require a lake of 10–200 acres. Even so, they raise only two chicks a season. That's if they are lucky: if the chicks survive predators and if the fledgling loons successfully make their annual migration to salt water. More and more, however, the chick-raising process is interrupted before it even gets to that stage. A single backpacker coming upon a nest and sitting down to watch the loons can — unknowingly and innocently — cause the adults to abandon the nest.

No responsible backpacker wants to interfere with the life cycle of the animals he enjoys watching. Unfortunately, it's all too easy to inadvertently interrupt mating, nesting, feeding, or childrearing. At first the results are barely noticeable: a drop-off in the birthrate of grizzly bears; an untended spotted owl's nest in the Pacific Northwest. In the long run, such interruptions can decimate a population.

In the desert, camp well away from water: Animals may be too shy to come past your campsite for their evening drink. Similarly, camp away from game trails. Use common sense: A mother grouse's broken wing display is, to be sure, fascinating to watch, but from a bird's-eye view, it's a matter of life and death. Don't get between a mother animal and her offspring. In the best case, you are creating a trauma for the animals; in the worst case, you are putting yourself in danger as well.

UNINVITED COMPANY

Even the most devoted animal lover has to concede that animals in the wild fall into two categories: the ones you want to see and the ones you don't. At a safe distance, the distinctions blur — I really don't mind seeing a rattlesnake if it is beyond striking range. The distinctions also blur at close quarters — at night, say, when you hear the sound of teeth on fabric coming from the direction of your backpack.

In highly used areas, animals sooner or later learn that a campsite means people, and that people mean a free meal. Even the most relentlessly conscientious minimum-impact hiker occasionally drops a noodle or two, and that's manna from heaven for a hungry mouse. In some sites, the sound of you zipping your tent for the night might as well be a dinner bell.

Nocturnal visitors will generally be of the harmless variety: mice, chipmunks, and the like, although occasional visits from skunks, porcupines, and raccoons are common enough. In some areas, bears are a real nuisance.

Animals have one thing in mind when they visit you in camp, and it isn't interspecies communication. They are interested in getting their paws and teeth on something that tastes good. Usually, that means food, but some animals crave salt (which they will find not only in your spice kit, but also in your boots, your socks, and the sweatband of your backpack). Others are attracted by sweet-smelling toiletry items like toothpaste. Animals are generally not interested in your gear, but they will chew through it if that's the way to get to your food. Occasionally, you might find the nesting material of a mouse or a chipmunk in some snug corner of your backpack.

Most hikers ultimately acquire one or two pieces of equipment that show the marks of little — and sometimes big — teeth. The most common memento is a food bag with a dime-sized hole in it, courtesy of a hungry mouse. But I've also seen a backpack mauled by a bear, a sock shredded by a mouse, boots destroyed by porcu-

The best way to prevent the clever and dexterous raccoon from making successful nightly forays is to keep all edibles safely stashed in a bag hanging from the branch of a tree.

pines, the lining of a rain jacket gnawed by a marmot, and a T-shirt chewed by a deer. The sock was mine.

THE ANIMAL-PROOF CAMPSITE

Your Food

In places where bears are not a problem, many hikers keep their food in the vestibules of their tents. This is controversial: Food in a tent will attract animals. I have to admit that I frequently sleep with food in my tent vestibule, and as far as I know, I've never lost any to nocturnal marauders. I have, however, heard plenty of anecdotes to the contrary, so be forewarned.

The best way to avoid an encounter with things that go munch in the night is to hang your food from a tree branch. Suspending food in this way is absolutely necessary in bear country, but it's also a good strategy if you are concerned about keeping your GORP and granola safe from smaller critters. In rainy climates, be sure your food is in a waterproof stuff sack; for added protection, you might want to line the sack with a garbage bag.

The backcountry shelters or cabins such as those found along the Appalachian Trail, on Vermont's Long Trail, or in the Adirondacks of northern New York are regularly visited by porcupines, raccoons, skunks, weasels, chipmunks, and mice. Usually you can hang your food and equipment from nails sunk into the beams and rafters. In some shelters, you'll find a homemade mouse barrier made of string, a stick, and a can. Believe it or not, they actually work.

Your Pack

Everyone knows that brand-new gear eventually becomes beat-up old gear, but there's no need to accelerate the process. Before you go to bed, remove anything edible from your pack and unzip all the zippers so curious critters can look around to their heart's content. In a shelter, hang your pack from a nail. Outside, put the rain cover on and, if possible, hang the pack from a tree branch. If you go off for a view or a swim, ask your hiking partner to keep an eye on your pack. Better yet, hang it up.

Boots

Sweat-soaked boots are another animal delicacy. Porcupines, particularly, love the taste of salt, and they can destroy a pair of boots overnight. On a clear night, or in a shelter, I tie my boots together and hang them up. On rainy

Although less aggressive than their grizzled cousins, black bears should not be underestimated. When taken by surprise, they can be unpredictable, and a sow with cubs is dangerous.

nights, they go in the vestibule.

Clothes

One afternoon in Glacier National Park, a ranger showed up in the middle of nowhere. He checked our permits and then warned us to beware of — the grizzlies? the black bears? hypothermia? No. It was the local deer he was worried about: They supplemented the salt in their diet by chewing on sweaty clothes. We had already been warned about hanging up our food, using stoves instead of fires, the difficulty of the terrain, the possibility of rain. Now we were supposed to be on the alert for deer? "Give us a break," we muttered to ourselves.

We had a chance to rethink our nonchalance that evening when the deer showed up, one of them carrying someone's long-stolen T-shirt in its teeth. He displayed intense interest in our clothesline, and we quickly moved all of our belongings into our tent. The moral of the story? Listen to the rangers and be prepared for anything.

BEAR COUNTRY

Perhaps no animal causes more excitement — or fear — than a bear seen in its natural habitat. There are two kinds of bears in the contiguous United States: black bears and grizzly bears. South of Alaska and Canada, grizzlies are found only in the northern Rockies, in parts of Idaho, Montana, and Wyoming. You're most likely to encounter them in places that are strictly protected (for instance, Glacier and Yellowstone National Parks), or in places that are very remote (like Montana's Bob Marshall and Scapegoat wilderness areas). Black bears (which can, in fact, be any color) are much more adaptable and much more common, living comfortably in a wide variety of environments: the arid mountains of New Mexico, the dense wet forests of the Great Smoky Mountains, the remote wilderness of California's High Sierra, and even the suburbs of New Jersey.

Experienced hikers who have camped in both black bear and grizzly country sometimes affect a little bit of nonchalance when talking about black bears. You'll hear them say that they don't bother to hang up their food; that black bears aren't really dangerous. And indeed, it is true that black bears are less aggressive than their grizzled cousins. My most common photograph of a black bear consists of a furry backside disappearing into the bushes. Still, it's not a good idea to be too casual on the subject. Bears, even small bears, are a lot bigger than you are, and any bear can be dangerous if provoked. Bears that are surprised are dangerous; mother bears with cubs are dangerous; bears protecting a food source are dangerous, even if it's yours; bears that have lost their fear of humans are dangerous.

Staying Safe in Grizzly Country

Mutual avoidance is the key. Experts recommend making noise as you walk to warn bears of your presence. Some people carry bells with them; others consider this unnatural, and prefer to talk or sing. In either case, the sounds of wind or a rushing river can completely wash over any noise you make. Be aware of your surroundings: of rivers and streams, of food sources like berry patches, of tracks and animal scat on the trail. Grizzlies often cache food, so if you smell something rotting, it's possible that you're close to a bear's larder — which he will defend. Leave your radio at home: You need to be paying attention to what's going on around you.

If you do see a grizzly, stay calm and keep your distance. Watch the bear's reaction (without, however, challenging him by looking him directly in the eye). If the bear sniffs the air (either standing normally on all fours or upright on hind legs), it means that he is aware of you and checking you out. If he exhibits signs of stress — perhaps by turning sideways to make himself look bigger, or moving his head from side to side, or popping his teeth and yawning — he is probably inviting you to leave. Do so, quietly and slowly. You should also be looking around for trees to climb, because adult grizzlies don't climb trees. (This bit of information is, however, scarcely reassuring in the lodgepole-pine forests of the West, where the average tree is about as climbable as your average telephone pole.)

Never, under any circumstances, run — not even if the grizzly charges. Running invites the grizzly to think of you as something to run after, and an adult grizzly can do upward of 40 miles an hour. You cannot. Often, the charge will be a bluff. If there are two or more of you, stand together to look like a bigger target. (Note: There is tremendous safety in numbers. There are no documented cases of a grizzly bear attacking a party of more than four people.)

In bear country, a combination of airtight (therefore odor-tight) containers and bear-bagging — hanging all food from the branch of a tree some 20 feet off the ground — is highly recommended.

In the last resort, play dead. The logic here is that a grizzly charges not to hunt you, but to remove you because you are a threat. If you play dead, the bear has achieved his purpose, and will probably leave you alone. (I must admit that, like the business about climbing trees in lodgepole forests, this advice has never sounded very reassuring to me. Grizzly bear experts, however, are unanimous on the best way to survive a grizzly mauling: Roll yourself into a ball. Draw up your knees to protect your torso and vital parts and cover your neck with your hands. And stay very, very still.)

In the last few years, a bear-repel-lent product called Counter Attack, made from capsicum pepper, has come on the market. The anecdotal evidence is that it's for real, but there are several drawbacks. If you carry it, it must be imme-diately available — like a gun in a holster — or it does no good. Do not succumb to the tempta-tion to let down your guard: The spray is not foolproof. Wind coming from the wrong direction can blow the spray away from the bear — and toward you. Also, for the spray to be effective, you need to be at extremely close range — less than 20 feet. Some people who have been bluff-charged by grizzlies laugh at the idea that they would have had time to dispense the repellent.

Camping in Bear Country

A bear (chances are that it's a black bear) that comes into your camp is almost always after your food. Often, the culprit will be a camp bear that has lost some of his fear of humans and has learned to associate humans with leftovers. In some popular areas,

HOW TO BEAR-BAG

Find a tree with a branch about 20 feet off the ground. The process is a lot easier if the branch doesn't have too much foliage. The ideal branch is one that is too thin to support the weight of a bear. (Adult black bears climb trees; adult grizzlies do not.)

❶ Tie a rock to the end of your rope. Hint: The thicker the rope, the less likely it is to get tangled.

❷ Toss the rope over the branch. The weight of the rock should bring it down, but if not, jiggling the rope will do the trick.

❸ Untie the rock and tie your food bag to the rope. (If you have several food bags, tie a carabiner to the rope and hang the food bags from the carabiner.)

the problems are almost epidemic. Shenandoah, Great Smoky Mountains, Kings Canyon, Sequoia, and Yosemite come immediately to mind. In fact, in the California national parks, woodlore has it that the bears walk with their noses in the air to identify food in trees; that mothers too heavy for the branches send their cubs out on mid-night raids; and that no food is safe anywhere. I tend to believe the stories: I once awoke to find a black bear standing on his hind legs under the branch where my food was hung, pawing at the air. He didn't seem too impressed or concerned when we started banging our pots and pans and throwing rocks at him. (Note: This

④ Pull the food bag all the way up to the branch. Tie a counterweight (usually a second food bag) to the other side of the rope, as high up on the rope as you can reach. Knot, coil, or tuck away the excess rope.

⑤ Push the counterweight up with your hiking stick until the food bag and the counterweight are several feet below the branch and at least 10 feet off the ground.

Instead of using a counterweight, you can tie the rope off on the tree trunk. But be warned: Bears in high-use areas know all about this trick, and have learned to bite or claw through the rope.

incident took place in Yosemite, where rangers encourage hikers to adopt an aggressive attitude toward bears. Do not do this unless local experts approve, and under no circumstances, ever, bang your pots or otherwise threaten a grizzly bear.)

There are a few things you can do to avoid losing your beef Stroganoff to an ursine organized crime family. In places with reputations for bear problems (the High Sierra and New Jersey, to name two disparate places where too many people and too many bears have been having too many arguments in recent years), you may find large metal lockers that are chained to trees or boulders. These are food-storage

DID YOU KNOW

Want to see animals in the desert? Try looking when the sun goes down. Many desert animals confine their activities to the cool desert nights. During the day, they hide from the heat, either by sleeping in the shade or by burrowing or diving a few inches underground, where the temperature can be 10–15 degrees cooler.

It's better to sit in one place and watch soundlessly than to night-hike: You'll see more animals if you remain quietly in one place. If you do walk at night in the desert, you should be concentrating on where you put your feet. Like the other denizens of the desert, rattlesnakes are out and about when the sun isn't.

lockers: Use them! Or you can try portable bear-resistant food containers, which are made especially for backpackers. These plastic containers are expensive (around $75) and heavy (about 3 pounds). They hold about 6 person-days of food, and prevent bears from smelling food odors. If you're going to be spending a lot of time in bear country, they're worth considering.

Bears know where hikers congregate, and they know that every night a

new stuff sack filled with goodies will be hanging, in all likelihood, from exactly the same tree. In some areas, bears become aggressive; they have learned that if they growl and threaten, humans tend to abandon their food. For these reasons, I prefer to camp in less frequently used areas in bear country, on the assumption that the bears are less acclimated to humans and their food. But if you camp in a pristine area, remember that it is your responsibility to see that it remains pristine when you leave.

Food smells attract bears, so don't cook right next to your tent. Go 100 feet away to cook and choose yet a third place — the farther away the better — to hang up your food. Hint: Select your tentsite first, your food-hanging site second. Flat spots and good bear-bagging trees take some effort to find. You can cook any old place.

Hang up all of your food as well as anything with an odor. This includes your toothpaste, your deodorant (assuming you carry any), soaps, sunscreen, and other toiletries.

Stay near your pack when taking a break. Many bears are introduced to human food as a result of chancing upon a pack left unattended. If a bear gets your pack, he considers it his, and he'll defend it. You can make noise and try to scare him off, but if push comes to shove and you find yourself face-to-face with an angry bruin, remember the law of the wild. He is bigger than you are. And stronger. Discretion is the better part of valor — as well as survival.

FINDING
YOUR WAY

Hiking has a pleasant, almost hypnotic, rhythm to it. At the end of a day, I often find myself surprised to realize that I haven't the foggiest idea of what I've been thinking about for the last several hours. It's easy to get lost in your thoughts — and that makes it easy to get lost in the backcountry. Getting unlost is a different matter entirely.

It is possible to hike thousands of miles without ever learning to use a map and compass. If you stay on well-marked trails, if you depend on the expertise of a more experienced partner, or if you limit your adventures to trails described in guidebooks, you may manage to avoid learning to navigate altogether.

However, knowing how to navigate does come in handy: If, for instance, your more experienced partner drops dead of a heart attack. If an off-season snowstorm covers all the trail blazes in a blanket of white. If a member of your party sprains an ankle and you need to find a shortcut to the road. An emergency is no time to be fumbling with the compass dial trying to remember whether it's the red end or the black end that points north.

Nor is navigation only for emergencies. Knowing how to use a map and compass can add to your enjoyment of the backcountry and allow you to explore off-trail whenever the fancy strikes. It is essential if you are heading to places where trails and junctions are unmarked.

GUIDEBOOKS

Your first and most basic tool is the written trail guide — assuming it is widely: Some offer exhaustive detail on every single landmark and tell you where to find water, where to camp, and where the nearest towns are when the trail crosses a road. Others throw in bits and pieces of natural history and local trivia. Many contain only the basics, like the mileage from shelter to shelter or trailhead to trailhead. Some

It takes practice to read a map. Get to know maps by using them on dayhikes along well-marked trails so that when you need one, you'll have the confidence to make good use of it.

available for the area where you plan to hike. This may consist of a few sheets of paper that you pick up at a ranger station, or it may be a small book of a hundred pages or more, which you can buy through mail order or at an outfitter. The quality and comprehensiveness of trail guides vary are clearly written; others are not. Usually, a guidebook also contains directions to the trailhead, instructions for parking and permits, information pertaining to local conditions (dangerous animals, hunting season, weather), and contacts for local hiking clubs, park service offices, ranger stations, emergency services, and the like.

If the trail you are following is well marked, a guidebook is probably all you'll need, if only to tell you how far it is from one place to another. The problem with a guidebook is that, usually, it covers only what's on the trail. If a side trail intrigues

A good time to practice map reading is when fog, mist, or rain alters the appearance of the landscape, even along familiar, marked trails.

you, you're on your own. If a shortcut looks attractive at the end of the day, the guidebook probably won't tell you if it's a steep slide down a mountain face or a gentle walk through a field. And — most important — if you wander off the trail by mistake, you've wandered out of the guidebook, too.

MAPS

Even if you're not planning to use your map and compass to navigate, bring them along. Some guidebooks are poorly written, or — commonly — out of date, and checking what the map has to say can resolve confusion. A map can help you navigate around unexpected obstacles: A recent example for me was the aftermath of an ice storm in southern Virginia

where so many thousands of trees were down that my intended route was utterly impassable. Whether you're facing an emergency, or you simply want to change your plans, a map gives you options. It also adds enjoyment: It's fun to be able to identify the mountains, lakes, and other features on your route. And finally, maps open up a whole new world of backcountry experience by giving you access to trails that are not described in guidebooks, and hence are more remote and less crowded.

Types of Maps

Choosing the type of map you need depends on where you are going. If you are headed cross-country to the back of beyond, you'll want maps that show good detail. If you're going to be

Being lost begins with the nagging feeling that you're not where you're supposed to be.

using the well-maintained trails that are typical of national parks and wilderness areas, a map showing more area but less detail may be perfectly adequate. In winter, you need to plan for bad weather; it's a good idea to have a map that shows side trails, roads, and nearby towns, so you can get out in case of an emergency.

Some guidebooks contain maps of the trails they cover. But check them out before you go; sometimes these maps are inferior, illegible copies. Another problem is that guidebook maps may show only a mile or two on either side of the trail, giving them the same flaw as the guidebooks: They are useful only if you stay on route.

TOPOGRAPHIC MAPS. So-called "topos" are the wilderness traveler's most important navigational tool. The more

remote your journey, the more important your map — and your ability to read it. Topos contain information common to all maps: roads, rivers, political borders, and so on. But for the backpacker, their most important feature is a system of contour lines that show the lay of the land: cliffs, passes, mountains, depressions, ridges, and ravines.

The standard for topographic maps is set by the U.S. Geological Survey (USGS), which will send you a free index of its maps for every state. Most backpackers prefer 15-minute maps (1 inch on the map equals 62,500 inches on the ground, or about 1 mile), but these are being phased out in favor of $7^1/_2$-minute maps (1 inch on the map equals 24,000 inches on the ground, or about $^2/_5$ of a mile). The $7^1/_2$-minute maps show much more detail, but they don't cover as much terrain, so you have to carry more of them: You can walk across several maps in a day, especially if your trail cuts across a corner or two.

Excellent topographic maps are also produced by companies such as Trails Illustrated, whose waterproof maps note features of particular interest to hikers, like campgrounds, ranger stations, and backcountry campsites. These maps are available for many well-traveled, popular areas.

NATIONAL PARK MAPS. You receive a free visitor's map when you enter a national park, but these are more appropriate for people touring the park by automobile than on foot. Some park maps note trails and may be sufficient for short dayhikes. Topographic maps showing contour lines are available for sale at most National Park Service visitor's centers.

FOREST SERVICE AND BLM MAPS. Both BLM and USFS maps cover large areas: The scale is ⁵/₈ of an inch per mile for Forest Service maps and ¹/₂ an inch for BLM (Bureau of Land Management) maps. These maps do not contain topographic information, so they are not usually sufficient for cross-country travel — unless you are traveling in wide-open country with easy landmarks, or unless you have a lot of tolerance for being lost. Dan and I carry Forest Service maps in winter and when traveling cross-country, in addition to our topos, because they list road numbers and trails, and because each one covers a lot of territory.

Two problems to watch for: First,

Forest Service maps are often out of date and even those with recent revision dates may not be thoroughly current or complete. Second, some of the cartographic decisions are political. For instance, a ranger once explained to me that the reason that an obsolete road in a wilderness area was not marked on the map was that wilderness areas weren't supposed to have roads! In another case, a road wasn't mapped because it was closed to vehicular traffic. And often, old trails that have long since been abandoned continue to show up on government maps.

HIKING CLUB MAPS. Local hiking clubs often maintain local trails and publish the guidebooks and maps associated with those trails. Some of these publications are excellent, drawing on a well of local information and lore, but sometimes the maps are not up to professional standards. If the trail is well marked, this won't be a problem. You might want to check with a local contact before you head out.

PROFILE MAPS. Finally, there are profile maps, not to be confused with contour (or topographic) maps. Profile maps show the ups and downs of the trail, expressed graphically as elevation gained or lost per mile. These maps tell you mileage between landmarks (usually campsites, road crossings, springs, mountains, and the like) and the grade and length of climbs and descents. Many hikers use them to plan their daily itinerary.

Reading a Map

It takes a while to get comfortable with

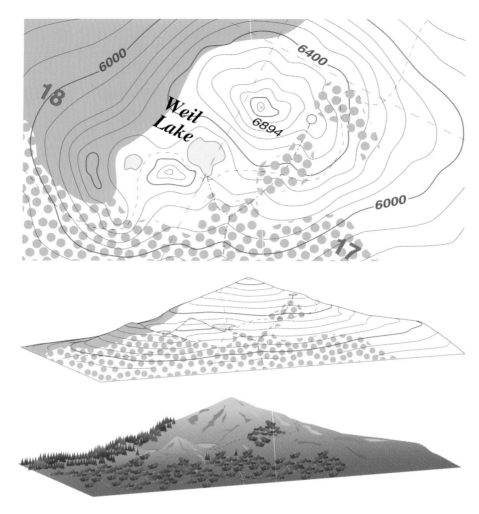

Small portion of a typical 15-minute series topographic map (top) shows the contour lines that describe the terrain you're crossing. At first the lines appear meaningless, but with practice, they will begin to reveal peaks and valleys (middle). When you learn to recognize the many USGS symbols, you can gain an idea of certain details of the landscape (bottom) including rivers, lakes, trails, and vegetation. Note that the contour interval on this map is 80 feet, meaning that each line represents a change in elevation of 80 feet.

maps and to be able to read them as easily as you read a book. Part of this is a function of perspective: The lines and squiggles would make a lot more sense if we were looking down on the terrain from a helicopter.

The best way to get comfortable

with maps is to make them part of your everyday hiking. Take a map and a compass along on a well-marked trail and consult them regularly. On an exposed ridge, try to figure out which peak is which, and where your route goes. Compare what it looks like on

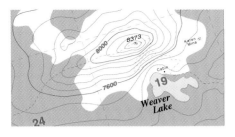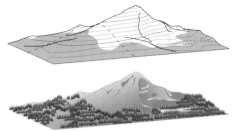

In this example, a trail follows the ridgeline to an 8,373-foot peak, then abruptly descends a steep face of the mountain in a series of switchbacks to the shore of Weaver Lake, more than 1,000 feet below the peak.

the map to what it looks like on the ground. At lunch, reconstruct what you've seen that morning and check out what it looks like on the map.

The basic building block of the topographic map is the contour line. Always check the legend for the contour interval, because it can range from 10 feet to 100 feet — and (rarely) even to 100 meters. In the typical $7\frac{1}{2}$-minute USGS map, the contour interval is 40 feet, which means that every contour line represents an increment of 40 feet of elevation. You'll notice that every fifth contour line is heavier than the others. This makes it easier to count the intervals in order to ascertain elevation. Lines very far apart mean that the terrain is flat, or gentle; lines extremely close together indicate steep slopes or cliffs. In addition, there are several common configurations of contour lines that every map user soon learns to recognize.

Inevitably, you will find that there are some discrepancies between maps and terrain. A beginning map reader calls these "mistakes." Experienced map users come to expect them. Some of them are, indeed, mistakes. Others

merely reflect the scale of the map: A map using 100-foot intervals for its contour lines will not show a 99-foot-high bluff, whereas the same bluff would stand out readily on a map with 10-foot contour lines.

Another reason for discrepancies is time. Always check the date on the map before you start to use it. I don't know about maps of urban or populated areas, but many USGS maps of remote areas tend to be 20 or 30 years old — and sometimes much older. In remote parts of southern New Mexico, the USGS sells a topo map (also called a "quad" for quadrangle) that was published by the War Department back when the U.S. Army was chasing Pancho Villa more than 75 years ago! USGS maps include the date of the original map and the revision date, if any, on one of the bottom corners of the map. The revision date is marked in purple, as are any changes on the map itself.

The date is important because the landscape is not static, something you'll appreciate when you try to use an outdated topographic map. Roads and power lines are built, trails fall into

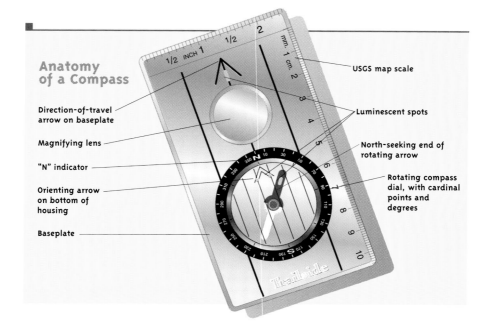

Anatomy of a Compass

Direction-of-travel arrow on baseplate

Magnifying lens

"N" indicator

Orienting arrow on bottom of housing

Baseplate

USGS map scale

Luminescent spots

North-seeking end of rotating arrow

Rotating compass dial, with cardinal points and degrees

disrepair. A mudslide dams a stream to create a new lake, a rockslide obliterates a footway, sand dunes roll over each other and the roads underneath them. A good map reader does not just read a map: He interprets it, finding reasons for the discrepancies between map and terrain. The date of the map is the most common reason for these discrepancies.

USING A COMPASS

Knowing how to use a compass allows you to do four things:
1) If you know where you are, you can use a compass to identify landmarks like peaks, passes, lakes, or ridges.
2) If you don't know where you are,

you can use your map to identify the features and landmarks surrounding you, and then use compass bearings to determine your position.
3) You can use a compass to give directions to someone else. (For instance, "Follow the creek 0.2 mile upstream to the junction with four trails. Take the one that follows a bearing of 270 degrees.* Go 0.1 mile to a fence. After crossing the fence, follow a bearing of 100 degrees 200 yards cross-country to the campsite.")
4) Finally, you can use a compass to follow a directional bearing to a place that you cannot see.

There's no real difficulty in learning to use a compass. There is,

* Because a compass uses a circle as its basis for measurement, it is (like any other circle) divided into 360 degrees: 0 degrees is north, 90 degrees is east, 180 degrees is south, and 270 degrees is west.

however, a great deal of difficulty in describing the use of a compass to someone who is not holding one in his hand. If you read this section without a compass, it will seem hopelessly confusing. Do yourself a favor: Get a compass. Any compass.

First things first. You already know that the compass needle points north. (Which end of the compass needle should be fairly obvious: It should be distinguished in some easily visible way — red or gold paint, or with an arrow at the tip.) Next, there is the

Learning to use a compass is simple IF you have one in your hand and use it. Go and buy a compass and perform the exercise on page 179, "Following a Bearing." It's actually good fun.

minor matter of declination. Declination — more simply expressed as the difference, in degrees, between where your compass says north is and where north really is — is the result of the fact that the earth has two North Poles. The magnetic pole, to which your compass points, is actually several hundred miles away from the geographic, or "true," North Pole. (To further complicate matters, magnetic north moves around from year to year — although not generally enough to affect the kind of navigation we are discussing in this chapter.) True north is where the northern axis pokes out of your globe at home; true north is also the frame of reference for your map. Meanwhile,

Adjusting for Declination

To adjust for declination, first review the three parts of the compass that work together to tell you which way is north and which way you want to go: The "N" indicator is found on the compass dial, the direction-of-travel arrow is fixed on the compass housing, the needle always points to magnetic north (see "Anatomy of a Compass," page 174).

❶ Hold the compass so that the needle, the N indicator, and the direction-of-travel arrow are all pointing in the same direction (magnetic north).

❷ Now turn the entire compass until the needle is pointing to the degree of declination indicated on your map (in this example 30 degrees east). Note: Be sure to turn the entire compass. Do not rotate the compass dial.

After you have turned the compass the needle will be pointing to magnetic north — but the N indicator and direction-of-travel arrow are pointing to true north on your compass. The angle between the two is the declination.

your compass stubbornly points to the other, "wrong" North Pole. In order for your compass and your map to agree on which way is north, you need to make an adjustment. The amount of the adjustment — the declination — is noted on your map, and it changes from place to place.

Note: You have two choices when adjusting for declination. You can adjust for declination right at the beginning, or you can shoot your bearing using magnetic north, and then add or subtract the declination. I find the first method easier (among other

things, it eliminates a whole lot of arithmetic). But either method is valid, providing that you don't forget to make the adjustment, and that you make the adjustment in the right direction. Whatever you do, be consistent! In this chapter, we adjust for declination first.

Using Map and Compass Together

To use a map and compass together, spread the map on the ground (when you get more confident, you can cut corners — for most purposes, I just hold the map in front of me). Put the

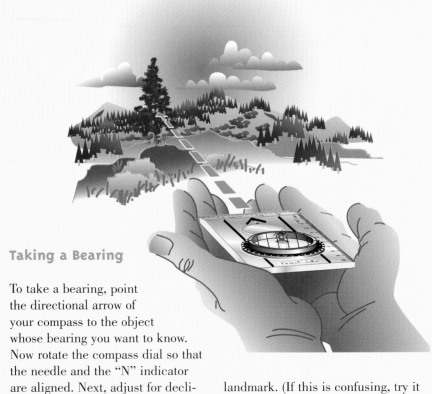

Taking a Bearing

To take a bearing, point the directional arrow of your compass to the object whose bearing you want to know. Now rotate the compass dial so that the needle and the "N" indicator are aligned. Next, adjust for declination. The "N" indicator is now pointing to true north; the needle, as always, continues to point to magnetic north; and the directional arrow tells you the bearing of your landmark. (If this is confusing, try it out wherever you are reading this book. Even if you are indoors— shoot a bearing from the couch to the television set, or bookshelf, or the kitchen door.)

compass on the map, and orient it to true north. Now rotate the map under the compass so that the legend that shows true north is lined up with true north on your compass. When you have done this, the map, the compass, and the terrain will all be aligned with each other.

If you know where you are, and you want to identify a landmark, take a compass bearing of the landmark. When you have done this, the directional arrow will be pointing not north, but to the landmark. Put the compass back down on the map, making sure that the line of the directional arrow runs through your current position on the map. The arrow itself will point

second landmark. The point at which the two directional lines intersect is your current location.

LOST AND FOUND

There are different kinds of being lost, ranging from momentary disorientation to the complete, all-out, am-I-even-on-planet-Earth variety. What most hikers experience as being lost is somewhere in between. Some people don't mind being lost: They like roaming around in the wilderness, and as long as they can find water and, eventually, a way out, any old trail will do. Others have no particular destination, or possess a high tolerance for uncertainty. This section is written for hikers who want to know where they are.

Losing Your Way

Being lost begins as a nagging feeling that you're not where you're supposed to be. The trail doesn't seem right. It could be anything: You expected to pass a lake, and there is no sign of one. The last junction said it was 2 miles to a shelter, and you've been walking for more than an hour on easy terrain. The warning signs depend on

To use map and compass together, put the compass on the map and orient it to true north. Then rotate the map under the compass so that the true north legend is lined up with the true north on your compass. Now you can triangulate to pinpoint your position.

toward the landmark. (It will also point to an infinite number of other things on line with the landmark, but the distance and shape of the landmark should identify it for you.)

TRIANGULATING. If you don't know where you are, you can try triangulating, a process that is a lot easier than it sounds. Arrange the map and compass so that they are aligned with the terrain (as above). Now, take a guess as to where you might be. Study the map to see if you can match shapes to the landscape. Are there prominent features? A knob on a mountain? A steep notch? Take a bearing of the landmark. Now place your compass on the map, with the directional arrow pointing to the landmark. Your current position is somewhere along the line of the directional arrow. Next, repeat the process with a

Following a Bearing

Let's say that you have directions that tell you to follow a bearing of 270 degrees for a mile. First, rotate the compass dial so that the directional arrow is pointing to 270 degrees. Now turn yourself (and the compass) until the "N" indicator points to true north. (Remember to adjust for declination.) Once the compass is aligned, the directional arrow will point to 270 degrees. Hold the compass up to eye level (some more expensive compasses have notches or slits to look through) and identify a prominent feature on your exact heading. Now all you have to do is walk. When you reach that feature, take another bearing and continue. In open country, your bearing may be a peak several miles away; in dense forest, you may be going from tree to tree. Make sure you know which tree you are heading toward, especially if you have to go around an obstacle.

Using many bearings requires special care because errors can compound themselves.

PRACTICING WITH YOUR COMPASS

The best way to become confident in the use of a compass is to practice with it. Try the following exercise.
- Go to an open field and stand in the middle. If you want to be sure you've done the exercise correctly, leave something behind at the starting point—a book, a daypack, or an accommodating friend.
- Take a bearing of 90 degrees.
- Walk 20 paces in that direction.
- Take a bearing of 225 degrees.
- Walk 28 paces in that direction.
- Take a bearing of 315 degrees.
- Walk 28 paces in that direction.
- Take a bearing of 45 degrees.
- Walk 28 paces in that direction.
- Take a bearing of 180 degrees.
- Walk 20 paces in that direction.

If you've used your compass correctly, you should find yourself approximately back where you started.

the terrain: On the Appalachian Trail in western Maine, I start wondering if I've missed a turnoff if the footway is easy for more than 10 minutes!

A warning for people with a good sense of direction: Don't trust it! Having a bad sense of direction may actually be a blessing in the backcountry. I'm one of those people who sit around at night scratching their heads while the sun sets in what I would have sworn was an eastern corner of the sky. But that means that I know better than to trust my instincts. Conversely, people with a generally good sense of direction get into trouble when they trust their gut. Small mistakes compound into big ones. Sometimes they, too, end up at night watching the sun set in the east.

It is entirely possible to become thoroughly lost even while paying close attention to your surroundings. Let's say that you are following a dry streambed to its source, and you turn up a side gully by mistake. It may not occur to you that you have taken a wrong turn — even if you are experienced, and even if you have been paying close attention. Indeed, it is precisely this assumption — that you are where you think you are — that is going to get you into trouble. You go on. The map doesn't quite exactly match the terrain, but you're not concerned: You know that discrepancies are common. You continue, still assuming that you are on the right track, committing yourself to your current course by virtue of the miles you walk on it. You check your map, looking for confirmation; indeed, you find it. The map suggests that you'll see another gully, and you do — never mind that it doesn't exactly bend in the right direction; never mind that it looks less like a gully than an old game trail. And so on and so forth, until you end up at the bottom of a ravine, when you're supposed to be on top of a ridge.

Avoidance, as always, is the best strategy. Pay attention: to your surroundings, to your map, and especially to that nagging feeling. If the trail is marked frequently (with paint blazes, signs, ax cuts on trees, or piles of rocks) and the marks suddenly stop, or if the trail is generally up to a certain standard and it suddenly deteriorates, con-

sider the reasons: Did you change jurisdictions? (National park trails, for instance, are better maintained than national forest trails.) Have you crossed into a wilderness area where trail markings are less frequent? Where did you last see one? Was there anywhere else the trail might logically have gone?

If you can't figure out the answers, stop your group. This takes some confidence, because groups have momentum. Some parties seem drawn to a particularly self-defeating kind of logic: "Oh, let's just keep going and see what happens." This approach should be undertaken only by people who don't mind walking extra miles.

If you stop the minute you think there might be a problem — when the sum total of your mistake has been missing one turn — all you have to do is retrace your steps. But if you've gone a fair distance, you may have blundered through some additional junctions. And the path might look different when you start going backward. All of a sudden, you've stopped being disoriented and have become truly lost.

Often, your hiking partners can answer your questions. Someone else might have seen a blaze that you missed just a minute ago. Then again, they might confirm that there is a problem: "Yeah, I was kind of wondering about that myself...."

If no one in the group can definitively resolve your concerns (definitively does not mean: "I just have a feeling this is the way we're supposed to go"), you'll need to pull out your map and guidebook to see what they

When reading maps and using a compass become second nature, you'll enjoy plotting a day's course. You'll also have the confidence and know-how to hike anywhere without fear of becoming lost.

can tell you. The guidebook may say, for instance: "At 1.6 the trail deteriorates due to frequent flooding for 0.2 mile, then ascends Slippery Rock Mountain." If you're on a deteriorated floodplain with Slippery Rock Mountain looming over you, you'll have the answer to your questions. If the guidebook doesn't give you any indication (which is most often the case — guidebooks usually don't give tenth-of-a-mile by tenth-of-a-mile detail), it's time to consult your map.

Getting Unlost

Careful! Stop! Caution! Here's where you can compound your initial error. For some reason, it seems to be human

nature to misinterpret the map based on what you expect it to say rather than what it actually does say. It's almost as if we believe that we can remake the landscape by insisting on our preconceptions.

Before you look at your map, take a good, clear look at your surroundings. What are the prominent features? If the terrain is densely forested or featureless, what was the last thing that stood out? A mountain? A long climb or descent? A stretch along a river?

Now look at the map. Where did you last know where you were? How long ago was that? How many miles, approximately? What happened since then? Usually, you'll find that by the

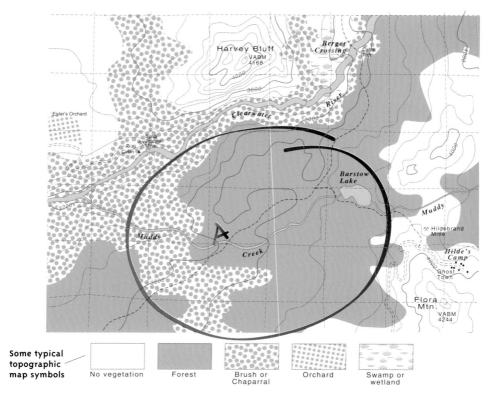

Some typical topographic map symbols

| No vegetation | Forest | Brush or Chaparral | Orchard | Swamp or wetland |

You last knew you were on the trail where it crossed Muddy Creek (A) an hour ago. Draw a circle on your map using your last known location (A) as the center and the distance you've walked as the radius. You're in that circle somewhere.

time you think through your route, you can easily identify where you are — and whether it's where you are supposed to be. Any mistakes become clear in retrospect: You missed a stream crossing and instead continued on an old trail that isn't maintained anymore. You took a wrong turn at the junction to Muskrat Pass; you should have gone toward Muskrat Mountain. If you still don't know where you are, try triangulating (explained above).

If, in fact, you are really and truly lost — if, after a thorough inspection

of the map, review of your route, and examination of landmarks, you still find it impossible to ascertain that you are even on the map — DO NOT PANIC! First, no matter what the illusion of wilderness, chances are that you are no more than 10 or 20 miles from a road. Second, you're unlikely to be as lost as you think you are. Don't start trying to remember the survival tips you learned in your scouting days, or head off to follow the nearest river back to civilization. That worked in Daniel Boone's day, but today our wildernesses are no longer as big as they once were, and while following waterways will undoubtedly take you out, it may be the long way. On occasion, when Dan and I are bushwhacking through difficult country, we follow streambeds to creeks and creeks to rivers, but we find that traveling cross-country along waterways makes for fiendishly difficult walking through canyons, rocks, vegetation, and deadfall. Before you set out to play nineteenth-century mountain man, sit down. Have something to eat. And let your brain do the walking.

Getting unlost is a process that is different each time you find yourself somewhere other than where you're supposed to be. Mostly, it's a matter of creatively using the information that is available to you.

Let's take an example: You have finally responded to a nagging little voice that tells you that if you were on course, you would have come to a prominent cliff a half hour ago. The last time you remember knowing your exact location was at your lunch stop an hour ago at Muddy Creek (see illustration, left). There has been no cliff, and looking ahead, you see no sign of any cliff-type formations. You notice several other discrepancies.

First, identify where you last knew absolutely for a fact that you were. (In this case, the crossing of the creek.) How far have you walked since then? (Multiple your approximate hiking pace by the number of hours you've been walking.) Now, draw a circle on your map using your last location (A)

as the center and the distance you've walked (or a little farther) as the radius. You're in that circle somewhere. It's unlikely that you walked in completely the wrong direction, so concentrate on the part of the circle that points in the direction you thought you were going in.

Now, take a look at what the map says is in that circle. Does anything look familiar? If you had been on course, what might you have seen? What do you remember seeing instead?

Look around at the terrain. Are there any prominent landmarks? Is there a high point of land you can climb to for a better look? You can try a few forays; usually, they will turn up enough information to help you identify your position. But heed this: Don't go anywhere without your pack! Being lost with your pack is not a major calamity; being lost and losing your pack is.

Let's say you are still unsure of your location. Look for big landmarks on your map that would be easy to identify if you were near them. Ridges or rivers are best, because they follow a generally linear course for several miles.

In this example, you are lost somewhere in the circle, but you can't tell exactly where. You do know, however, that no matter where you are, a course of due north will take you to the river — or to the trail you are looking for.

Once at the river, it will be an easy matter to pinpoint your exact location: You only need to take a bearing from a single, identifiable landmark somewhere along the river. In dense or monotonous country, this might be difficult, in which case there's another strategy you can use: deliberate miscalculation. In this case, the river intersects the route you want to follow (but have somehow lost). Once you reach the river, you'll need to know whether to turn left or right to get back on route. In order to do that, you make a deliberate, identifiable mistake — and then correct for it. In this example, the river is north of the circle in which you are lost. The trail you want to find intersects the river to the northeast of the circle. Therefore, from anywhere in the circle, you know that a bearing of due north will take you to the river. You also know that it will take you west of where you want to be. Once you get to the river, all you have to do to get back on route is follow the river eastward until it intersects with the trail. Voilà! You're back on track and on your way.

Not all examples are as clear-cut as this one. Sometimes the terrain requires more complicated thinking, especially if steep mountains, cliffs, or dense forest make cross-country travel difficult. But you'll usually use the same kinds of strategies to find your way back on track. Think about what you've seen. Try to reconcile the terrain with your map. Reason out what might have happened. Use all the tools available to you in as many creative ways as you can: your map, your compass, the terrain — and, most important, your mind.

DID YOU KNOW

Backpackers now have the technology of the United States Department of Defense at their fingertips. The new global positioning system uses 24 satellites to tell you where you are, accurate to about 50 feet. It can also calculate compass bearings to your destination, distances, and your rate of travel. The gizmo weighs in at 18 ounces. Prices range from $500 to $1,500. But before you throw away your compass, take heed: It's never wise to depend on a piece of equipment to do what you should be able to do yourself. The GPS is a helpful tool, but it's no substitute for knowing how to read a map and use a compass. After all, what if the batteries went dead?

SHARING
THE
ADVENTURE

Backpacking is a marvelous adventure, and once you get going, chances are you will want to share your experiences with family and friends. Introducing others to the woods is special, whether you are an enthusiastic beginner or an old-timer who regularly leads others. But there are pitfalls, into which even the most experienced backpacker can occasionally stumble.

A successful hiking partnership begins with communication. What kind of experience do you want to have? Is it the same experience your partners anticipate? People go into the backcountry for dozens of different reasons: to photograph flowers; to meander; to push themselves physically; to get in shape; to identify mosses and lichens; to sit by a lake with nothing to do but daydream. Before you head out, it's important to think about the kind of experience you want to have, and to talk about it with your hiking partners.

COUPLES

When Dan and I began hiking together, he already had some 15,000 miles of long-distance backpacking under his belt. I wasn't exactly sitting on a couch all the way at the other end of the spectrum — I had been on dozens of weekend trips, had taught

Just one of the sweet rewards of hiking the entire length of the Appalachian Trail with a partner! Distance hiking can create (or destroy) long-term bonds.

at an outdoor education center, and had volunteered as a weekend trip leader for a local Sierra Club chapter — but I had never hiked more than 50 miles at any one time. I completely overestimated my strength on our first long trip together — a 250-mile trek through the High Sierra. Because there was nowhere to resupply, we carried 17 days' worth of food — and 58-pound packs. The trip just happened to be our honeymoon, and we learned some valuable lessons! (One of the most important: You can slow down and cut back on your mileage. We ended up doing 200 miles, not 250, and that made all the difference in the world.) We've since gone on to hike many thousands of miles together.

DISCUSS THE CHALLENGES. If you are the more experienced partner, be up front about the physical challenges of backpacking, and talk about what to expect. If you happen to be blessed with better-than-average strength or endurance, don't assume that your partner will be able to keep up if he just pushes a little harder. Discuss what you'll do if it turns out your plans were too ambitious.

SEE THE TRAIL THROUGH YOUR PARTNER'S EYES. Remember that your novice partner has less experience to draw from. Beginners gasp as they make their way up their first 3,000-foot climb, convinced it will never end; you, on the other hand, know how to pace yourself and know that you can make it to the top. Don't forget that a 3,000-foot mountain might look insurmountable to someone who has never climbed one. (On my first really big climb, I actually refused to believe that we were going up to an obvious pass, even though it was the only place to go, and even though the map left no doubt on the subject. Until we were halfway up, I kept insisting, "No, they can't be sending us there!" To me, the idea of actually climbing up that THING was simply inconceivable.)

START SLOW! If you are the more experienced hiker, don't trust your partner's early burst of enthusiasm and energy. I once hiked with a friend who actually burst into song ("La-da-di, la-da-da, a knapsack on my back," as I recall) on her first hike. That lasted approximately 3 miles, until the beginning of the first climb. There was no more singing after that. If you are the less experienced partner, don't overcommit to high mileage. Nothing is fun if you are too exhausted to enjoy it. A slow start of 7 or 8 miles a day will help you break in and have fun. If you find that mileage easy, you can always hike farther the next day.

SHARE YOUR EXPECTATIONS. Discuss how you like to hike, or, if you've never hiked before, try and imagine an ideal. Are you an early riser? Do you like to stop for frequent breaks? Do you prefer to get the bulk of your miles done before lunchtime? Do you want a detailed itinerary, or do you just want to see what happens? Are you willing to change your plans if you or your partner is tired? If it's raining? If

there's a spectacular sunset?

DON'T TRY TO HIKE AT YOUR PARTNER'S PACE. Probably the most nagging partner problem stems from the fact that each person's pace is different. Other issues involve communication, or compromise, or flexibility, all of which can be negotiated. But pace is a physical fact; most people have difficulty straying too far from their natural gait. In physically mismatched partnerships, the slower person feels pushed; the faster person feels held back; and no one is happy or comfortable. Sometimes, hiking partners are forced to stay together, as in winter, on difficult terrain, or when hiking with map and compass off-trail.

When sharing a shelter with others, be considerate of their need for a modicum of privacy.

> 66 Hikers have a saying, 'Hike your own hike.' But when my husband Bob and I finished hiking the entire Appalachian Trail together, we both felt that we had hiked each other's hike. Bob likes the physical challenge of backpacking, but he never got to really stretch himself because he always felt he had to hold back for me. I wanted an easier, slower hike—but I always felt that I had to do more miles than I wanted to. Bob actually went back and redid the AT two years later—alone, so he could have the experience of a hike that was as physically demanding as he wanted it to be. 99
>
> — Dorlyn Williams, age 49, Harper's Ferry, West Virginia

But if you're on good, clear trail — as you probably will be at least the first few times you go out — try splitting up for a while and meeting at a predetermined point. Not only will you get to hike at your own speed, you'll also be more likely to see wildlife and to enjoy the special solitude of hiking alone.

TRAIL ETIQUETTE

With no finish line, no referees, no one right way to do it, hiking is perhaps the quintessential sport for anarchists.

Against a world of corporate ladders, bosses, obligations, E-mail, voice mail, and schedules, the freedom of the backcountry stands out in sharp relief. That does not, however, mean that there is no such thing as etiquette in the wilderness. As more and more people take to the woods, common courtesy has become increasingly important to the backcountry experience.

IN SEARCH OF PEACE AND QUIET. The wilderness is not, strictly speaking, a very quiet place. True, there is a distinct lack of noise: car alarms, telephones, door buzzers, beepers, honking horns, TV chatter, blaring music (one hopes!), and the like. But there is no shortage of music: wind, water, birds; the calls, bugles, and howls of loons and coyotes and elk. And sometimes, at night, there is silence, punctuated only by an occasional hoot from an owl or the insistent cry of a whippoorwill. One of the most common reasons people go into the woods is to enjoy both the sounds of wildness and the sound of silence. Be aware of how much noise you're making when you pass someone else's campsite, especially if you are traveling in a group.

SHARING SHELTERS. Even if you appreciate solitude, you might find yourself camping with other backpackers — especially if you are hiking on well-used trails or in places that require you to stay at designated

Introduce young kids to backpacking on dayhikes to interesting places like this beach.

Groups of 6 or more should be especially conscious of low-impact methods. Locate campsites away from water sources and popular sites along the trail, making sure, however, not to trammel rare or delicate plants in the process.

campsites. Enjoy these interactions; over time, you'll make many new friends as the result of a chance trailside encounter. Unfortunately, not every encounter is positive: Sometimes, you'll arrive at a shelter after a day of wet, cold hiking to be welcomed with a curt, "The shelter's full." (You should carry a tent to insure against such situations.) But as far as the business about the shelter being full is concerned, we agree with the Appalachian Trail hiker who said, "The shelter is full when everyone who needs shelter is in for the night." Established camping and shelter sites are for everyone. If you use them, welcome newcomers and make room.

If you're the newcomer, be considerate, especially between sunset and sunrise. When Dan and I hike on weekends, we sometimes find ourselves arriving at the trailhead after dark on a Friday night and walking in a few tenths of a mile to a shelter. We know that hikers are likely to be asleep soon after sundown, so if the shelter is occupied, we pitch our tent. We also use our tent if we intend to get up before sunrise because we've learned that it simply isn't possible to pack up and get going without waking everyone up. Some hikers insist that they have the "right" to come in as late as they like, or get up as early as they want. But having the right to do something doesn't make it the right thing to do.

SHARING CAMPSITES. In crowded areas, where the campsites are well established, people often expect to share a site, particularly if there are several fire rings and obvious flat spots. We usually look around when we arrive at a campsite and pick an unobtrusive spot off in a corner. If we really want to be alone, we make an effort to go off-trail somewhere. In the bigger and more remote wildernesses of the West, where it is possible to camp out of sight (and, even more important, out of earshot) of other hikers, most backpackers try to keep some distance between their camp and that of their neighbors.

GROUPS AND SHELTERS. It only takes one night camped with 40 people jammed in and around a shelter built for 12 for a backpacker to question whether groups should be permitted to use trail shelters. Minimum-impact ethics would suggest not. The National Outdoor Leadership School, which pioneered the idea of minimum-impact camping, takes thousands of students into the backcountry each year, but in the field, NOLS groups do everything possible to avoid even being seen by other wilderness users. Even a well-organized and well-led group can diminish the experience of other hikers, and the bigger it is, the bigger its impact — something to think about when planning your group excursion to the backcountry. A group of more than 6 hikers should split up while walking during the day. If possible, keep group sizes to fewer than 10 people — including the leaders.

STICK TO PREARRANGED PLANS. If you are hiking with one or more partners, don't go off alone without telling someone what you're doing and when you intend to come back. If you agreed to camp together at a certain place, don't make a spur-of-the-moment decision to camp somewhere else — your companions might hurt themselves if they get worried and go looking for you in the dark.

ON THE TRAIL. Each person has a pace that is naturally most comfortable for him. If someone behind you has caught up, his pace is faster than yours: Step aside and let him pass! This is so obvious as to be almost ridiculous, but over the years I've seen plenty of people who speed up the minute someone comes up the trail behind them. The problem is, the slower hiker can't sustain the faster pace; eventually, he slides back into his normal pace and the faster hiker catches up again — at which point, the process is repeated. Don't ask me why, but my informal and highly unscientific survey suggests that this happens most frequently when the would-be passer is a female and the won't-be passee is a high-school-aged or young-adult male.

WOODSWOMEN

I may be slightly prejudiced on this subject, but I'm not alone in thinking that women are often more successful backpackers than their male counterparts — even though we are outnumbered. Certainly, women can hike as far and climb as high as men. In addition, backpacking rewards endurance rather than strength, and emotional flexibility rather than goal orientation, and it punishes those who would push too far and too fast for too long. Clichés about tortoises and hares apply. Not that men can't be flexible and women can't be strong, but there do seem to be marked (if somewhat stereotypical) differences in the attitudes of men and women in the backcountry. These differences seem to work in favor of women, particularly over the long haul.

Why, then, a separate section for women? Partly for encouragement, to override the chorus of voices that tell women they can't or shouldn't do something, that the outdoors is a place for men, that smaller means weaker and somehow less competent. And partly to address the two major issues that are most likely to keep women out of the woods: menstruation and safety.

Most women soon learn that, while they're just as happy if they don't have to deal with monthly periods in the backcountry, they can easily make do with adequate supplies and a few extra Ziploc bags for the associated trash. At a recent gathering of long-distance hikers, a group of women compared personal supplies, but the only general consensus seemed to be to use whatever you're most comfortable with. Just remember that you have to pack out the trash (consider using tampons without applicators) or, if you have a fire, burn it thoroughly (this requires a large, very hot fire). Carry a little extra water for washing up. Finally, don't be surprised if your periods become irregular: Backpacking is physically stressful, and many women experience changes in their monthly cycles.

A more important issue for women is that of safety (which applies both to men and to women, but not equally). The fact is that, like everywhere else in the world, the wilderness is a safer place for men than it is for women. Keep your guard up: You don't need to be afraid of people, but you do need to check them out. It's probably true that you are safer in the woods than in your hometown (I know that's true for me), but it's also true that occasionally a few crazies, drunks, or nuisances wander into the backcountry.

Women are, if anything, better adapted to long-distance hiking than men. In any event, women can ignore all talk of the advantages of men's strength in the outdoors. Enjoyable, safe backpacking is not about displays of strength.

TIPS FOR HIKING SAFELY

● Don't Appear to Be Alone. If necessary, invent a hiking partner: "My husband's waiting for me, I've got to go catch up" is a good one. One woman I know wears a wedding ring, even though she is determinedly single.

● Trust Your Instincts. If someone makes you feel uncomfortable, keep going. Don't tell strangers where you intend to camp — either specifically or by implication. But if you find yourself making friends with other hikers on a populated trail, see if you can arrange to camp with or near them.

● Camping Alone. If you prefer to camp alone, avoid obvious and frequently used campsites and go off-trail where you can't easily be seen.

● Leave an Itinerary. Make sure someone at home knows where you intend to go and when you intend to be back.

● Cars. Don't leave valuables in your car. Car vandalism has recently become such a problem in the East that many hikers no longer park at trailhead lots. Instead, make arrangements to park at a local motel or business, and then arrange a shuttle to the trailhead. Local trail guides may provide information. If you are hiking in the East anywhere near the Appalachian Trail, call Appalachian Trail Conference

(ATC) headquarters (see Sources and Resources) for a list of people who shuttle hikers.

● Theft. Usually, the farther you get from a road, the safer you and your gear are. I sometimes console myself with the thought that in order to steal my pack, someone is actually going to have to carry it out, and they're not likely to do that if I'm far from a road. But we hikers tend to have a linear perspective, and we may not be aware of side trails that provide easy access to our belongings. No matter how dirty, scruffy, or beaten up they may be, packs do get stolen. Keep an eye on yours, especially near road crossings. Don't leave it unattended, even if you think you've got it well hidden. Thieves know where to look.

● About Guns. A fellow hiker who is also an NRA member says, "Guns don't belong on the trail. First, you need to be prepared to shoot a person if you pull a gun on him. Do you really want to enter the hiking community with that kind of attitude? And second, in order to be of any use to you, a gun has to be available at all times: You can't carry it in your pack. It has to be at your side. If you go to a spring, you have to take it with you. If you go to check out a view, you have to take it with you. What does that say to fellow hikers? Leave your guns at home."

When hiking with young children, don't be too ambitious, and stop to pitch your tent early, so that there's plenty of time to explore and no anxiety about settling in before dark.

KIDS

Coming down from the summit of Maine's Katahdin at the end of my Appalachian Trail through-hike, I ran into a man hiking with his two sons, ages twelve and sixteen. He wore a smile that went ear-to-ear. (Allow me that impossible cliché; it's how I remember him.) I had met the family earlier in the week, so I knew that each summer for the last four years, they had hiked several hundred miles. Now, less than a mile short of the summit, they were about to complete a lifelong dream and finish the Appalachian Trail.

Talk about quality time! No MTV, no telephones, no video games, no interruptions. Not to mention the sense of achievement and the wonder of the experience itself.

Kids thrive in the out-of-doors, no matter how young they are. I'm not an expert on backpacking with very small children, but I've put in quite a bit of

time with schoolkids, ranging in age from six to sixteen. Working as an outdoor education instructor, I had the opportunity to see, week after week, the delight and joy a child takes in the natural world: particularly if someone is there to explain its mysteries.

People who hike with kids caution that a family backpacking experience is very different from that of the average solo hiker. Everything takes longer, from getting up in the morning to walking from point to point. Kids are less likely to be able to continue and not complain when the going gets tough; they don't much see the point of suffering, of being tired, or hot, or wet, or miserable. Considerable effort has to go into forestalling crankiness (a condition to which we adults, too, are susceptible).

A few suggestions:

START WITH DAYHIKES. They'll help you get a feel for your child's pace, level of interest, and endurance. You'll also test your own patience, not to mention your ability to carry the child when that last mile back to the car is just too far.

DON'T BE TOO AMBITIOUS. For most families, a night in a campsite a mile or two from a road will require quite enough planning and cooperation. Remember, the point is not to get somewhere — it's to have fun. The first few times you camp, stay within easy walking distance of your car — maybe a quarter to half a mile. There's immense security in knowing that you can just pick up and leave if everything goes wrong.

INVOLVE YOUR CHILD IN PLANNING. A child who knows what to expect is likely to be more excited about the trip. A neat destination like a waterfall or a special rock formation offers a special reward for the day's walk.

EXPECT TO PUTTER. A small child's walking pace may be a half mile an hour. Adults tend to be goal oriented and concerned with getting where they are going. But your child may not understand or care about something as intangible (and unimportant) as a destination when there are all sorts of things to explore here and now: bugs, mushrooms, mosses, flowers, water, rocks, roots. Take advantage of what your child is teaching you. You, too, can learn to slow down and appreciate the everyday magic of the natural world.

TAKE TURNS WITH YOUR SPOUSE. A whole day at a small child's dawdling pace is enough to make almost anyone ready to pump out a 20-mile day, if only from repressed energy. Take turns with your spouse — if you have a couple of kids, trade off who goes with whom — and wait for each other at prearranged lunch spots or breaks.

GAMES. Several books contain suggestions for games in the outdoors. Or you can make up your own. Keep lists of animal tracks, birds, or flowers. Ask kids if they can figure out where an owl

lives. Or a porcupine. Can they figure out what a moose is doing when he sticks his head underwater? Almost anything can turn into a game outdoors.

HAVE A PRACTICE NIGHT OUT. The backyard is fine. Sometimes, kids become afraid in a new environment, and a tent certainly qualifies. Camping out close to home is a reassuring, stress-free introduction to life beyond walls — for both children and their parents.

The subject of kids in the backcountry requires another book, and several are available. For specifics, ranging from diapers to long-distance backpacking with infants and small children, check out some of the books listed in Sources and Resources at the end of this book.

OTHER USERS IN THE BACKCOUNTRY

Like it or not, the backcountry is becoming ever more crowded — and not only with backpackers. As more and more of us flock to what is left of our wild places, user conflicts increase between snowmobilers and cross-country skiers, mountain bikers and backpackers, anglers and river rafters and hunters and dirt bikers and ATV users and youth groups and horseback riders and llama packers and wildlife photographers.

Like any other user group, backpackers sometimes think that the best way to avoid conflicts is to ban all the other users. But before you subscribe to that theory, you should know that in some parts of the country, recreation

GAMES FOR KIDS

WHAT ANIMAL AM I?
This game works like "20 ques-tions." Write the name of an animal on a piece of paper and pin it to a child's back. The child then asks "yes," "no," or "maybe" questions about the animal he is supposed to be.

SCAVENGER HUNT
The normal scavenger hunt can be adapted to make kids think cre-atively about the natural environ-ment. Make up a list based on where you are. Things to collect might include "Something that will grow up and become a tree" (an acorn), "Ten pieces of litter" (to be packed out, of course), "Something a mouse could eat," "Something pretty," "Something a bird could use for its nest."

HUG A TREE
Blindfold the child and lead him to a tree. Let him spend a few minutes touching the tree. Then spin him around and lead him back to a cen-tral place. Remove his blindfold. Can he find his tree again?

use — and that means all kinds of recreation — is an economic motive for land preservation. You might consider this argument merely a variation of the old "lesser of two evils," but most backpackers would agree that it's far better to share terrain with mountain bikers than it is to hike through a clear-cut or a cow pasture. (As for ATVs and dirt bikes, I'm not so sure....)

If you do see other users, remember that they have a right to be there, and that problems rarely develop between people of goodwill and common sense. As a backpacker, remember that you can always retreat to wilderness areas, where mechanical means of transportation are prohibited. In addition, roads are not permitted in wilderness areas, so access is limited to those who are willing to walk.

A final tip: Avoid any area that has gotten recent publicity as one of the last "undiscovered" great hiking places. If you see it described in a newspaper or magazine, it is no longer undiscovered!

GOING FARTHER

I t starts innocently enough: You're on a marked trail and you have a sudden urge to ascend a peak off to the side somewhere. Or an out-of-season snowfall surprises you, and you find not only that you stayed warm and dry, but that the woods were exquisite all covered in white. A few more trips and you start wondering what Yellowstone looks like in March, or whether Nepal is all it's cracked up to be.

Of course, you may be one of the millions of backpackers who are quite content to stay in the three-season temperate zone without the need for a passport, a winter tent, or a crash course from Berlitz. Certainly, you could spend your whole life hiking and never run out of trails. But then again, you could be one of those who responds to the lure of places that are a little higher, a little colder, a little more remote. A little wilder.

WINTER

January in Wyoming: A nationwide cold spell had turned Grand Teton National Park into a deepfreeze. For nine days, the thermometer never rose above zero, and at night temperatures plummeted to –20 and –30 degrees: the kind of numbers that lose their meaning. But the first night was the worst. Dan and I and our fellow hikers had just arrived in the park, and hadn't had time to finish making camp before dark. As I lay huddled in my sleeping bag surrounded by a brittle, icy silence, I wondered just what I thought I was doing in the middle of winter in the wild country of Wyoming, separated from the cold outside by nothing more than a nylon tent.

Today, it's a toss-up whether winter or fall is my favorite season to hike. I like the winter woods: the silence and solitude, the prettiness, the quiet drama of daily survival. I like the feel of cold snow squeaking underfoot, and the way the sun angles as it slouches across the southern sky.

But it's not all pretty pictures. Snow and ice and cold are treacherous companions. Winter deserves a healthy respect. A few stalwart companions help. And if your pack has a couple of extra pounds of clothing, so much the better.

You don't necessarily need a whole new wardrobe for winter, but you do need to take more gear, especially clothing. A three-season tent can sometimes suffice, if it's not one of those that are mostly made of mosquito netting. In really severe conditions, however, you may want to upgrade to a winter tent,

BUILDING YOUR SKILLS

When the urge strikes to go beyond, there are a few things you need to consider before you buy more gear and head for places unknown. Do you have the skills to deal with navigation problems, solo hiking, and winter travel? Don't be discouraged if the answer is no: There are many ways to learn what you need to know.

● Ease into more challenging adventures. Introduce yourself to winter slowly, by hiking a little earlier — or later — in the year than usual. Climb a couple of lower mountains before you head off for a high-altitude trek. Or learn to travel solo by starting out on a well-used trail where help is readily available.

● Other hikers are a terrific resource. Local clubs may offer slide shows on the kind of trek you are dreaming about. They may even sponsor a trip (or at least be able to recommend one).

● Take a class. Where I live, hiking shops frequently offer courses, as do the Adirondack Mountain Club and the Appalachian Mountain Club. If you're a little more ambitious, you might consider one of the big national wilderness schools, such as the National Outdoor Leadership School and Outward Bound (see Sources and Resources), which teach everything from whitewater kayaking to rock climbing and glacier travel.

cold. Some are essential, including a full-length mattress pad, gaiters (for keeping snow out of boots), and ski poles (for keeping your balance). Also available are candle lanterns, ice axes, lightweight snow shovels, down booties, pile socks, layering systems for your hands, and insulating parkas for water bottles. Just remember that each piece of gear weighs something. It's not hard to fill a winter pack beyond your carrying capacity.

Winter travel with a pack is best handled on snowshoes. If

Dawn start for a climb, Palisade Glacier in California's Sierra Nevadas. Bulky clothing and clumsy, cold fingers make everything take longer in winter, so you must allow extra time.

which is designed to better handle snow loads and wind and may have nifty adaptations like cooking vents and a gizmo from which to hang your candle lantern. As you get more involved in winter camping, you'll find many other gadgets that help you deal with the

you fancy skiing, try it out at home first: Maneuvering on skis while carrying a pack takes some practice. Another option for skiers is to use the hut-to-hut systems available in some mountain ranges so you won't have to carry as much gear.

TIPS FOR WINTER

GROUP SIZE. A winter party should include at least four members, especially if you are going above treeline.

REGISTRATION. The rigors of winter hiking make it all the more important that someone knows where you are. If there is a registration box at the trailhead, sign in. And as always, leave your itinerary with a friend or family member.

STAY WARM AND DRY. Your full-time job in winter camping is to stay warm and dry. Constantly adjust your clothing layers. While hiking, you want to be wearing enough so that you stay warm without overheating. (If you are feeling hot, you are sweating too much, which means your clothes are getting WET!) As soon as you stop, take off your sweaty clothes and put on new layers of dry ones.

KEEP YOUR HEAD WARM. Remember that the layering principle works for your head. Your hat is your most important piece of gear: the first layer to put on when you are cold, and the first to remove when you are hot. In really cold weather, try using a balaclava and a hat. Still cold? Add the hood of your waterproof jacket.

AVOID TOUCHING LIQUIDS. Don't let your skin come into contact with any liquid, particularly fuel, that remains liquid far below 32 degrees Fahrenheit and which can cause instant frostbite. Also avoid touching metal fuel canisters with bare hands, since the metal will be as cold as the fuel inside it. Skin can actually stick to a super-cooled fuel bottle. Rolling some duct tape around the fuel bottle helps (and also provides a stash of tape for emergency repairs).

ALLOW EXTRA TIME. Everything takes longer in winter. It takes more time to start a stove with clumsy cold fingers or while wearing gloves. It takes longer for freezing-cold water (or snow) to come to a boil. It takes longer to take a tent down, since you'll have to stop to warm your hands and remove condensation that makes the poles stick to the tent fabric. The only thing that happens fast in winter is sunset: Make sure you reach camp early enough to get your chores done before dark.

HANDS AND FEET. Pay attention to your extremities: The winter gear I am most grateful to have includes pile socks and down or synthetic-fill booties to keep feet warm at night, and pile mittens, over-mitts, and polypropylene glove liners (bring two pairs of liners).

KEEP GEAR FROM FREEZING. The sweat in your boots will freeze overnight, and in the morning you'll feel like you're wearing blocks of ice. Sleep with boots (and anything else that can freeze) stuffed at the bottom of your sleeping bag. In temperatures that hover around zero, this includes batteries and your fuel bottle — the fuel won't freeze, but warm fuel works better than cold fuel.

ABOUT WATER. Water left in pots will freeze; so will water in your canteen. In temperatures slightly below freezing, turn the water bottle upside down so that ice forms at the bottom and not near the mouth. Some winter camping experts recommend burying your water bottle in the snow. Snow is a good insulator, and the temperature in a snow bank isn't cold enough to freeze the water. Or so they say: I've never done this because I like to keep my water near me so I can drink during the night. Never leave water in a water bag overnight. If the water freezes, the bag becomes useless.

You can't use it until the water melts, and in the meantime, the ice can tear the plastic liner.

PLAN SHORT DAYS. In northern climes, it may be dark for 16 hours or more, leaving you a mere eight hours to strike camp, travel, make camp, and cook. Winter mileage is invariably shorter than summer mileage, and if you're traveling on snowshoes, it's much slower, too.

MAKING CAMP. If you're camping on snow, you'll need to tamp it down so that you have a firm, even base to sleep on. Stomp out a tent pad while wearing your snowshoes or skis. If anyone in your group is a little chilly, this job might help warm him up.

SLEEPING BAGS. Make sure your bag is warm enough for the conditions. If in doubt, take along a vapor barrier liner or a bivvy sack, each of which adds a few degrees of warmth.

HYPOTHERMIA. Never forget that hypothermia can kill.

SOLO

Solo hiking is a completely different way to appreciate the outdoors. In the crowded East, or on very popular western trails, you may not notice much difference at first, especially if you stay in lean-tos or in campsites likely to be populated by other hikers. But in a truly remote area, hiking solo offers an intensity that is hard for other

outdoor experiences to match.

For one thing, there is the freedom. Freedom to get up when you like, to go as fast or as slow as you like, to stop to rest once every few minutes or every few hours. Hiking partners need to negotiate and compromise on every little detail: who carries what, how far to go, whether to eat lunch at this viewpoint or go on a little

Even a minor injury like a sprained ankle can become serious, especially if it is coupled with bad weather. The risks of going solo are obvious: Make sure you are competent to take them. And be sure someone has a copy of your itinerary.

THE JET SET

In Jamaica, hiking opportunities include a strenuous two-day trip to the top of 7,402-foot Blue Mountain Peak. In Europe, you can take your pick

Before pitching your tent on snow, tamp the snow down so that you have a firm, even base to sleep on, a blessing for backpackers accustomed to trying to find comfort between rocks and roots.

farther. Solo hikers are free of all that.

On crowded trails, solo hikers take few additional risks. In the event of an injury or a fall, someone is likely to come along and help. There is, of course, the occasional yahoo. Women, as usual, need to be especially wary. But most competent backcountry users adhere to the code of the wilderness: that it is everyone's responsibility to help someone in need. In remote places, hiking solo requires extra care.

of hundreds of hiking trails. Go hut-to-hut in the Slovakia's Tatras Mountains, or embark on a two-month-long adventure on the spine of the Pyrenees from the Atlantic Ocean to the Mediterranean Sea. In east Africa, you can add on to the traditional safari with a backpacking trip: The circumnavigation of Mount Kenya is one of the most spectacular hikes in the world. Even hikers on a tight budget will find that hiking abroad is affordable. After all, your major expense is airfare.

How do you find out about international hiking trails? Magazines focusing on backpacking or adventure travel routinely run features on exotic locations, as does the travel section of the Sunday *New York Times*. Also, check out a bookstore that is well stocked with travel books. The Lonely Planet guides are written with adventure travelers in mind. As always, recently returned travelers are a good source of information; they will most likely be delighted to show you their 50 rolls of film of Icelandic hot springs or Patagonian fjords. Where do you find such adventuresome people? Try your local hiking club, or attend the annual gathering of the Appalachian Long Distance Hikers Association.

THE LONG HAUL

Have you ever noticed that the blazes — and the trails — keep going? Have you ever wondered where they lead? Have you ever met a long-distance hiker, muscled and fit and hard after two or three months on the trail?

A weekend trip, a weeklong trip...suddenly, you're frantically saving vacation days so you can complete a major trail like Vermont's Long Trail (265 miles) or California's John Muir Trail (213 miles).

And then there are "the big ones." The Appalachian Trail is 2,150 miles long. The Pacific Crest Trail is 2,638. The Continental Divide Trail is not yet fully constructed, but it is anticipated that its final length will be 2,800 miles

from Mexico to Canada. A couple of thousand people set out each year to walk one of the three major national scenic trails (by far the majority of them choose the AT). Only a couple of hundred succeed.

John Viehman (left) and a friend along New Zealand's Milford Track. What better way to see a foreign land than far from the crowds and with the independence that backpacking affords.

Why, if hiking is so wonderful, is there such a high attrition rate among through-hikers? The reasons vary. Some people drop out because of lack

TIPS FOR THE JET SET

IMMUNIZATIONS. Third World travel generally requires a few shots. Check well in advance, because some courses of medication need to be started a few weeks before you go. Also check on whether you'll need to take malaria pills, and if so, what kind.

YOUR HEALTH. Discuss your trip with your doctor. Make sure your basic immunizations (polio; measles, mumps, rubella; and tetanus) are up-to-date. Also, make sure you have an adequate supply of any prescription drugs you need, along with a copy of the prescription. Ask your doctor to prescribe a general antibiotic such as tetracycline and a prescription-strength painkiller for emergencies. Finally, do not even think about getting on a plane without paying a farewell visit to your dentist!

MAPS. Depending on where you are going, you might want to write away for maps in advance. Some guidebooks tell you whether and how to do this. In Europe, maps are readily available locally, although English-language publications may be hard to find. Surprisingly, you don't need to bother with maps if you're headed to trek in Nepal: You can get English-language maps and guidebooks to your heart's content in Kathmandu!

FOOD AND SUPPLIES. You'll usually need to bring your gear with you (an exception again is Kathmandu, where climbers departing the Himalayas dump their gear; you can rent or buy almost anything). Food can be a challenge in Third World countries. Quick-cooking prepared foods are sometimes available in big cities, but almost never in the bush. You might want to bring some freeze-dried or prepared dinners along.

STOVES. Make sure you have a multi-fuel stove. You won't be permitted to check fuel with your luggage, and finding white gas in an unfamiliar city is enough to frustrate even the most resourceful traveler. The MSR XGK II is probably the best bet for unpredictable fuel sources in foreign countries. Ours burned well on dry-cleaning fluid purchased in Nairobi and kerosene from Kathmandu.

BEFORE YOU GO. Read up on the culture to try to learn a few words of the language. Some of the backpacker's most magical moments come from interactions with other people. But to make the magic work, you'll need to avoid the traveler's greatest pitfall: offending someone inadvertently.

PHOTOGRAPHY. If photographs are important to you, take extra film and batteries and, if possible, a small backup camera. The more remote your destination, the less likely you'll be able to buy even basic supplies.

The Weasel River Valley, Baffin Island, in the Northwest Territories of Canada. Have you ever wondered how far you could go if you kept going? Where the trail leads? Long-distance hikers cannot resist the urge to answer such questions.

of money or because of family obligations; others become injured. But many hikers simply find themselves overmatched. They didn't know what they were getting into, and they find that they don't love hiking enough to push through the dreary days of rain or heat or bugs. Through-hiking is not for everyone, but those who take to it usually consider it the experience of a lifetime.

There's an easier way of experiencing a long-distance trail. You don't have to take six months out of your life, or endure the aches and pains of a through-hike. So-called section hikers nibble at a long-distance trail by hiking one section at a time, year after year. Some finish by doing big chunks of a few hundred miles at a time.

Others take many years to do a long-distance trail, but when they finally do finish, their achievement and sense of accomplishment are no less. Another advantage to this plain is that section hikers can schedule their trips so that they hike each part of the trail at its optimum time of year.

LEADING OTHERS

As you continue to gain expertise, you will probably want to introduce your friends and family to the magic of the outdoors. In small informal groups, a leader usually emerges — someone who does the initial planning and answers questions about what to bring and what to leave at home. Generally, the leader is the person who has the

As you become an accomplished hiker, you may want to introduce others to the special world of the trail by volunteering as a leader. Before doing so, however, you must honestly assess your skills.

most experience, but each group will evolve differently. In situations where several or all of the group members are experienced outdoors people, leadership may be fluid, changing to reflect the different strengths and weaknesses of each member. Dan and I do this without even thinking about it: I'm better at navigation; he has more climbing experience. So when it's a compass, I'm in charge; when it's crampons, he calls the shots. We both trust the other's judgment — and we both feel free to ask questions and make our own suggestions.

If you intend to hike on a well-marked trail in good weather, you may not need a leader to do much more than announce what time to meet at the trailhead. But under more challenging or dangerous circumstances — at altitude,

in snow, off-trail — leadership becomes increasingly important, as does the willingness of group members to balance their individuality with responsibility to others.

If you are a member of a hiking club, you may find yourself interested in volunteering as a leader. Outing clubs usually check out potential leaders before letting them take a group of novices into the woods. At the very least, you should have current first aid training. You should also be a competent outdoors person. Yes, this should go without saying, but it is depressingly common to see groups of youngsters or even adults led by someone who clearly shouldn't be in charge of anyone in the backcountry. Before you volunteer to lead a trip, honestly assess your skills. Consider brushing up with a class, either through a local hiking club, at a college, or through one of the wilderness education organizations. It's impossible to know too much!

As a leader, your responsibilities begin when you announce a description of your outing on an outfitter's bulletin board, in your hiking club newsletter, or in the paper. Describe the trip as clearly as possible: the terrain, your intended mileage, whether the hike is "an easy amble" or "a challenging scramble" or somewhere in between. Then be prepared not only to answer questions of prospective hikers, but to ask them as well. It's your job to make sure that you gather together a group of people who understand the nature of the trip — and have the adequate preparation and gear for it.

Groups and Gear

You'll also need to provide a gear list. Before Dan and I head out to the trail, we have a ritual that we call the gear dump. The process varies according to the participants: With an informal group of experienced hikers, we usually just discuss the gear, item by item. Do we really need two stoves for three people? (No.) Is one water filter enough for six hikers? (Yes, if everyone carries his own supply of chemical purifiers for emergencies.) Does everyone really need his own army knife, pot scrubber, pot holder.... (No.) But do be sure that your group is committed to staying together if you're going to be sharing essential gear.

If we've been on the trail awhile, we'll know if our gear has been ade-

quate for local weather conditions, so we'll be able to tell companions who are joining us down the line whether or not they really need those three sweaters, a down jacket, and two layers of polypropylene.

In extreme conditions, and with novices or with children, we actually go through equipment piece by piece. In the past, we've found economy-sized bottles of shampoo, a bath towel, blue jeans, a week's supply of cotton underwear, and even a battery-operated razor. (And all of those items were in adult hikers' packs!)

Experienced backpackers appreciate the gear dump ritual. One friend actually did a little jig with her pack on when she discovered that the monster was a good 10 pounds lighter than she had expected. But that was because she knew down to her muscles and bones the advantage of getting rid of extra weight. Novices, on the other hand, may resist, because they've never felt the burden of a too-heavy pack. If you are trying to help someone pare down his pack weight, be sensitive, especially to newer backpackers, who, after all, did make a decision to pack those particular supplies — however ridiculous they may seem to you. Before throwing an item into the riddance pile, ask what it was for, explain why it isn't necessary, or suggest a lighter replacement.

Group Safety

There is safety in numbers in the out-of-doors. The Adirondack Mountain Club recommends that winter camping groups always number four or more. There has never been a documented grizzly bear attack on a group of more than four. Groups can sometimes perform self-evacuations in cases of emergency, and at the very least, they can send runners for help without leaving an injured victim alone. Finally, in emergencies, the average group tends to make better decisions than the average individual if the members discuss alternatives and listen to each other (something for leaders to remember).

But a group is only as strong as its weakest member, and a group trip can keep going only as long as no one sprains an ankle, or finds himself overmatched by weather, terrain, or mileage, or gets sick on the trail. The bigger the group (and the longer the group is out), the greater the chance that someone will have some sort of problem. Two tips: First, make sure someone in your group has a large area map in case you do need to change your plans and find a quick way out. Second, the leader should ask each member of the group to fill out a form listing any medications or health problems, especially things like heart trouble, respiratory problems, susceptibility to knee injuries, or epilepsy.

TRAIL VOLUNTEER WORK

Trails need constant work to stay open, and much of that work is done by volunteers. Cutting back brush, painting blazes, putting in water bars, building bridges, and replacing rotten puncheons (those plank bridges that span New England bogs) are hard jobs often done by a community of people who care about the outdoors and want to contribute to their sport. The work may be hard, but it's anything but drudgery. Working outdoors with a group of like-minded people is a great way to spend the weekend, and the work itself is a good substitute for a few hours at the gym. Local hiking clubs can put you in touch with local trail tenders.

While hiking the Appalachian Trail, I met a volunteer in Georgia who was planning his own AT through-hike, but first wanted to put 500 hours into trail work. "I enjoy hiking and this is a way to put something back. The trail wouldn't exist without the volunteers. Plus, it's fun." A retired gentleman on a trail crew in Tennessee stopped swinging an ax long enough to tell me, "Well, I guess I've come full circle. I liked messing around in the mud as a kid, and I still like it!"

Some volunteers become fiercely protective of their stretch of trail, especially when it becomes threatened by development or land use. Protecting trails often means protecting the land surrounding them; trail quality depends on the quality of the surrounding environment. Your local trail club can tell you what projects it's working on to ensure that its trails continue to offer a place of peace, removed from the drone of traffic, the buzz of machinery, and the clutter of everyday life. Trails are an opportunity to interact with the natural world, to slow down enough to notice the things we usually rush past, and to live simply with only what we can carry. You can help to keep them that way.

SOURCES & RESOURCES

What's next? Get some gear, pick a location, plan your trip. Following are organizations to contact, more books to read, and ideas about acquiring equipment.

After reading this book you may be ready to set foot onto a local trail and start a new hobby — or perhaps a new obsession. If, however, you seek company, you should have no trouble locating organizations teaching skills and leading group trips. There are so many such organizations, in fact, that we cannot possibly list them all or give information that will stay current. However, we can get you started.

LEADING HIKING CLUBS

When seeking a hiking club, a good place to begin, besides local bulletin boards, is the American Hiking Society and its member associations. The society has nearly 120 affiliated clubs. These groups are involved in education, leadership, and trail protection and maintenance. Many publish excellent trail guides to their regions. Most important, their members—many with years of experience hiking and back-packing—lead hikes and are a valuable source of advice and knowledge. Here are some of the largest clubs, many of which are mentioned in the text:

AMERICAN HIKING SOCIETY
P.O. Box 20160
Washington, D.C.
703-255-9304
Fax: 703-255-9308
Write or call for the society's complete list of affiliated clubs to find the one nearest you.

APPALACHIAN MOUNTAIN CLUB (AMC)
5 Joy Street
Boston, MA 02108
617-523-0636
Fax: 617-523-0722
Almost 55,000 members; the club offers numerous hiking programs from 2-5 days; also publishes many excellent guides to the outdoors.

APPALACHIAN TRAIL CONFERENCE (ATC)
PO Box 807
Harpers Ferry, WV 25425
304-535-6331
Helps coordinate maintenance of the 2,000 mile Appalachian Trail; excellent source of current information on hiking activities.

COLORADO MOUNTAIN CLUB
2530 West Alameda Ave
Denver, CO 80219
303-922-8976

**CONTINENTAL DIVIDE
TRAIL SOCIETY**
3704 N. Charles Street #601
Bethesda, MD 21218
410-235-9610

**FLORIDA TRAIL
ASSOCIATION (FTA)**
PO Box 13708
Gainesville, FL 32604
904-378-8823

GREEN MOUNTAIN CLUB
Route 100, Box 650
Waterbury Center, VT 05677
802-244-7037
*Coordinates up-keep and protection
of and publishes guide to the Long
Trail, which runs the length of Ver-
mont and includes many shelters.*

KEYSTONE TRAILS ASSOCIATION
PO Box 251
Cogan Station, PA 17728
717-322-0293

THE MOUNTAINEERS
303 Third Ave, W.
Seattle, WA 98119
206-284-6310

**NEW YORK-NEW JERSEY
TRAIL CONFERENCE**
232 Madison Avenue, #908
New York, NY 10016
212-685-9699

**PACIFIC CREST
TRAIL CONFERENCE**
PO Box 2040
Lynnwood, WA 98036
503-686-1365

**POTOMAC APPALACHIAN
TRAIL CLUB**
118 Park Street, S.E.
Vienna, VA 22180
703-242-0693

**WASHINGTON TRAILS
ASSOCIATION**
1305 Fourth Avenue #512
Seattle, WA 98101
206-625-1367

TOUR OPERATORS
In addition to regional trail
associations, these organizations and tour operators offer
hiking programs, or can recommend other sources to you:

BACKCOUNTRY
PO Box 4029-A114
Bozeman, MT 59772
406-586-3556
Fax: 406-586-4288
*Offers a catalog of trips and free
information packets on how to
query outfitters.*

BACKROADS
1516 5th Street, Suite A200
Berkeley, CA 94710-1740
800-462-2848
Fax: 510-527-1444
*Considered one of the foremost
active travel tour operators in
North America; write or call for
full-color catalogs.*

ECOTOURISM SOCIETY
PO Box 755
North Bennington, VT 05257
802-447-2121
*Keeps an eye on the environmental
viability of programs others
sponsor.*

**HOSTELLING INTERNATIONAL-
AMERICAN YOUTH HOSTELS**
733 15th Street N.W. #840
Washington, D.C. 20005
202-783-6161
Fax: 202-783-6171
*American and European group
programs for all ages.*

MOUNTAIN TRAVEL SOBEK
6420 Fairmont Avenue
El Cerrito, CA 94536
800-227-2384
510-527-8100
Fax: 510-525-7710

NATIONAL AUDUBON SOCIETY
950 Third Avenue
New York, NY 10022
212-979-3000
*The Audubon Society and its local
chapters sponsor a wide variety of
programs. Call for your nearest
chapter's offerings.*

THE NATURE CONSERVANCY
1815 North Lynn Street
Arlington, VA 22209
703-841-5300
*Oversees 1,100 wild preserves and
safeguards millions of acres. Ask
for your local chapter information.*

**RAILS-TO-TRAILS
CONSERVANCY (RTC)**
1400 16th Street N.W. , Suite. 300
Washington, D.C. 20036
202-797-5400
800-888-7747
Fax: 202-797-5411
*50,000 members; promotes
conversion of railways to trails
for public use.*

SIERRA CLUB
730 Polk Street
San Francisco, CA 94109
415-981-8634
*This esteemed environmental group
has 56 chapters & publishes an
annual guide to family outings in
its house publication,* Sierra. *Current information on trips is available by calling 415-923-5630.*

**STUDENT CONSERVATION
ASSOCIATION (SCA)**
PO Box 550
Charlestown, NH 03603
603-543-1700
Fax: 603-543-1828
*Places students in volunteer
positions with government outdoor
agencies.*

**TREKS FOR LIFE & BREATH
AMERICAN LUNG ASSOCIATION**
1701 18th Street N.W.
Washington, D.C. 20009
3-9 day backpacking trips.

**OUTDOOR RECREATION
COALITION OF AMERICA (ORCA)**
PO Box 1319
Boulder, CO 80306
303-444-3353
Fax: 303-444-3284
*Promotes outdoor sports legisla-
tively and has trade councils for
different sports; also publishes an
annual outdoor events guide.*

ELDERHOSTEL
75 Federal Street
Boston, MA 02210-1941
617-426-7788
Fax: 617-426-8351
*Elderhostel's programs for older
persons include a variety of outdoor sports and activities.*

OUTDOOR ADVENTURE SCHOOLS

These leading educational organizations are considered the best in the field:

NATIONAL OUTDOOR LEADERSHIP SCHOOL (NOLS)

Dept. R
288 Main Street
Lander, WY 82520
307-332-6873
NOLS trains future guides, year-round, even for college credit, all over the world.

OUTWARD BOUND (OB)

Route 90
R2, Box 280
Garrison, NY 10524
800-243-8520
Almost all Outward Bound participants consider their experiences with the school far more than an outdoor adventure — the learning experience is often spiritual as well. With 31 schools worldwide, OB is a school staffed by experts, with a solid reputation for safe and professional wilderness courses.

FIRST AID TRAINING

For first aid and CPR classes call the American Red Cross and ask for local chapter information:

AMERICAN RED CROSS NATIONAL HEADQUARTERS

431 18th Street N.W.
Washington, D.C. 20006
202-737-8300

MAGAZINES

The established outdoor magazines can both thrill and lend assurance to novice adventurers. They are chock full of techniques, recommendations, and usually ample sections with advertisements for outfitters, schools, and trips.

BACKPACKER

Rodale Press, Inc.
33 East Minor Street
Emmaus, PA 18098
Subscriptions: 800-666-3434
You can also read this popular outdoor magazine on your computer by sending to America Online for the software, 8619 Westwood Center Drive, Vienna, VA 22182-9806. Backpacker's annual guide to equipment is a must.

OUTSIDE

Mariah Media Inc.
400 Market Street
Santa Fe, NM 87501
505-989-7100; subscriptions: 800-678-1131
All active outdoor sports, practically invented adventure travel, environment, annual gear guide.

OUTSIDE KIDS

Mariah Media Inc.
400 Market Street
Santa Fe, NM 87501
505-989-7100; subscriptions: 800-937-9710
More outdoor sports and adventure from the people at Outside magazine, this time for and by kids involved in active sports—including in-line skating, snowboarding, roller hockey, and more.

FAMILY CAMPING

Rodale Press, Inc.
33 East Minor Street
Emmaus, PA 18098
Subscriptions: 800-666-3434
From Backpacker, *the magazine of wilderness travel, comes a new magazine to help families considering trips in the great outdoors.*

SIERRA

Sierra Club
730 Polk Street
San Francisco, CA 94109
415-776-2211
This conservation and outdoor magazine publishes an annual outing guide each January; Sierra is also available online, with special-interest forums and message-boards. Call 800-269-6422 for information.

WALKING MAGAZINE

Walking Inc.
9-11 Harcourt Street
Boston, MA 02116
617-266-3322
A place to start: recreational and fitness walking.

WILDERNESS TRAILS MAGAZINE

Wilderness Trails, Inc.
712 Satori Drive
Petaluma, CA 94954
707-762-8839
A mix of adventure and environmentalism.

WOMEN'S SPORTS & FITNESS

2025 Pearl Street
Boulder, CO 80302
303-440-5111
Keeping fit in various ways, including walking & hiking, with advice on women's particular needs.

ON-LINE SERVICES (The Internet)

Services and information available through the Internet change rapidly, but these sites we can recommend at the time of publication, and they are fun: for general information, *news:rec.backcountry,* and *http://www.gorp.com.* You'll find many linked sites with photographs and maps, clubs, etc. Search and order from Adventurous Traveler Bookstore through their web site, *http://www.gorp.com/atbook.htm.*

There are lots of folk putting photographs on the World Wide Web, a great many of themselves on top of a mountain. Check out *http://io.datasys.swri.edu* for a menu of documents that will tell you everything from how to start a fire to evaluations of equipment to a list of ways... well, find out for yourself!

For those considering subscribing to a commercial on-line provider, America Online has a number of outdoor services.

TRAILSIDE: MAKE YOUR OWN ADVENTURE

Trailside's service can be accessed via keyword "Trailside" or through *Backpacker's* section "Trailside TV." The Trailside service provides information from the television series' program guides and station listings as well as an active bulletin board, Campfire Chats, Trailside Outfitter, Maps and Snaps, New and Reviews, and complete gear lists from ongoing Trailside adventures.

OUTDOOR ADVENTURE

This travel and recreation service lists outfitters, organizations, and providers of lodging. It also has an active message board for travelers.

AMERICA ONLINE

By subscribing to America Online you can access *Backpacker* magazine as well. To subscribe, call 800-827-6364, Ext. 10380. The software will be provided to you free.

BOOKS

If you like to read or feel better easing slowly into this new venture, here are some suggestions. There are excellent series, both of trail guides (with maps) and techniques for managing outdoors, and many new books coming out each year.

BACKPACKING TECHNIQUES & CONCERNS

As Far As the Eye Can See, David Brill. 1990. $14.95. Rutledge Hill.

Backpacker's Handbook, Chris Townsend. 1993. $14.95. Ragged Mountain/McGraw Hill.

The Backpacker's Photography Handbook: How to Take Great Wilderness Pictures While Hiking, Climbing & Skiing, Charles Campbell. 1994. $19.95. Watson-Guptill.

Backwoods Ethics: Environmental Issues for Hikers & Campers, Laura & Guy Waterman. 2nd rev. ed. 1993. $13.00. Countryman.

The Complete Buyer's Guide to the Best Outdoor Recreation & Equipment, Kevin Jeffrey. 1993. $14.95. Foghorn.

The Complete Walker III, Colin Fletcher. 3rd ed. 1984. $22.95. Paper. $19.00. Alfred Knopf.

Desert Hiking, Dave Ganci. 3rd ed. 1993. $13.95. Wilderness.

Hiker's Companion: 12,000 Miles of Trail-Tested Wisdom, Ross & Gladfelter. 1993. $12.95. Mountaineers.

Knots for Hikers & Backpackers, Frank & Victoria Logue. 1994. $4.95. Menasha Ridge.

Modern Backpacker's Handbook, Glenn Randall. 1994. $14.95. Lyons and Burford.

Mountaineering: The Freedom of the Hills, Don Graydon, ed. 1992. $32.00. Paper $22.95. Mountaineers.

NOLS Wilderness Guide, Peter Simer & John Sullivan. 1993. $10.95. Simon & Schuster.

Trail Design, Construction & Maintenance, Robert Proudman & William Birchard, Jr. 1981. $5.80. Appalachian Trail Conference.

Trailside's Hints & Tips for Outdoor Adventure, editors of *Backpacker* magazine, John Viehman, ed. 1993. $9.95. Rodale Press.

The Two Ounce Backpacker. A Problem Solving Manual for Use in the Wilds, R. S. Wood. 1982. $4.95. Ten Speed Press.

Wilderness Ethics: Preserving the Spirit of Wildness, Laura & Guy Waterman. 1993. $13.00. Countryman.

Words for the Wild: The Sierra Club Trailside Reader, Ann Ronald, ed. 1987. $12.00. Sierra Club.

FOOD & COOKING

Cooking in the Outdoors: The Basic Essentials, Cliff Jacobson. 1989. $5.99. ICS.

Edible Wild Plants & Useful Herbs: The Basic Essentials, Jim Meuninck. 1988. $5.99. ICS.

Gorp, Glop, & Glue Stew: Favorite Foods from 165 Outdoor Experts, Yvonne Prater & Ruth D. Mendenhall. 1981. $10.95. Mountaineers.

The NOLS Cookery: Experience the Art of Outdoor Cooking, National Outdoor Leadership School Staff. 1991. $6.95. Stackpole.

The One-Burner Gourmet, Harriett Barker. 1981. $14.95. Contemporary Books.

Simple Foods for the Pack: The Sierra Club Guide to Delicious Natural Foods for the Trail, Claudia Axcell, et al. 1986. $9.00. Sierra Clubs.

Trailside's Trail Food, editors of *Backpacker* magazine, John Viehman, ed. 1993. $9.95. Rodale Press.

The Trekking Chef: Gourmet Recipes for the Great Outdoors, Martin, Claudine. 1989. $14.95. Lyons & Burford.

The Well-Fed Backpacker, June Fleming. 1986. $9.00. Random House.

Wild Foods Field Guide & Cookbook, Billy J. Tatum. 2nd ed. 1985. $8.95 Paper. $7.95. Workman.

WOMEN IN THE OUTDOORS

The Basic Essentials of Women in the Outdoors, Judith Niemi. 1990. $5.99. ICS.

The Outdoor Woman: A Handbook to Adventure, Patricia Hubbard & Stan Wass. 1992. $14.95. MasterMedia Limited.

HIKING WITH CHILDREN

Backpacking with Babies & Small Children, Goldie Silverman. 1986. $10.95. Wilderness.

Best Hikes with Children: a series published by The Mountaineers Books.

Sharing Nature with Children, Joseph B. Cornell. 1979. $7.95. Dawn Publications.

Travel with Children, Maureen Wheeler. 2nd ed. 1990. $10.95. Lonely Planet.

WINTER CAMPING & WILDERNESS SURVIVAL

AMC Guide to Winter Camping, Stephen Gorman. 1991. $12.95. Appalachian Mountain Club.

Harsh Weather Camping in the Nineties: Secrets, Suggestions, Tips & Techniques, Sam Curtis. 1993. $12.95. Menasha Ridge.

The Outdoor Survival Handbook: A Guide to the Resources & Material Available in the Wild & How to Use Them for Food, Shelter, Warmth, & Navigation, Raymond Mears. 1993. $13.95. Saint Martin's Press.

Wilderness Skiing & Winter Camping, Chris Townsend. 1993. $17.95. McGraw-Hill.

Winterwise, a Backpacker's Guide, John M. Dunn. 1989. $12.95. Adirondack Mountain Club .

WHERE-TO GUIDES AND TRAIL GUIDES

The Active Travel Resource Guide, Dan Browdy, ed. Ultimate Ventures, $19.95. The latest edition lists 85 organizations and the tours they offer, dates, prices, and all.

Appalachian Mountain Club guides and maps. Compact books to carry with you when hiking in New England, with great pull-out maps.

Appalachian Trail series, published by the Appalachian Trail Conference, with guides and maps to the great trail.

Camper's Guide to U. S. National Parks, Morava and Little. Gulf. Two volume set on camping opportunities, including hike-in. $18.95 each.

Climber's and Hiker's Guide to the World's Mountains, Michael Kelsey. 3rd ed., $34.95. Kelsey Pub.

The Complete Guide to America's National Parks, $14.95. Fodor's Travel Publications.

Discover the Adirondacks series: published by Countryman Press.

50 Hikes series, written about Eastern states, published by Countryman Press.

Hikers Guide to series: popular guides to favorite regions of the U.S.

Lonely Planet: a wonderful series of guides for traveling and trekking abroad.

100 Hikes series, published by the Mountaineers as guides to the Northwest.

SOFTWARE

Best Foot Forward databases, with guides to trails in five states, are available from Grizzlyware, 16837 N.E. 176th Street, Woodinville, WA 98072 (800-258-4453).

HIKING SOME OF THE PLACES MENTIONED IN THIS BOOK

Along the Colorado Trail, John Fielder & M. John Fayhee. 1992. Westcliffe.

Appalachian Trail Backpacker, Victoria & Frank Logue. 1994. $10.95. Menasha Ridge.

Appalachian Trail Companion, Joe & Monica Cook, eds. 1995. $5.95. Appalachian Trail Conference.

Journey on the Crest - Walking 2600 Miles from Mexico to Canada, Cindy Ross. 1992. $21.50. Peter Smith.

The Thru-Hiker's Handbook 1995, Dan W. Bruce. $10.95. Center for Appalachian Trail Studies.

Uncommon Places, David Muench. 1991. $39.95. Appalachian Trail Conference.

Walking the Appalachian Trail, Larry Luxenberg. 1994. $16.95. Stackpole.

Where the Waters Divide: A Walk Across America Along the Continental Divide, Karen Berger & Dan Smith. 1993. $23.00. Crown.

MAP & COMPASS

Be Expert with Map & Compass: The Complete Orienteering Handbook, Bjorn Kellstrom. U. S. Geological Survey & Orienteering Services. 1994. $15.85. Macmillan.

Map & Compass: The Basic Essentials, Cliff Jacobson. 1988. $5.99. ICS.

The Outward Bound Map & Compass Book, Glenn Randall. 1989. $8.95. Lyons & Burford.

Staying Found: The Complete Map & Compass Handbook, June Fleming. 2nd ed. 1994. $10.95. Mountaineers.

SAFETY & FIRST AID

Emergency Medical Procedures for the Outdoors, Patient Care Publications Staff. 1987. $6.95. Menasha Ridge.

Field Guide to Venomous Animals & Poisonous Plants, Steven Foster. 1994. $22.95. Paper $15.95. Houghton Mifflin.

First Aid for the Outdoors: The Basic Essentials, William W. Forgey. 1988. $5.99. ICS.

Hypothermia, Frostbite & Other Cold Injuries: Prevention, Recognition, Pre-Hospital Treatment, James A. Wilkerson, et al, eds. 1986. $11.95. Mountaineers.

Medicine for Mountaineering & Other Wilderness Activities, James A. Wilkerson, ed. 4th ed. 1992. $16. 95. Mountaineers.

Medicine for the Backcountry, Buck Tilton. 2nd ed. 1994. $12.99. ICS.

Mountaineering Medicine: A Wilderness Medical Guide, Fred T. Darvill, Jr. 13th rev. ed. 1992. $5.95. Wilderness Press.

NOLS Wilderness First Aid, Tod Schimelpfenig & Linda Lindsey. 1992. $12.95. Stackpole.

Rescue from the Backcountry: The Basic Essentials Of, Buck Tilton. 1991. $5.99. ICS.

Simon & Schuster Pocket Guide to Wilderness Medicine, Paul G. Gill, Jr. 1991. $9.95. Simon & Schuster.

Standard First Aid, American Red Cross Staff. 1993. $6.00. Mosby-Year Book.

VIDEOS

Our own Trailside series of videos which aired on public television are perhaps the best inspiration we can offer to the novice hiker. Included are tips and techniques from experts and professionals, led in each video by John Viehman, executive editor of *Backpacker* magazine and Trailside's host and series editor. These videos and others in the Trailside series may be purchased by calling 800-TRAILSIDE (800-872-4574). Catalog available.

Backpacking in Tennessee: an introduction to hiking — to the highest peaks of the Great Smoky Mountains — surrounded by the colors of fall.

Bear Country: hike & camp in Alaska, with great advice about understanding and staying safe in the bears' own country.

Family Camping in Virginia: with just a short hike, camp in the wilderness. Great ideas for games, too, amid scenes of Shenandoah National Park.

Rainforest Hiking In Puerto Rico: an introduction to wet weather hiking in the El Yunque rain forest.

Winter Camping in Montana: learn how to snowhoe and build a snow shelter inside Glacier National Park.

Alpine Hiking on the Appalachian Trail: learn to tread carefully through blooming alpine tundra.

A SAMPLING OF OTHER VIDEOS:

Backpacking Made Easy: an everything-you-need-to-know video.

Hiking the Olympics: eight hikes in the varied country of Washington's Olympic Peninsula.

Hiking Yosemite: seven hikes in Yosemite National Park.

John Muir Trail: history, how-to, suggested guides and side trips, as well as views from Mt. Whitney to Yosemite Valley.

Land of One Season — the Basics of Mountain Safety: wilderness survival techniques.

Medicine for the Outdoors: bees to bumps: medicine with Dr. Auerbach.

Tahoe Yosemite Trail: a 180-mile trail, connecting to the John Muir Trail, plus practical information and help.

MAIL-ORDER SOURCES OF BOOKS & VIDEOS:
ADVENTUROUS TRAVELER BOOKSTORE
PO Box 577
Hinesburg, VT 05461
800-282-3963 or 802-482-3330
Fax: 800-282-3963 or
802-482-3546
E-mail: books@atbook.com; on the World Wide Web —
http://www.gorp.com/atbook.htm — search their full selection of 3,000 titles by keyword. Largest supplier of worldwide adventure travel books & maps.

BACKCOUNTRY BOOKSTORE
PO Box 6235
Lynnwood, WA 90836-0235
206-290-7652
Books and videos on all outdoor activities, as well as knowledgeable staff.

VIDEO ACTION SPORTS, INC.
200 Suburban Road, Suite E
San Luis Obispo, CA 93401
800-727-6689
805-543-4812
Fax: 805-541-8544
Catalog available.

L.L.BEAN
Casco Street
Freeport, ME 04032
800-727-6689
Retail store in Freeport, outlets and catalog sales. Books, videos and audio tapes.

MAIL-ORDER SOURCES OF MAPS
Libraries are a good place to start for maps. Your local outfitters will also carry some. We recommend a fascinating book, *The Map Catalog,* edited by Joel Makower, 1992, $18.00, Vintage Books. This invaluable source describes the wide range of maps published and where to order them. *Trails Illustrated* is a series published by a group of the same name, with topographical maps for major parks and mountains in the U.S. The *Delorme Atlas/Gazeteers* have large-scale maps of most states with trails and campsites.

You can order topographical maps from the following government agencies: (Hikers in the western half of the country may also wish to contact their regional Bureau of Land Management for maps of 3,600 miles of marked trails. Also, try your state department of natural resources, state parks, or transportation authority.)

MAP DISTRIBUTION

U.S. Geological Survey
Box 25286, Federal Center
Denver, CO 80225
800-USA-MAPS
publishes a list of current maps

OFFICE OF PUBLIC INQUIRIES

National Park Service
Room 1013
Washington, D.C. 20240
202-208-4747
maps and folders for national parks, forests, seashores, and historical sites

U.S. FOREST SERVICE

Public Affairs Office
2nd Floor
Auditors Building
14th & Independence Ave, S.W.
Washington, D.C. 20250
202-205-1760
155 national forest maps

MAIL-ORDER SOURCES OF EQUIPMENT

These stores offer catalogs and mail-order sales of backpacking gear, clothing, and a full line of accessories.

CAMPMOR

810 Route 17 North
PO Box 999
Paramus, NJ 07652
800-526-4784

DON GLEASON'S CAMPERS SUPPLY

Pearl Street
Northampton, MA 01060
413-584-4895

L. L. BEAN

Casco Street
Freeport, ME 04033
800-221-4221

RAMSEY OUTDOOR

226 Route 17 North
Paramus, NJ 07652
201-261-5000

REI

Dept. N5001
Sumner, WA 98352-0001
800-426-4840, ext. N5001

WILDERNESS EXPERIENCE

20675
Nordhoff Street
Chatsworth, CA 91311
800-222-5725

MAIL-ORDER SOURCES OF FOOD

ADVENTURE FOODS

Route 2
Whittier, NC 28789
704-497-4113

ALPINE AIRE

PO Box 926
Nevada City, CA 95959
800-322-MEAL

BACKPACK GOURMET

PO Box 334-C
Underhill, VT 05489
802-899-5445

INDIANA CAMP SUPPLY

125 East 37th Street
PO Box 2166
Loveland, CO 80539
303-669-8884

MOUNTAIN HOUSE

Oregon Freez Dry, Inc.
PO Box 1048
Albany, OR 97321
800-547-4060

TRAIL FOODS

PO Box 9309-B
N. Hollywood, CA 91609-1309
818-897-4370

UNCLE JOHN'S FOODS

Box 489
Dept B994
Fairplay, CO 80440
800-530-8733

MANUFACTURERS OF EQUIPMENT

Who makes the gear you need? A great many manufacturers, most of whom will send you a catalog and/or product information and a list of dealers if you call. Some sell from their factories.

ADIDAS AMERICA

No factory sales
541 N.E. 20th Street
Suite 207
Portland, OR 97232
800-423-4327
boots, outdoor sports clothing

ALICO SPORT

75 dealers; no factory sales
PO Box 165
Beebe Plain, VT 05823
800-475-4266
boots

ALPINA SPORTS CORP.

No factory sales
PO Box 23
Hanover, NH 03755
603-448-3101
boots

AMERICAN TRAILS/MZH, INC.

1,200 dealers; no factory sales
80 E. Rt. 4
Paramus, NJ 07652
800-221-7452
sleeping bags

ARC'TERYX

275 dealers; no factory sales
170 Harbour Avenue
North Vancouver, BC
Canada V7J 2E6
800-985-6681
packs

ASOLO FOOTWEAR

400 dealers; no factory sales
139 Harvest Lane
Williston, VT 05495
802-879-4644
boots

BIBLER TENTS

40 dealers; factory sales
5441-D Western Ave
Dept BG
Boulder, CO 80301
303-449-7351
tents, stoves, sleeping bags

BOREAL
No factory sales
PO Box 7116
Capistrano Beach, CA 92624
714-248-5688
boots

**CAMP TRAILS/JOHNSON
WORLDWIDE ASSOCIATES**
No factory sales
1326 Willow Road
Sturtevant, WI 53177
800-848-3673
*packs, tents, sleeping bags, outdoor
gear and clothing*

CAMPING GAZ/SUUNTO USA
2,000 dealers; no factory sales
2151 Las Palmas Drive
Carlsbad, CA 92009
619-931-6788
stoves, water filters

CAMPMOR, INC.
retail store; catalog sales
28 Parkway
PO Box 700
Saddle River, NJ 07458
800-525-4784
full line of outdoor gear

**CARIBOU
MOUNTAINEERING, INC.**
1,800 dealers; factory sales
PO Box 3696
Chico, CA 95927
800-824-4153
packs, sleeping bags

CASCADE DESIGNS, INC.
1,000 dealers; no factory sales
4000 First Ave S.
Seattle, WA 98134
800-531-9531
packs, sleeping bags, sleeping pads

CLIMB HIGH
600 dealers; factory sales
1861 Shelburne Road
Shelburne, VT 05482
802-985-5056
*packs, stoves, sleeping bags, full
line of outdoor gear & clothing*

CLOUD 9/MZH, INC.,
see American Trails/MZH, Inc.

DANA DESIGN
180 dealers; factory sales
1950 N. 19th Street
Bozeman, MT 59715
406-587-4188
packs

DECKERS CORP
1140 Mark Ave
Carpinteria, CA 93013-2998
805-684-6694
Teva sandals

**EASTERN MOUNTAIN
SPORTS (EMS)**
55 retail stores; no factory sales
One Vose Farm Road
Peterborough, NH 03458
603-924-6154
full line of outdoor gear & clothing

**EUREKA!/JOHNSON
WORLDWIDE ASSOCIATES**
see Camp Trails/Johnson Worldwide Associates

FABIANO SHOE CO.
Factory sales
850 Summer Street
S. Boston, MA 02127-1575
617-268-5625
boots

FEATHERED FRIENDS
50 dealers; factory sales
2013 Fourth Ave
Seattle, WA 98121
206-443-9549
sleeping bags & repairs

GARUDA
34 dealers; factory sales
PO Box 24804
Seattle, WA 98124-0804
206-763-2989
tents

GENERAL ECOLOGY, INC.
No factory sales
151 Sheree Blvd.
Exton, PA 19341
800-441-8166
water filters (First Need)

GREGORY MOUNTAIN PRODUCTS
Factory sales
100 Calle Cortez
Temecula, CA 92590
800-477-3420
packs

HI-TEC SPORTS USA, INC.
2,000 dealers; no factory sales
4801 Stoddard Road
Modesto, CA 95356
800-521-1698
boots

INTEGRAL DESIGNS, INC.
324 dealers; factory sales
PO Box 40023
Highfield P.O.
Calgary, AB
Canada T2G 5G5
403-640-1445
tents, sleeping bags

JANSPORT
5,000 dealers; no factory sales
10411 Airport Road SW
Everett, WA 98204
800-552-6776
packs, sportswear

KATADYN
400 dealers; no factory sales
Geneva Road
Brewster, NY 10509
800-431-2204
water filters

KELTY, INC.
800 dealers; no factory sales
1224 Fern Ridge Pkwy.
St. Louis, MO 63141
314-576-8069
packs, tents, sleeping bags

LEKI-SPORT USA
60 Earhart Drive
Williamsville, NY 14221
716-633-8062
hiking poles

L.L. BEAN
main strore; outlets; catalog sales
Casco Street
Freeport, ME 04032
800-221-4221
*full line of outdoor gear &
clothing*

LOWE ALPINE SYSTEMS
400 dealers; no factory sales
PO Box 1449
Broomfield, CO 80038
303-465-0522
packs

MADDEN MOUNTAINEERING
Factory sales
2400 Central Ave
Boulder, CO 80301
303-442-5828
packs

MARKILL/BERGSPORT INTERNATIONAL
170 dealers; factory sales
PO Box 1519
Nederland, CO 80466
303-258-3796
stoves

MARMOT
240 dealers; no factory sales
2321 Circadian Way
Santa Rosa, CA 95407
707-544-4590
sleeping bags, outdoor sports outerwear

MERRELL FOOTWEAR
1,200 dealers; no factory sales
PO Box 4249
Burlington, VT 05406
800-869-3348
boots

MONTBELL AMERICA
250 dealers; factory sales
940 41st Ave.
Santa Cruz, CA 95062
800-683-2002
packs, sleeping bags

MOONSTONE MOUNTAINEERING
500 dealers; no factory sales
5350 Ericson Way
Arcata, CA 95521
800-822-2985
sleeping bags

MOSS, INC.
300 dealers; no factory sales
PO Box 577
Camden, ME 04843
207-236-0505
tents

MOUNTAIN EQUIPMENT, INC.
No factory sales
4776 E. Jensen Avenue
Fresno, CA 93725
209-486-8211
packs

MOUNTAIN SAFETY RESEARCH/MSR
1,200 dealers; factory sales
4225 Second Ave. S.
Seattle, WA 98134
800-877-9677
stoves, water filters

MOUNTAINSMITH, INC.
350 dealers; factory sales
18301 W. Colfax, Bldg. P
Golden, CO 80401
800-426-4075
packs

NEW BALANCE ATHLETIC SHOE, INC.
4,000 dealers; no factory sales
61 N. Beacon Street
Boston, MA 02134
800-253-SHOE
boots

NIKE, INC./A.C.G.
4,500 dealers; no factory sales
One Bowerman Drive
Beaverton, OR 97005-6453
800-344-6453
boots, sportswear

THE NORTH FACE
450 dealers; no factory sales
999 Harrison Street
Berkeley, CA 94710
800-447-2333
packs, tents, sleeping bags, outerwear

ONE SPORT, INC.
350 dealers; no factory sales
1003 Sixth Ave. S.
Seattle, WA 98134
800-826-1598
boots

OPTIMUS/SUUNTO USA,
see Camping Gaz/Suunto USA

OSPREY PACKS
125 dealers; factory sales
PO Box 539
Dolores, CO 81323
303-882-2221
packs

PATAGONIA
retail and catalog sales
PO Box 8900
Bozeman, MT 59715
800-336-9090
outdoor sports clothing

PEAK 1/THE COLEMAN CO.
Factory sales
PO Box 2931
Wichita, KS 67202
800-835-3278
packs, stoves, sleeping bags

PUR
900 dealers; factory sales
2229 Edgewood Ave. S.
Minneapolis, MN 55426
800-845-7873
water filters

QUEST
1500 dealers; no factory sales
569 Charcot Ave.
San Jose, CA 95131
800-875-6901
packs, tents

RAICHLE MOLITOR USA, INC.
No factory sales
Geneva Road
Brewster, NY 10509
800-431-2204
boots

RECREATIONAL EQUIPMENT INC./REI
41 dealers; no factory sales
PO Box 1938
Sumner, WA 98390-0800
800-426-4840
full line of outdoor gear & clothing

REEBOK INTERNATIONAL
2,000 dealers; no factory sales
100 Technology Center Drive, Annex 2
Stoughton, MA 02072
800-843-4444
boots, outdoor sports clothing

RIDGE REST,
See Cascade Designs, Inc.

THE ROCKPORT CO.
4,000 dealers; no factory sales
220 Donald Lynch Blvd.
Marlboro, MA 01752
800-343-WALK
boots

SALOMON NORTH AMERICA, INC.
500 dealers; no factory sales
400 E. Main St.
Georgetown, MA 01833
800-225-6850
boots

SIERRA DESIGNS
800 dealers; factory sales
1255 Powell Street
Emeryville, CA 94608
800-736-8551
tents, sleeping bags

SLUMBERJACK
3,000 dealers; no factory sales
PO Box 7048A
St. Louis, MO 63177
800-233-6283
sleeping bags, sleeping pads

STEPHENSONS-WARMLITE
1 dealer; factory sales
22 Hook Rd.
Gilford, NH 03246-6745
603-293-8526
packs, tents, sleeping bags, sleeping pads

SWEETWATER, INC.
600+ dealers; no factory sales
4725 Nautilus Ct. #3
Boulder, CO 80301
800-557-9338
water filters

TECNICA USA
No factory sales
19 Technology Drive
West Lebanon, NH 03784
603-298-8032
boots

TEVA SANDALS,
see Deckers Corp.

THERM-A-REST,
see Cascade Designs, Inc.

THE TIMBERLAND CO.
No factory sales
11 Merrill Industrial Drive
Hampton, NH 03842
603-926-1600
boots, outdoor sports clothing

TRANGIA/MSR
1,200 dealers; factory sales
PO Box 24547
Seattle, WA 98124
800-877-9677
stoves

TRIGON
50 dealers
306 Westlake Ave #313
Seattle, WA 98109
206-624-4453
packs

VASQUE
No factory sales
314 Main Street
Red Wing, MN 55066
612-388-8211
boots

WALRUS
150 dealers; factory sales
PO Box 3875
Seattle, WA 98124
800-550-8368
tents

WESTERN MOUNTAINEERING
40 dealers; factory sales
1025 S. Fifth Street
San Jose, CA 95112
408-287-8944
sleeping bags

WILD COUNTRY LTD.
300 dealers; factory sales
230 E. Conway Road
Center Conway, NH 03818
603-356-5590
packs, tents

JACK WOLFSKIN,
see Camp Trails/Johnson Worldwide Associates, which imports Jack Wolfskin

PHOTO CREDITS

RICHARD BAILEY: 206
DUGALD BREMNER: 17 (TOP), 46, 68, 78, 85, 93, 175
JOHN CANCALOSI/TOM STACK & ASSOCIATES: 139
DENNIS COELLO: 6, 27
JOE AND MONICA COOK: 110, 125, 141, 145, 170, 187, 192
DAVID M. DENNIS/TOM STACK & ASSOCIATES: 153
CHESS EDWARDS: 203
E. EVANS: 52
STEVE HOWE: 14, 22, 42, 50, 54, 66, 91, 96, 143, 178
T. KITCHIN/TOM STACK & ASSOCIATES: 106
FRANK LOGUE: 15, 19, 24, 30, 34, 36, 38, 89, 131, 181
BECKY LUIGART-STAYNER: 11, 37, 41, 45, 53, 57, 63, 69 (BOTH), 70 (ALL 3), 74, 79, 80, 87, 88, 90, 95, 101, 113, 135, 167, 185, 197
RON LUXEMBURG: 13 (BOTTOM), 18
JOE MCDONALD/TOM STACK & ASSOCIATES: 149
SYD NISBET: 94, 117, 144, 169, 186
GALEN ROWELL: 13 (TOP), 39, 59, 82, 190
ROB SIMPSON/TOM STACK & ASSOCIATES: 151
DANIEL R. SMITH 103, 120, 127, 130, 154, 202,
RICHARD HAMILTON SMITH: 12, 17 (BOTTOM), 21
RICHARD P. SMITH/TOM STACK & ASSOCIATES: 161
SCOTT SPIKER: 16, 60, 189, 205
ALEX THOMSEN: 75
GORDON WILTSIE: 33, 40, 104, 109, 163, 168, 194, 196, 199
ROBERT WINSLOW/TOM STACK & ASSOCIATES: 159
GEORGE WUERTHNER: 98, 111, 155

INDEX